A TREASURY OF
WHITE HOUSE
TALES

A TREASURY
—OF—
White House Tales

Webb Garrison

RUTLEDGE HILL PRESS

Nashville, Tennessee

Published in Nashville, Tennessee, by Rutledge Hill Press, 211 Seventh Avenue North, Nashville, Tennessee 37219

Typography by D&T/Bailey Typesetting, Inc., Nashville, Tennessee.

Library of Congress Cataloging-in-Publication Data

Garrison, Webb B.
    A treasury of White House tales / Webb Garrison.
        p.   cm.
    Includes index.
    ISBN 1-55853-382-6 (Paperback)
    I. Presidents—United States—Ancedotes.   I. Title.
    E176.2.G37 1989   89-6252
    973' .0992—dc20   CIP

Printed in the United States of America
4 5 6 7 8—99 98 97 96 95

Contents

Part Three—Wives and Mothers

Part Four—The Imperial Presidency

Part Five—Trail Blazers

Part Six—Money Matters

The Most Powerful Men
In the World

Today it is customary to refer to the president of the United States as the "most powerful man in the world." Long before that label came into vogue, national leaders and rank-and-file citizens alike were keenly conscious that—for them—the president really did exercise more power than anyone else.

No television idol, Olympic gold medal winner, head of an industrial dynasty, or star in the Super Bowl even approaches the president of the United States in influence on the lives and destinies of millions of people. Also, because of the overwhelming power of the office, those who are close to the chief executive by blood, marriage, or appointment take on great significance as well.

Textbook information about presidents of the United States and their intimates is easily available. Not so ready at hand are accounts of unusual and off-trail aspects of their lives. In coming to focus upon colorful, little known, and sometimes bizarre aspects of the strangely heterogeneous group of men who have been presidents of the United States, *A Treasury of White House Tales* runs the gamut from the sublime to the ridiculous. Many of these men had extraordinary ability, and all were subject to the frailties of ordinary persons and the vagaries of fate.

Initially, I had thought of devoting one chapter to each of the thirty-nine chief executives who had served through 1988. (Grover Cleveland served two nonconsecutive terms and is counted as our twenty-second and twenty-fourth presidents.) As I wrote, it became obvious that our forty-first president would be in office before the volume would be published and that *A Treasury of White House Tales* would be published on the occasion of the Bicentennial of the American Presidency.

My original tentative plan was discarded early, for presidents, like other humans, vary widely. A few lived almost unbelievably dull lives despite their elevated position, and a few stand head-and-shoulders above their peers when it comes to generating stories of abiding human interest. The colorful characters appear frequently in *A Treasury of White House Tales*, while the others are mentioned only briefly.

Here you will learn about hairbreadth escapes from death that have affected the course of our nation. You will get glimpses at the secret lives and deeds of those who for a time guided the course of America. You also will discover that the much-decried "packaging" of the candidates in the 1988 election was not new; both William Henry Harrison and Abraham Lincoln were "packaged" with skill, long ago.

In *A Treasury of White House Tales* you will take quick glimpses at some of the women who most influenced presidents, and perhaps the awesome power of "the imperial presidency" will come home to you in a fresh way. You may be intrigued by tales of chief executives who have blazed trails, and you may be amused or astonished at the way money has affected the lives and accomplishments of others.

In short, from this collection you will become a little better acquainted with Americans who differ from you chiefly by the fact that ability or circumstances elevated each to a position of power in which all traits of character—every decision, whim, or fancy—took on magnified significance and abiding interest.

—Webb Garrison

A TREASURY OF
WHITE HOUSE
TALES

Part One

Close Calls

Primitive painter Edward Hicks captured George Washington's famous cocked hat and big white horse on canvas in 1776. [New York Public Library]

1

Miraculous Escapes Led George Washington to See Himself as "Special"

December 23, 1753, found a tall "district adjutant" slowly making his way toward "the forks of the Ohio," where Pittsburgh is now situated. Wearing what he called "an Indian dress," twenty-two-year-old George Washington, who had volunteered for the mission, pushed deeper into French-controlled territory every day.

Not yet a soldier, his mission was that of messenger empowered to deliver to the French an ultimatum demanding that they stop encroaching upon English-held territory.

At Will's Creek on the Potomac, Washington had recruited Christopher Gist to serve as his guide. With an interpreter and four frontiersmen, they pushed across the ridges of the Alleghenies where, writing to Governor Dinwiddie of Virginia, the young adjutant reported in November that "Waters were quite impassible without swimming our Horses."

Swollen rivers forced the tiny party of Englishmen to build a crude raft on which they hoped to float to French-held Fort Le Boeuf. When the raft turned over in icy waters, Washington was the only man in the party who could not swim. However, although thrown into ten feet of ice-filled water in the Allegheny River, he somehow escaped unhurt.

Later in the same expedition an Indian employed by Washington as a guide turned out to be allied with the French. Suddenly he ran fifteen paces ahead, then turned to fire at the tall Virginian. Historian James T. Flexner writes that "the bullet moved through utter emptiness without changing the history of the world."

Twice saved from death "by the grace of God and the skin of the teeth," the grateful young adventurer pondered the meaning of his strange deliverances. The first volume of his writings includes reflections that exclaim, "See the wondrous works of Providence! The uncertainty of human things!"

May 1754 saw the man who had survived against great odds volunteer to lead a company of men to establish an outpost against the French. Commissioned a lieutenant colonel, Washington led a surprise attack upon the enemy. During the sharp skirmish, one man close to him was killed; several others were wounded. Having deliberately exposed himself to enemy fire, Washington jubilantly wrote to his brother, "I have heard the bullets whistle, and, believe me, there is something charming in the sound."

Months later, British Colonials under Edward Braddock, with Washington as second in command, met the French head-on in the battle of Fort Duquesne. In the thick of fighting Washington's attention was caught by a firm yank upon his coat. Looking down, he found that the garment had been ripped by French bullets.

Still, he tried to persuade Braddock to let him lead their men forward and fight the enemy Indian style. Braddock shook his head but signaled that officers were to ride ahead of the tiny band of enlisted men. As they rode, Braddock was shot from the saddle, Washington's hat was knocked from his head by a bullet, and his horse was shot from under him.

When General Braddock died, Washington ordered him buried in the center of the road. Then he had wagons run back and forth over the grave to prevent the Indians from discovering it. Though unhurt during the campaign, Washington had to jump from the saddle twice when horses were shot from under him, and he counted at least four bullet holes in his clothing.

Rumor said that Washington had been killed, but when the twenty-three-year-old heard it, he wrote to his brother to deny the report.

Washington's awe and delight never became stale. Thirty years later, near the end of the American Revolution, he was still incredulous at "the miraculous care of Providence, that protected me beyond all human expectation."

Fighting in mid-September 1755, Washington's green troops turned and ran without firing a shot at the French and their Indian allies. Soon he was alone in a crossroad, with about fifty enemy soldiers advancing at a run from a distance of approximately eighty yards. Washington sat calmly, looking at them, until aides galloped up, seized the bridle of his horse, and hurried him from what appeared to be certain death.

While leading a rescue party on the same expedition, he was caught directly in the line of fire. His men were firing upon troops they

"Washington Crossing the Allegheny River," (Denison Kimberly engraving, 1842). Artist incorrectly depicted young Washington as accompanied on the raft only by Christopher Gist. [LIBRARY OF CONGRESS]

thought to be enemies, but Washington heard a familiar voice and realized that the targets were members of his own Virginia regiment.

Immediately, their leader dashed on foot between the two bands of men and used his sword to knock firearms upward. Bullets whizzed about his head so rapidly that before he made the two groups understand what they were doing, fourteen lay dead and twenty-four were wounded.

George Washington, who had been in the center of fire from both directions, had nary a scratch.

Ironically, Washington never knew of his most bizarre escape from death. In the 1940s Major Reginald Hargreaves spent many years "prowling through vast mazes of uncatalogued material in London's Public Record Office." When he turned his attention to "an especially dusty corner," Hargreaves uncovered a document that tells the story of that escape. Early American accounts of the Revolution include only a tantalizing hint about this, buried in volume four of John Andrews' *History of the Late War* (1786).

Heading mostly still raw recruits, Washington went on reconnaissance on September 7, 1776. He wanted to know whether units at Chad's Ford on Brandywine Creek would be able to stop British troops. In characteristic fashion, he mounted his easily recognized horse and with only one aide rode out to check his advance units.

British companies were encamped just four miles from the vital ford. Early on the morning of Washington's foray, three Redcoats were on patrol far ahead of their own lines.

Major Patrick Ferguson, in charge of the British band, was a famous sharpshooter, as well as the renowned inventor of a light breech-loading rifle. While demonstrating his weapon for King George III, Ferguson had hit the bull's-eye at 100 yards—lying flat upon his back. According to Ferguson's meticulously written account, the British spotted two Americans. One of the riders was recognized to be a man of great importance because he wore "a remarkably large cocked hat" such as no enlisted man or petty officer would be permitted to use.

Patrick Ferguson signaled to his men to shoot them as soon as they came in range. Suddenly and unaccountably, he changed his mind, stepping out and shouting a demand for surrender. At the sound of the Englishman's voice, the rider wearing the big cocked hat wheeled his horse and raced for cover.

"I could have lodged half a dozen balls in him," Ferguson wrote, "but it was not pleasant to fire at a man's back, so I let him alone."

George Washington, who did not recognize the peril, rode back to camp to continue his long uphill fight for American freedom.

Collectively, Washington's incredible deliverances had a powerful influence upon his life. Pondering the meaning of these incidents, he concluded that his marvelous escapes from death meant that Providence had special plans for him.

As a consequence, his diaries and letters are liberally sprinkled with comments about the way in which "Providence has saved us in a remarkable manner"—plus references to "the hand of Providence" and "the finger of Providence."

Never a devout churchman, Washington nevertheless said of his own leadership of the emerging United States, "At best I have only been an instrument in the hands of Providence." He even went so far as to register his belief that Americans fighting for independence were brought to "an awful crisis" so that the work of Providence in effecting deliverance would be more conspicuous.

Could George Washington have led untrained colonial troops to victory against seasoned veterans in British ranks if he had lacked a sense of having been especially chosen for divine guidance and protection?

That question—not subject to an unqualified answer—is seldom raised. But it is central to the story of the fight for American independence.

2

Andrew Jackson's Skinny Body and Loose Coat Saved His Life

"**Y**our conduct and expressions, relative to me of late, have been of such a nature and so insulting, that it requires and shall have my notice," began a formal letter penned on May 22, 1806.

Gen. Thomas Overton, an intimate friend of Andrew Jackson, the man who had written the words, hand delivered the message to swash-buckling young Charles Dickinson of Nashville, Tennessee.

Dickinson's insults—earlier directed largely against Rachel Jackson—"must be noticed and treated with the respect due a gentleman, although in the present instance you do not merit it," continued the message from the future president.

"I hope, sir, that your courage will be an ample security to me that I will obtain speedily that satisfaction due me for insults offered."

On what was then the brawling southwestern frontier of the United States, *satisfaction* meant only one thing: pistols at dawn.

Dickinson had hoped for weeks that his prodding would lead to a challenge. At age twenty-five—a dozen years younger than Jackson—he was rated an expert with the pistol. A recent lengthy visit to New Orleans had reputedly been spent largely in practice with hand guns.

Back in Nashville, Dickinson had picked up the *Impartial Review* newspaper and in it read a letter from Jackson to Thomas Swann. Challenged by Swann, the man destined to become the hero of the battle of New Orleans had refused to fight. Swann was not a gentleman, he said; hence, he was not eligible for an affair of honor.

Admitting that he had caned Swann, Jackson wrote that he did so because the youth was "the puppet and lying valet for a worthless, drunken, blackguard scoundrel"—his father-in-law, Charles Erwin, who purportedly had given Jackson worthless notes in payment for losses in a horse race.

Dickinson, who had been itching for a fight, took up the cause of Swann and Erwin. Through columns in the *Impartial Review* he called the older man "a poltroon, a coward, and a worthless scoundrel." His letter published on May 22 led to Jackson's challenge later that day.

Within hours, seconds were chosen. Harrison's Mill on the Red River in Kentucky was selected as the place of meeting. Nashville was buzzing with excitement; numerous bets were placed, with Dickinson heavily favored because of Jackson's known inferior marksmanship.

May 30 found the duelists and their seconds in a clearing near the Red River. General Overton offered Dickinson his choice of a matched pair of .70 caliber pistols that fired one-ounce balls. Then the prescribed distance of twenty-four feet was paced off and the principals took their positions.

Though the morning was warm, Jackson wore a coat nearly two sizes larger than was needed to cover his gaunt body. Shorter and thicker, Dickinson was snappily dressed in blue and gray.

"Fire!" commanded Overton, who had won the right to issue the command by drawing lots.

Regional lore insists that Dickinson had practiced snap firing at a string stretched twenty-four feet away, often cutting it in two with a single shot. At the command, he snapped his arm and fired while his pistol was still in motion.

Wincing and lifting his left arm to hug his chest, Jackson showed no emotion. Slowly and carefully he lifted his own weapon.

"God in heaven!" Dickinson cried. "Is it possible that I missed him?" He stepped toward his foe, but was halted by Overton.

"Back to position, sir!" shouted the general, brandishing his own pistol. Dickinson obeyed the command and stood full face toward his

Long after the famous Dickinson duel, Andrew Jackson remained "uncommonly skinny"—Nineteenth Century Broadside.

General Andrew Jackson, or "Old Hickory." [NATIONAL ARCHIVES]

foe. Andrew Jackson aimed precisely and then squeezed the trigger. His ball hit Dickinson in the abdomen and passed completely through his body. Blood spurting from the wound spelled quick and certain death.

Only then did Jackson's second notice that the challenger left a bloody print behind at every footstep. Upon being hit, he had clutched his chest in a futile attempt to staunch the flow of blood.

Jackson tried to dismiss his wound as trivial. In reality, it was nearly fatal. His foe's bullet lodged so close to his heart that surgeons refused to attempt to remove it.

Jackson survived that famous duel, analysts say because he was unusually skinny—and because he partly concealed his frame with that oversize coat. Dickinson hit the spot at which he aimed, but he misjudged the position of Andrew Jackson's heart by a fraction of an inch.

Still carrying Dickinson's ball next to his heart, Old Hickory started down the steps of the U.S. Capitol on January 30, 1835. Richard Lawrence, a house painter with a history of mental delusions, pushed to within a dozen feet of the president.

Lawrence deftly whipped out a single-shot derringer and pulled the trigger. His percussion cap exploded, but gunpowder in the weapon failed to ignite.

Jackson raised his cane to strike the assailant, but before he could do so Lawrence—now standing less then four feet away—whipped out a second derringer and fired again. For the second time the cap exploded, but the gunpowder did not ignite.

Weapons experts who examined the two pistols found both in working order. They calculated that the odds against two successive malfunctions were in the range of at least 125,000 to one.

No other chief executive matches the incredible record of the man from Tennessee. Twice marked for death from pistol shots, both times he beat what seemed to be impossible odds and died in his bed at the Hermitage in Nashville in 1845 at age seventy-eight.

3

A Simple Military Song
Saved John Tyler's Life

"**N**o doubt about it," said U.S. Secretary of the Navy Thomas W. Gilmer, "our new cannon will be heard around the world."

Gilmer's verdict, delivered just nine days after he assumed office in 1844, became legendary in Washington, D.C., as "one of those totally unexplainable premonitions."

Two or three hours after having voiced his views about the cannon called Peacemaker, Gilmer joined President John Tyler and a host of top dignitaries aboard the gunship *Princeton*. Moored in the Potomac River near the capital, it was to be the site of a vivid demonstration of America's new naval muscle.

Robert F. Stockton, a career naval officer and commander of the *Princeton*, had spent years developing bigger and better weapons. He had turned away from then-standard cast iron because the brittle metal would not produce ordnance capable of handling shot heavier than 32 pounds. However, wrought iron worked miracles, he reported.

In England, craftsmen followed Stockton's directions and managed to produce a smoothbore cannon that he named the Oregon. Using charges of 20 and 30 pounds of black powder, it fired 216-pound balls.

With the British-made weapon as a prototype, Stockton persuaded Philadelphia iron workers to forge another 12-inch gun designed to be recognized as "substantially more powerful than any other in the world." Dubbed the Peacemaker, the mighty weapon was installed on Stockton's vessel along with the Oregon.

More than 400 guests accepted Stockton's invitation to be present for a demonstration firing on the afternoon of February 28, 1844. They gathered in the stateroom below the deck, where a "sumptuous collation" was followed by a toast from President Tyler and impromptu songs by guests.

An announcement interrupted the merriment. Yielding to pleas of his friends, Captain Stockton had agreed to a third—and final—firing of the Peacemaker. Those who wished to be on deck for this salute to U.S. naval power would have to move promptly.

John Tyler signaled that he would be there at once. Because his military experience was limited to a few months of service in the Charles City, Virginia, Rifles, he had come under criticism from opponents. Furthermore, although he had never heard the whine of British bullets during the War of 1812, Tyler had accepted a veteran's bonus of 160 acres of land in what is now Sioux City, Iowa. Politically, therefore, it was highly important that he show full support of the nation's military effort in all its aspects.

His foot was on the bottom rung of the ladder leading to the deck when a familiar voice was heard. He paused, recognizing William Waller, who had married Tyler's daughter Elizabeth two years earlier in a White House ceremony. Waller had started to sing a brisk military ditty, and it would be an affront to climb to the deck before he finished the short song.

Thus the president rejoined the celebration clustered about his son-in-law. As Waller reached the line that ran, "Eight hundred men lay slain," a mighty roar from the deck served notice that he and other latecomers would not be present, after all, for the additional firing of the Peacemaker.

The words of Waller's song were so appropriate that listeners broke into applause. Then an officer blackened with powder dashed through a gangway and shouted, "Surgeons! All surgeons! To the deck at once!"

At the late afternoon blast of the big wrought-iron cannon, the breech of the Peacemaker had exploded and jagged chunks of hot metal had made the decks a scene of carnage.

Navy Secretary Gilmer lay dead, also Secretary of State Abel P. Upshur, who had approved construction of the *Princeton* and her super-

Captain Robert F. Stockton, who designed and fired the "Peacemaker."

Secretary of State A. P. Upshur died instantly when the big gun exploded. [LIBRARY OF CONGRESS]

guns. New York Senator David Gardiner had been killed instantly while Missouri Senator Thomas Hart Benton was wandering about in a daze, badly wounded.

Tyler's body slave, almost always at his side, was among the dead. So was Commodore Beverly Mascy, chief of construction for the U.S. Navy. Two seamen were killed on the spot; nine others received serious injuries.

About 4:20 P.M. the stricken *Princeton* reached Alexandria, Virginia. Tyler remained aboard with the dead until their bodies were removed to the East Room of the White House.

The president's bitter political rival, James G. Bitney of the Liberty Party, wrote, "our fair capital has seen nothing quite like the funeral services of Sunday, March 2."

Then he added; "Many mourners marvel that President John Tyler was not among the dead. It is incredible that a jolly military song should have delivered this man from crippling injury or sudden death."

All Washington—not simply Birney—knew that had Tyler's son-in-law not begun to sing precisely as the president started for the deck, he would have had a place of honor near the breech of the Peacemaker when it was fired.

Four months after his miraculous deliverance, Virginia-born Tyler stunned the capital for the second time. He took as his second wife Julia Gardiner, whose father had been killed in the explosion. Less than half the president's fifty-four years of age, the new first lady was just twenty-four. His fifteenth child, their daughter named Pearl, was born when the ex-president was past his seventieth birthday.

On May 5, 1861, Tyler again stunned the capital by accepting a seat in the provisional congress of the Confederate States of America. A few months later, the man whom fate spared from the Peacemaker's blast was elected to represent his congressional district in the permanent C.S.A. Congress—thereby becoming the only ex-president to hold office in the Confederacy.

4

A Senator and a Sculptress Saved Andrew Johnson's Presidency

J ohn F. Kennedy's *Profiles in Courage* gave Senator Edmund Gibson Ross a special niche in American history. There Kennedy reminded the nation that Ross cast the deciding vote by which President Andrew Johnson was cleared of trumped-up charges by political foes.

What Kennedy did not tell readers was the behind-the-scenes work of Vinnie Ream, a twenty-one-year-old sculptress who was born in Madison, Wisconsin. Oral tradition in Washington, D.C., credits her with having been the decisive person in the power struggle that rocked the nation.

After Andrew Johnson succeeded to the presidency upon the death of Abraham Lincoln, trouble began almost immediately. Announcing his intention of following a policy of "reconciliation along with reconstruction" for former Confederate states, Johnson pointed out that such a program was precisely what Lincoln had planned.

Congressman Thaddeus Stevens of Pennsylvania was outraged, however. "Slavocracy must be wiped out!" he thundered in a speech to his home-state followers. "Every plantation of 200 or more acres must be carved into many pieces. Forty acres should be given to every adult male slave who formerly worked the place for his master. Then the rest should be sold, and the proceeds should be used to reduce the national debt incurred during the War of the Rebellion."

Harsh words by Stevens and others who shared his views were accompanied by stern measures. Both in the House of Representatives and in the U.S. Senate, bill after bill was enacted to wreak revenge upon the defeated South.

When President Johnson began to voice mild protests at these legislative actions, Stevens attacked him in public. "Though he occupies the White House," said Stevens, "he is an alien enemy—a citizen of a foreign state [Tennessee]—and therefore not now legally the head of our government."

This distortion ignored Johnson's total commitment to preservation of the Union during the Civil War and his courageous service as military governor of Tennessee after Union victories brought much of the badly divided state under Federal control.

March 2, 1867, saw passage of three major bills, all of which are now generally considered to have been unconstitutional. One re-established martial law in the South. Another relieved the president of his role as commander-in-chief of U.S. armed forces. The third—infamous as the Tenure of Office Act—required Senate approval of any presidential decision to remove an office holder whose nomination had been confirmed by the Senate.

On August 5, 1867, President Johnson took the initiative. Realizing that Secretary of War Edwin M. Stanton of Pennsylvania opposed nearly everything he did, Johnson asked him to resign.

Stanton flatly refused to do so.

Andrew Johnson then suspended Stanton and named war hero Ulysses S. Grant as his successor. Soon pressure from powerful political leaders persuaded Grant to withdraw from the cabinet. Stanton then took physical possession of the War Department, refusing to admit to the building Johnson's new appointee, Major General Lorenzo Thomas.

Although two earlier attempts to impeach the man from Tennessee had failed, Johnson's foes were confident that they could win in the climate they had created. Sponsored by the Joint Committee on Re-

President Andrew Johnson of Tennessee. [NATIONAL ARCHIVES]

Persuasive Dan Sickles was waylaid by Vinnie Ream. [PENNSYLVANIA HISTORICAL SOCIETY]

construction, an impeachment bill passed on February 24, 1868, by a vote of 126 to 47. Congressmen, who had sole power to act on this measure, debated the bill for only two days.

Action then shifted to the Senate, which has total responsibility for conducting the trial of an impeached official. Conviction requires votes of "two-thirds of the Senate, sitting as a judicial body."

Eleven separate articles of impeachment were drawn up on the theory that the president was sure to be convicted upon at least one of them. Johnson insisted that "I want to be present, to state my own case and to answer all questions." However, during the formal trial he did not appear in the Senate chamber.

With Chief Justice Salmon P. Chase presiding, the hearing began on March 5, 1868. Since fifty-four Senators were then in office, conviction required thirty-six votes. Radical Republicans were sure of thirty; Johnson had the firm support of eleven. That meant that, from the start the verdict was clearly in the hands of twelve Senators—all Republicans. By mid-April, five of the twelve had indicated that they would vote for conviction.

Testimony ended on May 7, and the Senate took a four-day recess before reconvening to vote. Pressure on the seven uncommitted lawmakers mounted daily. By May 11, four of the seven had decided to support the president; managers of the anti-Johnson forces then succeeded in having the decisive vote postponed from May 12 until May 16.

Two more uncommitted men came out for acquittal during this period. Now everyone in Washington knew that thirty-five senators would vote for conviction and eighteen would vote for acquittal. One man, who had kept silent throughout the trial, would swing the decision.

That man was Edmund Ross of Kansas.

Appointed in 1866 to fill an unexpired term, Ross arrived in Washington as "an intense radical and an earnest opponent of Andrew Johnson." He uniformly supported radical measures for Reconstruction; but when Johnson was impeached, he let it be known that he advocated a fair trial, regardless of the president's political views. At first he leaned toward conviction, but the growing flood of letters and telegrams from Kansas demanding that he help to oust the chief executive made him uneasy.

When the Senate re-convened on May 15, Senator Benjamin Franklin Wade of Ohio, who was next in line for the White House, had already selected members of his cabinet. Radicals were positive that Ross, the only man whose vote was in question, would yield to the pressure of his colleagues. To make sure that he did, they chose as emissary a handsome and persuasive spokesman, Gen. Dan Sickles, who had lost a leg at Gettysburg.

Rumors about the impending mission of Sickles reached the Washington studio of a well-known young woman. Vinnie Ream had come to the capital with her family at age fifteen and soon had managed to find a job as a clerk in the Post Office Department.

Without formal training, she began executing strikingly beautiful works of sculpture. Her medallion of an Indian chief came to the attention of Abraham Lincoln, who consented to pose for her in the White House for half an hour a day. Over a period of many weeks, she worked on a bust of the president that was nearly completed when he was assassinated.

When it was finished, the bust was such a good likeness that on July 28, 1866, she became the first woman to win a commission to execute sculpture for the U.S. government. Upon completion of a satisfactory life-size statue of Lincoln, Vinnie Ream was to receive ten thousand dollars.

She was hard at work upon the statue during months in which political foes of Johnson pressed their unrelenting attack upon him. Vinnie was acquainted with nearly all top leaders of Washington and was on casual terms with many others. Of those who dropped into her studio frequently to relax and chat, her favorite was Ross of Kansas, "my special Senator," who held the swing vote.

Ross had told her of the increasing pressure upon him early in the trial of President Johnson and of his growing uncertainty in the light of that pressure. So when Vinnie Ream overheard a conversation that identified Dan Sickles as the man selected to persuade Ross to vote for conviction, she moved into action.

On the day of the fateful vote, the sculptress found Sickles near the Senate chamber. Somehow she persuaded him to go with her to her

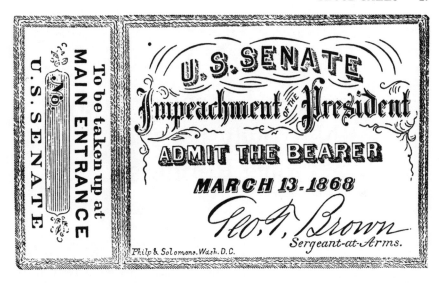

Ticket of admission to impeachment proceedings. [NATIONAL AR-CHIVES]

studio, "to give his opinion and advice about the Lincoln statue."

During the brief interval in which Sickles was with Vinnie Ream, Edmund Ross, pale with emotion, walked into the Senate chamber. There he cast the deciding vote of "Not Guilty!" by which Andrew Johnson escaped conviction.

Ross ended the trial of Johnson on charges that scholars now generally dismiss as false, flimsy, or both. His vote, however, ended his political career and he dropped out of public sight, finding work as a journeyman printer in New Mexico.

Angry and astonished foes of the president soon learned from Sickles why he had not performed as promised. Within a week after she had played a behind-the-scenes role in the hairbreadth escape of Andrew Johnson, Vinnie Ream was evicted from her studio.

Strangely, perhaps, it was Thaddeus Stevens of Pennsylvania who eventually rallied behind the girl who had helped to thwart his scheme. Stevens had Vinnie re-instated in her studio, where she made a plaster model which she took to Italy for veteran craftsmen to complete a white marble statue.

On January 25, 1871, in the rotunda of the Capitol, formal ceremonies were held. Many of the dignitaries who were present did not know that the statue they praised was the work of a Wisconsin girl who had helped to save Andrew Johnson from conviction by the U.S. Senate.

5

Abraham Lincoln's Body Narrowly Escaped Grave Robbers

Perhaps the strangest tale of a narrow escape by a chief executive revolves about events that took place on election night, 1876, when a gang of counterfeiters opened the tomb of Abraham Lincoln and almost seized his body as a hostage.

Had Patrick D. Tyrrell been a less persistent man, the final resting place of the man who issued the Emancipation Proclamation might be unknown today. Tyrrell, who headed the Chicago office of the U.S. Secret Service, had scored a coup by putting two notorious counterfeiters behind bars, but he believed that other members of their gang would not remain idle very long.

So Tyrrell sent a paid informer—a "mole" or "roper"—to infiltrate the gang believed to take orders from Big Jim Kinealy. Tyrrell's man, Lewis C. Swegles, made friends with the operator of The Hub, a saloon at 294 West Madison Street in Chicago.

Swegles, who had a record as a horse thief, boasted that he had bossed thieves who dug up cadavers and sold them to body-scarce medical schools. He didn't know that by gaining acceptance as "one of the best body snatchers in the midwest," he would be selected to take part in one of the most bizarre crimes on record.

Jack Hughes, ace passer of counterfeit money for the Kinealy gang, reached Chicago in midsummer and headed immediately for The Hub. There he conferred at length with the barkeeper, Mullen. Afterward, smiling behind his walrus mustache, Mullen told Swegles of their plan to steal the body of Lincoln.

Following Lincoln's assassination, the nation had mourned his death with an intensity unmatched even following the slaying of John F. Kennedy. Against the wishes of government officials, Lincoln's widow had insisted that her husband's body be interred in

Wealthy and influential Robert Todd Lincoln probably leaked word of the plot to kidnap his father's corpse. [DICTIONARY OF AMERICAN PORTRAITS]

Springfield, Illinois, rather than in the nation's capital.

Because there was little security at the cemetery, it would be almost absurdly easy for Hughes and Mullen to pry off a thin marble slab and extract the coffin underneath. When he heard the plan, Swegles agreed that a few good men could pull it off. But why?

Big Jim Kinealy wanted a hostage, someone whom the state of Illinois would want very badly. His men were running out of phony currency, and unless he could secure release of his engraver, Ben Boyd, who was beginning a ten-year sentence in the state penitentiary, one of the nation's biggest counterfeit rings would soon be out of business.

At his St. Louis headquarters Kinealy came up with the idea of seizing a hostage and swapping him for Boyd. At first he considered kidnapping a state official, but he knew it would be difficult and dangerous. Furthermore, kidnapping carried a stiff sentence.

Above every living person, the gang leader reasoned, *the state of Illinois treasures the body of Abraham Lincoln.* If Lincoln's body could be used as a hostage, it should be easy to work out an exchange that would free Ben Boyd.

It was this plot upon which informer Swegles stumbled in the course of what he had thought would be routine infiltration of a gang of counterfeiters. When he passed word along to Secret Service agents, they called him a liar and accused him of trying to work a doublecross.

Swegles persisted in his story and eventually convinced Patrick D. Tyrrell that he was telling the truth. Tyrrell, in turn, immediately conferred with Robert Todd Lincoln.

By then a prominent lawyer, Abraham Lincoln's son intimated that he had faith in the Secret Service's efficiency, but he called in operatives from the Pinkerton detective agency. He also probably was responsible for a news leak to the publisher of the Chicago *Tribune*.

Unaware that they had an informer in their ranks, the counterfeiters proceeded to develop detailed plans. They believed that a wagon carrying the body of Lincoln would attract absolutely no attention on the night of November 7, the date of a hotly contested presidential election. Gang members would travel from Chicago to Springfield by train, then wait until the cemetery attendants went home. Then they would snatch the body of Lincoln, cover it with straw, and use relays of drivers to reach Mount Pulaski, Illinois, before dawn.

Once turmoil over theft of the body subsided, it would be moved across the state line to the sand dunes of Indiana. Winds would soon obliterate all traces of activity, and the corpse could lie there—at an unmarked spot unknown to anyone outside the gang of conspirators—until Illinois decided to come to terms.

In St. Louis, Kinealy thought the plan to be so foolproof that he would no longer be satisfied by an even swap. In exchange for the body of the president, he would demand the release of Ben Boyd, plus "maybe $200,000 or so in used bills of $10 and $20 denominations."

Swegles listened to instructions brought from St. Louis, nodded, and occasionally offered suggestions. Such a job would require at least one more experienced man, he said. Billy Brown was just the right party for it; he'd taken part in many "resurrection" jobs.

Mullen and Hughes brought Brown in for drinks and questions; soon they agreed to use him. It wasn't until later that they discovered that Billy Brown was Agent Nealy of the U.S. Secret Service.

Mullen, Hughes, Swegles, and Brown left Chicago for Springfield at 9:00 P.M. on November 6. They rode the Chicago & Alton Railroad to their destination, then checked into a second-rate hotel without incident. As night approached, Billy Brown stole a horse and wagon, and behind a saloon Hughes found an axe he could use to break the lock off the tomb.

Leaving noisy election-night crowds behind, the would-be ghouls hurried toward the burial place of the slain president. Just as they had hoped, the large, unfinished monument was dark and deserted.

It took only a few strokes with the axe to break the padlock on the iron gate that barred passage in the vault. Once inside, Swegles flashed his bulls-eye lantern around and quickly located the sarcophagus.

By lantern light, Mullen pried off the slab of marble that served as a lid to Lincoln's resting place. Hughes and Mullen seized the heavy lead-lined casket and started to pull it out. Then they stopped to rest, ordering Swegles to bring up the wagon for the getaway.

This was the opportunity for which the informer had been waiting.

Nervously, he signaled men who were hiding behind the adjacent cenotaph.

Agent Tyrrell was in personal charge of the raid. With him were J. C. Power, custodian of the monument, two Pinkerton agency detectives, several Secret Service operatives, and a reporter from the *Chicago Tribune*. When Mullen and Hughes heard noises, they fled, dropping the coffin half out of the sarcophagus.

Having scored a complete scoop, next day the *Tribune* relegated election news to second place and ran on page one the story of the nearly successful attempt to steal Lincoln's body. In an era of conservative journalism, headlines of unprecedented size proclaimed:

HORRIBLE DASTARDLY ATTEMPT TO STEAL
THE BONES OF THE MARTYR–PRESIDENT

Few readers took the story seriously. Editors of a rival newspaper, the Chicago *Inter-Ocean*, called the account "a political concoction." At first the *Chicago Times* ignored the whole business. Within a few days, however, the Democratic paper was charging that Republicans had desecrated the grave of their party's great leader in order to say that Democrats had stooped to grave robbing on election night.

When a region-wide dragnet led to the arrest of both Mullen and Hughes, a shocked nation began to accept the truth. Belatedly, the *New York Times* published its first story about the case on November 22. Robert Todd Lincoln engaged noted attorneys to aid in prosecution of the criminals, and public indignation became so keen that there was fear of mob violence against the grave robbers.

Evidence against the conspirators was so overwhelming that there never was any doubt that the accused would be found guilty. . . . But *what* was their crime?

Illinois statutes made it a felony to sell a stolen cadaver, but there was no law against taking a body. The undertaker who had sold Lincoln's coffin testified that it was worth precisely seventy-five dollars.

As a result, on May 31, 1877, Mullen and Hughes were found guilty of "having conspired to steal a coffin belonging to the National Lincoln Monument Association." That brought each of them sentences of one year in the state penitentiary.

Given a few slight changes in a long chain of circumstances, the body of Abraham Lincoln might have been hidden in the sand dunes of Indiana and lost forever.

Present-day visitors to Oak Ridge Cemetery are shown a sarcophagus that proclaims, "Now He Belongs to the Ages." He really does, guides explain, for the sarcophagus is empty. As a safeguard against a repetition of events on election night 1876, the body of Abraham Lincoln now lies beneath ten feet of solid concrete.

CHAPTER
6

Teddy Roosevelt's Life Was Saved by a Speech

"**L**adies and gentlemen," announced Progressive Party aide Henry Cochems, his voice quavering, "I have something to tell you and I hope you will receive the news with calmness. Colonel Roosevelt has been shot!"

Hecklers in the Milwaukee, Wisconsin, auditorium shouted, "Fake! Fake!"

In response, Roosevelt pushed Cochems from the podium while unbuttoning his coat. As he whipped the garment open, persons sitting near the front saw that the whole lower half of his shirt was blood-stained. Many men gasped; one woman screamed.

"I am going to ask you to be very quiet," said the hero of San Juan Hill. "If you'll do that, I will do the best I can. . . ." Roosevelt spoke for eighty minutes—only occasionally referring to his text—then consented to go to Emergency Hospital for x-rays.

When Milwaukee physicians failed to locate the bullet, Roosevelt was moved to Chicago's Mercy Hospital, where he was placed under the care of the renowned Dr. John Murphy. Murphy's x-rays revealed that the trajectory of the bullet had been slightly altered by the thick manuscript of Roosevelt's speech and the edge of a spectacle case. Fired from a distance of six feet, the bullet plowed upward for about five inches and partly imbedded in Roosevelt's fractured fourth rib, about four inches from the sternum. It was described by Murphy as "much flattened and spread out of shape. It is crushed into the upper edge of the rib. Several small splinters of bone project near it."

Roosevelt's family physician, Dr. Alexander Lamber, examined the wound and the x-rays. "No doubt about it," he reported, "his speech saved the Colonel's life."

While the candidate was undergoing examination, authorities were learning about his assailant, John Flammang Schrank. According to Milwaukee police chief John T. Janssen, to whom he gave a voluntary

For ardent campaigner Theodore Roosevelt, the political rally was "a bully pulpit."

report, Schrank was born in Erding, Bavaria, and came to the United States at age thirteen.

"I have been personally acquainted with Roosevelt since he was police commissioner of New York in 1895," he said. "When I learned that he planned to start a third political party, I knew that spelled danger for the nation. He had already ruled the country from the White House for eight years. His plan to win a third term as president is a direct violation of principles laid down by George Washington."

Schrank, age thirty-six, talked fluently and freely. Reflecting upon comments made by his victim at the time of the shooting, fellow prisoner John Clanton said, "Schrank may have been insane at the time of the intended murder, but he is sane now. That is what every prisoner in this tier of the county jail thinks."

Experts disagreed with that verdict. Under their probing, the assailant had already told them of a series of strange dreams.

In a written statement he said that on September 15, 1901, at 1:30 A.M., he saw "President McKinley sit up in his coffin pointing at a man in monk's attire whom I recognized to be Theodore Roosevelt. The dead president [McKinley] said: 'This is my murderer—avenge my death.'"

Eleven years later, when Roosevelt launched his campaign for a third term in the White House as head of the Progressive or Bull Moose Party, Schrank began having frequent, vivid dreams. "Never let a third term party emblem appear on an official ballot," he wrote in a confession that he labeled a proclamation. "I am willing to die for my country. God has called me to be his instrument, so help me God."

At the bottom of the confession he penned the first lines of Martin Luther's hymn, "A Mighty Fortress is Our God."

As a result of a November hearing before Judge A. C. Backus of the Milwaukee municipal court, Schrank was ruled insane and was committed to a hospital for the insane in Oshkosh, Wisconsin, where he learned of Roosevelt's defeat by Woodrow Wilson. He expressed gratification and was prompted to demand the bullet he had fired into the candidate's body.

"That bullet is my property," he said. "In after years when I am regarded as a hero it will be valuable, so I want it to go to the New York Historical Society."

Schrank did not get his wish. Roosevelt carried the slug in his chest until his death in 1919. Because of the bullet's location, physicians had decided not to remove it at the time he was shot. It had never proved necessary to do so.

Writing about the bullet to his friend Charles G. Washburn on March 5, 1913, the former Rough Rider said of it, "I do not mind it any more than if it were in my waistcoat pocket!"

By then the full story of the attempted assassination was known. A long-time resident of New York City, Schrank had stalked his victim for more than a month, following him through six states before getting the right opportunity to shoot at close range.

On September 19 he wrote out a statement of his intention and hid it in the room he had rented in New York. Then he borrowed $350, bought a handgun, and took a train to Charleston, South Carolina, where Roosevelt was to speak.

From Charleston he followed the ex-president to Chattanooga, Tennessee, where he got within fifteen feet of the candidate, but lost his nerve. Schrank then trailed Roosevelt for several weeks through eight states and at least six times was on the verge of using his weapon. In Chicago on October 12 he had an opportunity for a clear shot, but he said he passed it up "because I didn't want to make the city look bad."

Checking Roosevelt's schedule as announced in newspapers, the would-be killer frequently preceded him to his next stop. Thus, he took a train to Milwaukee one day before Roosevelt was due to arrive and inspected the five-story Gilpatrick Hotel in which Roosevelt was to stay. Settling for a room in a smaller hotel nearby, Schrank registered under the name of Walter Scott and paid the bill of one dollar in advance.

When his quarry left the Gilpatrick for his car the following morning, Schrank was on the sidewalk waiting. He stood nearly motionless until Roosevelt was about six feet away, already standing in the automobile that was to carry him to the municipal auditorium for his scheduled speech.

A short man with thin lips and dreamy eyes, Schrank attracted no

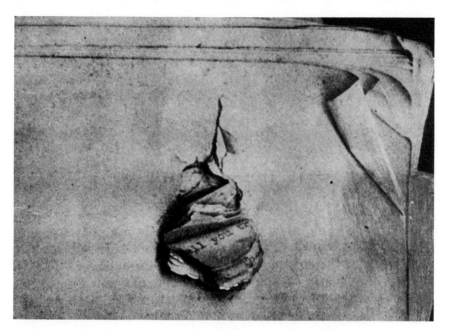

Manuscript of speech that saved Teddy Roosevelt's life.

attention until he fired his weapon. Ex-athlete Elbert Martin, the candidate's stenographer, tackled the gunman and bystanders pulled him to the pavement.

Roosevelt reacted by shouting, "He doesn't know what he is doing! Don't strike the poor creature!"

Members of the crowd ignored that message and began to shout, "Lynch him! Kill him!"

Roosevelt waved his arm and managed to restore a semblance of order. "He pinked me, Henry," he said to Henry Cochems, who handled details of his speaking engagements.

Knowing nothing about his assailant, the man running as a Bull Moose candidate signaled officers of the Milwaukee police force. "Take charge of this man," he directed, "and see that no violence is done to him."

At the auditorium, Dr. S. L. Terrill made a quick examination and insisted that Roosevelt return to his hotel. "You have lost considerable blood," he pointed out, "and we do not know where the bullet has lodged." Roosevelt shook his head and strode to the platform to interrupt Cochems and deliver his speech.

A year later Roosevelt was able to joke with friends about the 38-caliber bullet in his chest. "It's a good thing Teddy has poor terminal facilities," one friend laughed. "Folded, that manuscript added up to 100 pages." So Roosevelt became the only U.S. president whose life was saved because he never learned when to quit when he had a chance to speak!

CHAPTER

7

The Saga of White House Security

S ecurity for the nation's chief executive and for members of his family has been an up-and-down business. Punctuated by war and assassinations, two centuries of history have moved from no protection at all to as close to total security as can be provided. No aspect of the presidential story is more revealing of the profound changes in public attitudes and in the office of the presidency itself.

On April 7, 1791, George Washington set out on a long journey. Riding in a four-horse coach, he planned to visit major cities of the southeast, traveling southward along the coast and returning by an inland route that would take him through Augusta, Georgia; Camden, South Carolina; and Winston-Salem, North Carolina.

Secretary of State John Jay was worried about bad roads. "You should lower the hang of your carriage," he suggested, "and exchange your coachman for a pair of postilions." Under such an arrangement, two seasoned horsemen, presumably armed, would have been ahead of the coach riding lead animals.

President Washington demurred. He often used a postilion named Giles, but the fellow was "still too indisposed to ride the journey." So the president settled for a coachman and a valet. His only other attendants were men needed to care for the horses.

He rode through forests and swamps, stopped at whatever tavern or inn happened to be on the road, crossed rivers on flatboats, and drank whatever beverage his host for the night provided. For his journey of 1,887 miles he took along not one guard.

In contrast, no one knows for sure how many police, soldiers, and Secret Service agents were on hand to guard Ronald Reagan on March 30, 1981. However, hundreds of them proved unable to prevent John Hinckley, Jr., from wounding the chief executive and three other persons outside a Washington hotel.

Prior to Hinckley's attack, use of bullet-proof glass and other protective measures was already standard. After Hinckley managed to hit

Beginning with his inauguration, James K. Polk treated security measures casually, ordering that no armed guards be seen by the public—wood engraving. [THE ILLUSTRATED LONDON NEWS]

Reagan with a bullet from a cheap snub-nosed "Saturday night special" revolver, tighter measures were imposed. Unscreened persons were no longer permitted anywhere near the president at public or private functions. Guests at White House parties were required to pass through metal detectors to gain admission. Reporters were no longer given the president's daily schedule, as in the past. Persons closely acquainted with the president were able frequently to distinguish the outline of a bullet-proof vest beneath his suit coat.

Old Washington hands say Thomas Jefferson was the first president to give security a thought. In his plan for the grounds of what was then called the Executive Mansion, architect Jefferson provided for gate lodges in which guards could be—but were not—stationed.

War has always caused at least a temporary tightening of security. During the War of 1812, fearing the British attack that actually came to the capital, James Madison stationed a guard of 100 soldiers to protect his wife and the Executive Mansion. When the invasion of Washington actually occurred, the force was not strong enough to defend the place, and Dolley Madison had to flee to the Virginia countryside. No other first lady—or chief executive—has ever been in comparable danger from enemy forces.

Though an invading army no longer posed a threat, James Monroe tried to keep a guard or guards stationed in the vicinity of the White

House, given that name for the paint applied after the residence was burned by the British.

John Quincy Adams scoffed at such pretentious and undemocratic ways and did away with security. Andrew Jackson followed his example. At his first inaugural reception, hordes of persons pushed into the White House, roaming eagerly from room to room. An editor of the *Washington City Chronicle* wrote, "The noisy and disorderly rabble in the President's House brought to my mind descriptions I had read, of the mobs in the Tuileries and at Versailles" at the time of the French Revolution.

As in the days of John Quincy Adams, the Jackson White House was open to office seekers of all kinds. They simply walked in the front door and climbed the stairs to the office area. "No matter how dirty, how drunk, or how muddy, a citizen has a right to see his president," Jackson is said to have ruled. Military officers, politicians, farmers, lawyers, auctioneers, messengers, and a horde of nondescript others joined petitioners for office in elbowing their way to the president's desk.

Old Hickory claimed to have received at least 500 letters containing death threats. Not only did he ignore them, Congress did also. Not until 1948 did it become an offense punishable by a fine of $1,000 or five years' imprisonment, or both, to threaten the life of a president through the U.S. mail.

Jackson's hand-picked successor, Martin Van Buren, often walked into a church service unattended even by an unarmed servant. When riding about the capital on horseback he frequently—but not always—permitted a single servant to go with him. But he began the practice of stationing police at the door of the White House. When political foes ridiculed Van Buren for this undemocratic practice, he retorted by explaining that he simply wanted to keep "the mobocracy from intruding themselves at levees."

Public opinion was sharply divided on the issue of whether or not a police officer had any business trying to screen White House visitors.

During the tenure of John Tyler, Van Buren's security measures went by the board. A famous visitor, Charles Dickens, penned a detailed account of his initial call at the White House. Escorted by a friend, he "entered a large hall, and having twice or thrice rung a bell which nobody answered, walked without further ceremony through the rooms on the ground floor, as divers other gentlemen (mostly with their hats on, and their hands in their pockets), were doing very leisurely."

Dickens then wandered upstairs into what he called "a waiting-room" that held fifteen or twenty persons. Soon a black messenger escorted him into a smaller room in which the president sat behind a table covered with papers. No sentry guarded the door; no attendant stood behind the chief executive; no one asked the visitor to produce identification or even to state his business.

James K. Polk, Zachary Taylor, and, a bit later, Franklin Pierce perpetuated the relaxed mood of the Tyler administration. A visitor described the White House as "surrounded by labourers roughly dressed, who stand or lounge on the grass; there are no guards, no police; all are behaving themselves properly." Taylor habitually mingled with the public on the grounds of the executive residence. Both he and Pierce often strolled unattended along Pennsylvania Avenue.

Millard Fillmore was less democratic and more cautious. He sensed personal danger in mounting North/South tensions; so he had a guardroom erected "at the president's gate." From the Washington arsenal guards were supplied with "four musketoons fixed with bayonets, each supplied with 20 rounds of ammunition." Rules were established for the screening of visitors.

Franklin Pierce, who succeeded Fillmore, put a stop to the screening of visitors and permitted the public at large to promenade in the East Room. He reduced guards to two night watchmen who—together—were paid $1,000 per year.

By the time Lincoln won the White House with less than 40 percent of the popular vote, radical changes had taken place. Traveling to the capital for his inauguration, the president-elect slipped through Baltimore in the dead of night, with railroad bridges and trestles under guard.

Platoons of soldiers lined the route of the inaugural parade and guarded the president at most public and ceremonial occasions, but at the White House there were few security measures, in spite of Mary Todd Lincoln's nervousness. On most days the front door was open for fourteen hours, with the unarmed attendant often absent from his post. None of the parlors had watchmen on duty. Members of the public often walked in at night and wandered about, sometimes even going upstairs, without being challenged.

April 10, 1865, saw the president overrule officers of the Metropolitan Police. Instead of stopping crowds at the Pennsylvania Avenue fence, said Lincoln, anyone who wished to enter the grounds must be permitted to do so, to celebrate Robert E. Lee's surrender at Appomatox.

Four days later, on Good Friday, the president and his wife went to the theater to see a performance of *Our American Cousin*. When his sole bodyguard, a Washington policeman said to have been thoroughly drunk, stepped from the box to go into the alley for another drink, John Wilkes Booth had the opportunity for which he had been waiting: a clear shot at close range.

Hysteria over the death of Lincoln failed to bring tight security to his successor, however. Andrew Johnson's first levee, on February 27, 1866, was "a regular jam" at which officers soon gave up futile attempts at checking of visitors.

Three years later, an aide found Annie O'Neil lurking in a White House corridor with a double-barreled pistol. Questioned, she said, "I am sent by God Almighty to kill Andrew Johnson."

"Her old-fashioned weapon was not loaded," said a newspaper report of the incident, "but had it been, she'd have been there, anyway."

Soldiers were brought to the White House to aid policemen at the time of Johnson's last levee, on February 22, 1869. That gesture proved futile. "The crowd was so great that customary regulations could not be enforced. The mass of people became so dense as to be uncontrollable. Policemen stationed at doors were swept away by the throng and carried onward with the living tide."

For an hour a day, three times a week, Ulysses S. Grant ordered aides to admit the general public "male and female, without distinction of costume or color." After having shaken hands continuously for an hour, the chief executive customarily "took his constitutional walk to the Capitol and back"—often wholly unattended. However, yielding to pressure from advisors, he reluctantly consented to have a few plainclothes officers mingle with guests at receptions.

James A. Garfield inherited a relaxed White House and did nothing to change the mood. Only after his assassination were armed guards posted at the gates with instructions to admit no one without a pass.

Chester A. Arthur, the vice president who succeeded slain Garfield, stubbornly refused the services of a bodyguard. He was, however, the first chief executive to have a valet.

During the mid-1880s it was common knowledge in Washington that anyone who wished to do so could walk into the White House to shake the hand of Grover Cleveland. Benjamin Harrison, his successor, was "thoroughly alarmed" when a young male knocked down a doorkeeper and eluded another. Having heard the crashing of glass, the president hurried to see what was happening. He grabbed the intruder, pinned his arms to his sides, and held him until help came.

Grover Cleveland strengthened security at the White House, but he was virtually unguarded while on an 1887 speaking tour. [ATLANTA HISTORICAL SOCIETY]

A flood of threatening letters during Grover Cleveland's second administration frightened his wife so badly that she persuaded him to strengthen security. When guards were increased from two policemen to twenty-five patrolmen and two sergeants, many citizens were outraged. A Washington newspaper reported that "Mr. Cleveland not only keeps off the sidewalks; he seldom goes driving—and when he does so he is under the protection of two detectives who follow the White House carriage in another vehicle."

William McKinley was fatally wounded by a shot from a .32 Iver Johnson revolver on September 6, 1901. Only then, in the aftermath of the third assassination of a president in thirty-six years, were strong measures taken. Secretary of the Treasury Lyman J. Gage took matters into his own hand and assigned Secret Service agents to guard Theodore Roosevelt.

Since that time, the number of professional bodyguards assigned to the president and his family has increased in geometrical fashion. Yet Washington lore insists that Teddy Roosevelt put a gun in his own pocket "in order to have the chance to take down an assassin before he can shoot me" and tried to avoid the use of Secret Service personnel.

Although guards surrounded his carriage and armed soldiers lined the rooftops of nearby buildings during Lincoln's second inaugural, the artist carefully omitted these signs of tight security. [HARPER'S WEEKLY]

Whether that belief is true or not, the police unit assigned to guard the White House during his administration consisted of only six men, who spent part of their time frolicking with Archie and Quentin Roosevelt, the president's sons. When he went on horseback rides, the president ordered guards to remain far behind, barely in sight.

Because of World War I, security increased at the White House, yet Woodrow Wilson persisted in taking long solitary walks, even when streets were piled high with ice and snow.

Mrs. Florence Harding made a lasting innovation when she borrowed one of the president's Secret Service men for her own use, but she kept him so busy working as a messenger and general handyman that his vigilance was often relaxed. President Calvin Coolidge then added to the circle of those given Secret Service protection by demanding that Ed Starling be assigned as bodyguard for his son John Coolidge at Amherst College.

In the aftermath of the assassination of John F. Kennedy, and attempts upon the lives of Gerald Ford and Ronald Reagan, the president of the United States is today one of the most heavily guarded men in the world. Family members and presidential candidates are routinely assigned bodyguards, and the White House is largely closed to the public.

It is interesting to speculate how George Washington, Andrew Jackson, or even Abraham Lincoln would react to the changed mood of the country and the increased protection offered their successors today if they could get past security and wander incognito in the familiar halls of the White House.

Part Two

Undercover Stuff

Grover Cleveland served two non-consecutive terms, making him the twenty-second and twenty-fourth presidents.

CHAPTER

8

A Life and Death Drama
Took Place at Sea

Calling on millionaire investor Elias C. Benedict of New York, U.S. Secretary of War Daniel Lamont came directly to the point.

"The President needs the use of your yacht for several days," he said. Benedict, who shared a joint bank account with President Grover Cleveland in the era before political leaders were expected to put their assets into blind trusts while in office, asked no questions.

"Give me a few days to get things ready for him," responded the yacht owner whose friends frequently addressed him as Commodore. "I'll have the *Oneida* in the East River no later than June 30, if that is agreeable."

Lamont nodded assent, returned to the nation's capital, and called reporters to his office. Mrs. Cleveland, who was expecting her second child, was quite uncomfortable, he told them. Hence, the entire family would spend the five weeks before the coming session of Congress in their summer home at Buzzard's Bay, Cape Cod.

Almost as an afterthought, the cabinet member, who doubled as White House spokesman, added that "President Cleveland plans to relax a few days by taking a cruise with Commodore Benedict."

The announced plans were so routine that few newsmen were at the railroad station when the president and his family boarded their private car shortly after noon on June 30, 1893. All veteran reporters knew that Cleveland heartily despised them and preferred not to see them under any circumstances. He was particularly angry over their incessant buzzing around his pregnant wife, Frances, and his only daughter, Ruth.

Not yet two years old, Ruth had drawn so much attention that makers of candy were alleged to have cashed in on her name—by introducing the Baby Ruth candy bar.

With Ruth in tow, Frances Cleveland—who had made big news by her marriage to her long-time guardian, thereby at age twenty-one

By refusing to permit an autopsy of the dead president, Mrs. Warren G. Harding raised questions about his death that have never been answered.

becoming the youngest-ever mistress of the White House—proceeded to Cape Cod. With only Lamont accompanying him, the president drove to a Manhattan dock and boarded the waiting yacht *Oneida*.

Members of the crew had already been briefed. Cleveland was having trouble with two teeth, they were told. While aboard, he would have them extracted and would remain on the yacht a few days to rest and recuperate. "He has asked a few friends to join him for the cruise," Lamont added.

Early on the morning of July 1, "the president's friends" took off their business suits and donned surgical gowns. According to one account, the 250-pound chief executive was propped in a chair against a mast. He was about to undergo anesthesia, and it was feared that, if prone, his corpulence could cause complications.

A more credible story insists that despite his bulk, Cleveland was stretched upon an operating table below the deck, just under a skylight.

Whatever his position, the president insisted upon smoking one more good cigar before surgeons began their work. Neither he nor they realized that tobacco probably played a significant role in the cancer that had developed in the upper left section of his mouth.

Cleveland himself had discovered the rough spot, about the size of a twenty-five-cent coin. "Not a syllable must be allowed to reach the press," the president told his physician, Dr. R. M. O'Reilly. "Everyone knows that we are in a financial crisis; and I am expected to lead the nation out of it. If the public knew of my condition, business failures and foreclosures would quadruple in a matter of days."

Cleveland's assessment of the nation's mood at the height of the Panic of 1893 was probably correct. Already, a stock market crash had been followed by failure of 600 banks and at least 16,000 businesses. News that the president had cancer would have triggered new and desperate reactions.

So the surgeons operated behind closed doors. Two teeth close to the cancerous area were extracted in a matter of minutes. Joseph D. Bryant, Cleveland's personal physician, then presided over removal of the upper left jawbone. Once that procedure was completed, renowned dental specialist W. W. Keen of Philadelphia inserted a cheek retractor. Widely used in France, the device was relatively unknown in the United States.

Once Cleveland's jaw was carefully packed, it took close scrutiny to observe anything unusual about his appearance. To avoid leaving a visible scar, all surgery had been performed within the mouth.

Sixteen days later, surgeons again bent over the president, removing more tissue because examination suggested that they had failed to excise all of the cancer. As soon as healing began, Dr. Kasson C. Gibson inserted a temporary upper jaw made of rubber. This device caused Cleveland's face and voice to appear nearly normal. It was later replaced with a permanent cast of the removed jawbone. Attached to an upper dental plate, it could be taken out, cleaned, and inserted again with ease.

On September 9, 1893, less than sixty days after Cleveland's second surgery, Dr. Bryant again hurried to the White House. This time, he came in the role of obstetrician to preside over the delivery of Esther Cleveland, the first child born in the White House to a president.

In November, the still-recuperating chief executive won a congressional battle over legislation that many economists of the era credited with bringing the Panic of 1893 to an end.

So much national frenzy had focused upon fiscal affairs that few persons who came in daily contact with Cleveland even suspected that he had faced a personal crisis. However, someone who had been aboard the yacht at the time of the secret operation leaked a few details to Philadelphia reporter E. G. Edwards. Edwards wrote a vivid story, but even the editor of the *Public Ledger,* in which the news item appeared, indignantly denounced the account as "an infamous exploitation of a toothache." Other news media ignored Edwards's story or denounced it as a fabrication.

Grover Cleveland's cancer did not recur. He died of heart failure and had been in his grave for nine years when Dr. W. W. Keen decided to go public with a graphic account of the secret operation. When it appeared in the *Saturday Evening Post* in 1917, the nation finally learned what had taken place in secret at sea.

Much earlier, White House aides shut the door to newspaper reporters and members of the general public when Abraham Lincoln came down with smallpox. Especially virulent during the winter of 1863–64, it claimed a great many lives. To avoid public panic, Lincoln's secretary casually announced that the president was "suffering from a mild attack of varioloid, causing him to be indisposed for a few days."

Since no other member of the White House family or staff contracted the often-fatal disease, it is believed that Lincoln was infected while visiting sick and wounded soldiers in Washington hospitals.

When Woodrow Wilson suffered a paralytic stroke in 1919, it was impossible to pretend that he was hale and hearty, but a lid of secrecy was clamped down tightly. Except for Mrs. Wilson and a few physicians and intimates, no one else knew the president's condition.

This time, the closed-door policy backfired. Rumors proliferated: zeal in campaigning for the League of Nations had caused the president to lose his mind; he had become the victim of venereal disease; marital strife had reached such a peak that Wilson had attempted suicide to escape his domineering second wife.

Only when Wilson recovered sufficiently to walk haltingly with a cane did it become generally recognized that he had, indeed, been incapable of exercising the powers of his office for weeks or even months.

Wilson's successor, a very ill Warren G. Harding, was taken from a train in San Francisco in early summer, 1923. His sickness had developed in Seattle, where food poisoning was suspected, but San Francisco doctors said that he seemed to have a severe case of pneumonia.

Precisely what caused the president to die soon after will never be known, however. Mrs. Harding refused permission for an autopsy. (Even though Abraham Lincoln had been shot in public, an autopsy was performed.) Mrs. Harding's main preoccupation at the time of her husband's death seemed to be to obliterate the scandals of his administration by burning as many of his personal papers as she could.

Quite a different kind of secrecy was practiced during the administration of Franklin D. Roosevelt.

A victim of polio in 1921, through great effort he had first learned to drag himself crablike across the floor to escape his greatest fear, that he might be trapped by fire. Later, in therapy at Warm Springs, Georgia,

Rare wheelchair photo of Franklin Roosevelt from FDR's Splendid Deception. [THE FDR LIBRARY]

he learned to walk a short distance using leg braces or crutches.

As president, Roosevelt often wore a braid-looped Navy cape cut unusually long to conceal his braces. Of course, Americans in general, and the press in particular, knew that the chief executive was severely crippled. However, all during Depression and wartime years an informal and unwritten code of "open secrecy"—without parallel in modern times—developed among the press corps. Reporters seldom referred to Roosevelt's physical handicap and, though they regularly had opportunities to do so, few photographers included his brace-gripped legs or his wheelchair in their shots.

CHAPTER

9

Three Strikes . . . And In!

A TERRIBLE TALE

A child was born out of holy wedlock. Now ten years of age, this sturdy lad is named Oscar Folsom Cleveland. He and his mother have been supported in part by our ex-mayor, who now aspires to the White House. Astute readers may put the facts together and draw their own conclusions.

Greatly condensed here, that front-page story appeared in the Buffalo, New York, *Evening Post* on July 21, 1884. According to the detailed account, the local leader who had received the Democratic nomination for the presidency on July 8 had long been involved with a woman of questionable reputation, Maria Halpin.

Buffalo tradition holds that agents working for Republican nominee James G. Blaine came to the city within days after Cleveland said he considered himself ready for the White House. It took them only a short time to discover that gossip linked the Democratic nominee with others who visited the home of Maria. Whether or not her "sturdy lad" was actually called Oscar F. Cleveland is uncertain.

When wire services began to pick up the story, national leaders of the Democratic party held a hasty conference. They then wired their nominee for instructions. His telegram became a classic in the annals of American politics.

"Tell the truth," Cleveland instructed.

The truth, it soon developed, was that Cleveland had visited the woman regularly, along with several other Buffalo men. When she became pregnant, gallant Cleveland, the only bachelor in the group, stepped forward to protect his married friends and took partial financial responsibility for the child.

"The boy could be mine," he confessed. "I do not know."

Editorial writers and cartoonists had a field day. Republican money subsidized mass production of a campaign song that bore the name of H. R. Monroe. Identity of the writer has never been positively established, but he was widely believed to have been then-popular song writer Monroe H. Rosenfeld. Issued by the National Music Company of Chicago under the title "Ma! Ma! Where's My Pa?" the song had four stanzas and a chorus:

Little Tom Tid was a frolicsome kid,
A cute little cuss, I declare,
With eyes full of fun,
And a nose that begun
Way up in the roots of his hair.
Jolly and fat was this frolicsome brat,
As he played thro' the livelong day,
But one eve, to his cost,
His papa got lost,
And he and his ma sang a lay, Oh,
CHORUS
Ma! Ma! Where is my Pa?
Up in the White House darling,
Making the laws, working the cause,
Up in the White House, dear.
Ma! Ma! where is Papa?
Up in the White House, darling:
Making the laws, working the cause,
Up in the White House, dear.

Verses dealing with Little Tom Tid "in the folds of his loose-fitting dress" who "cried for his daddy in vain" made it impossible for any informed voter to be unaware of scandal in Cleveland's past. It was the chorus, belted out with special enthusiasm, that really caught the public imagination. Many political pundits agreed: "Cleveland has had it; he's finished."

Just to make sure he was properly polished off, political foes dragged another skeleton out of the big man's closet. During the Civil War, Cleveland had resorted to provisions of the Conscription Act of 1863 under which he paid $150 to hire a substitute to serve in the Union army while he stayed comfortably at home.

What he did was legal, and most voters knew it. But the implied cowardice constituted a second, and perhaps fatal, strike against the man who had stepped to the political plate with bat in hand.

Grover Cleveland made no serious effort to inform the public about his actions during the Civil War. At the time he had bought his way out

*Frank Beard's 1884 cartoon was calculated to bar Grover
Cleveland from the White House.* [PUCK MAGAZINE]

of the army, he already had two brothers in uniform and a mother and
two sisters at home to support, but he seldom spoke of these matters
even under fire.

His casual response to the second charge was characteristic. Unlike
modern candidates, Cleveland never mounted a serious campaign. He
made few public appearances and gave fewer speeches. While charges
of scandal echoed and re-echoed in newspapers, he stayed at his desk
in Albany and worked at the job of governor.

In some major cities, Democrats tried to capitalize on the first item
in the smear campaign. Using the same melody, they transformed the
refrain and in their torchlight parades sang it like this:

Ma! Ma! where's my pa?
Gone to the White House,
  Ha, Ha, Ha!

Experts on both sides of the bitter contest conceded that while
Cleveland had a chance to carry the solid South, the pivotal state was

New York. Hence it was there that Cleveland's rivals pulled out and used their third fast ball.

Practically unknown nationally until nominated for the presidency, the man from Buffalo was dubbed "Grover the Good" by his admiring followers.

"How can a hangman be called 'good' under any circumstances?" countered Republican leaders. To make that question memorable, they issued broadsides telling the story that constituted a capsule biography of Cleveland.

In 1872, as sheriff of Erie County, New York, Cleveland had taken personal charge of the hanging of Patrick Morrissey, condemned to death for stabbing his mother. Five months later, on February 14, 1873, the sheriff again presided over an execution. This time the victim was Jack Gaffney, a professional gambler convicted of committing murder during a brawl over a card game.

Regardless of the felons' offenses, two hangings served as a hook on which to hang an emotion-charged nickname, the "Hangman."

While broadsides about the "Hangman" were being distributed, political foes made one last desperate effort to capitalize on the paternity issue. Just one week before the election, his opponent, James G. Blaine, met with New York clergymen who were indignant that a man of questionable morals might go to the White House. During the meetings the Reverend S. D. Burchard of Murray Hill Presbyterian Church, referred to the Democratic Party as "the party of Rum, Romanism, and Rebellion."

Candidate Blaine made no objection to the allusion. As a result, Rum, Romanism, and Rebellion made headlines in most New York newspapers on October 29 and 30.

Reacting to the slur, angry Irish Catholics turned out to vote in record numbers, and their last-minute rally put the state in the Cleveland column by 1,149 popular votes. Nationally, in the electoral college Cleveland took 219 votes to Blaine's 182.

When he learned that his opponent had conceded, the scandal-plagued candidate called reporters to his Albany office and joked about having been the first man in American politics to experience three strikes—and in!

"I am glad that those who smeared me so professionally have conceded," the big man said. "Very glad. There will be no trouble. If they had not conceded, I should have felt it my duty to take my seat anyhow!"

CHAPTER

10

Though Woodrow Wilson
Appeared Strong,
He Was Fragile As a Reed

Washington, D.C., 5 April 1919
To: Admiral Cary T. Grayson
  In my opinion the President must in some dramatic way clear the air of doubts and misunderstandings and despair which now pervade the whole world situation.
  He must take hold of the situation with both hands and shake it out of its present indecision, or political sabotage and scheming will triumph. Only a bold stroke by the President will save Europe, and perhaps the world.

Woodrow Wilson's private secretary was responding to an urgent cable from the president's personal physician in Paris. Having been asked what could be done to get favorable publicity about the "Big Four" conference then under way, Joseph P. Tumulty laid the burden of action squarely upon the shoulders of the man he adored.

In a message to Congress on January 8, 1918, Wilson had made public his carefully prepared ideas about a treaty to bring the Great War [World War I] to a formal close. His famous Fourteen Points had been announced with the realization that France and England did not share the same goals for the peace as those of the United States.

Then Wilson left for France to meet with Lloyd George of Great Britain, Georges Clemenceau of France, and Vittorio Orlando of Italy, as the Big Four, to dictate the terms of peace to the Central Powers.

"I have come here to make peace on the basis of my Fourteen Points

Publicly ebullient, Woodrow Wilson agonized in private.

and on no other basis," the President of the United States had told foreign reporters upon arrival in Paris. He then issued an oblique warning to the Allied prime ministers, saying that he would withdraw from the conference and cut off U.S. economic assistance unless they reached agreement upon "just terms with Germany."

Now suddenly and unpredictably, the strong-willed chief executive seemed to have had a collapse of nerve. On April 7, he was committed to fight for his beliefs; on the following day he capitulated on one of the central issues: reparations to be exacted from defeated Germany. Warned by another telegram from Tumulty that "a withdrawal at this time would be a desertion," he continued to take part in discussions, but never again with the fire and determination shown earlier.

William C. Bullitt, a member of the American Peace Commission who subsequently resigned because of objections to the Treaty of Versailles, was present at the epoch-making conference. He later collaborated with Sigmund Freud, the father of modern psychoanalysis, in a volume that analyzed Woodrow Wilson's emotional and mental life.

"Wilson preached magnificently, promised superbly, then fled," the two scholars wrote in 1966. His flight from his stated position, which amounted to sudden surrender, had drastic effect upon world history. Abandonment of his Fourteen Points eventually fueled skyrocketing inflation in Germany, which led to economic collapse of the defeated nation and the rise of the Nazi movement that produced Adolf Hitler and World War II.

What happened to Woodrow Wilson at so crucial an hour? Bullitt and Freud speculated that the man whom citizens regarded as having a will of iron simply wilted under pressure. They attribute this to a brief nervous breakdown similar to longer ones he experienced both before and after the Paris conference.

According to the authors, Wilson suffered at least fourteen periods in which "nervousness, dyspepsia and headaches became so severe as to interfere seriously with his work." Collectively, these intervals of breakdown amounted to approximately eight years of his fifty years of adult life.

Numerous accounts of Woodrow Wilson's life note, in passing, that he was plagued by indigestion from childhood and that, as a result, he regularly used a stomach pump upon himself while he was president of Princeton University and later in the White House.

According to Sigmund Freud, some of Wilson's early problems stemmed from being regarded by his peers as "a laughed-at 'mama's boy.'" He never participated in sports or games of any kind and, when queried on this topic, he fended off questioners by saying that he was sickly, nervous, and had poor eyesight.

Originally planning to become a Presbyterian minister, young Woodrow Wilson had to withdraw from Davidson College because of severe indigestion. The same thing happened at the University of Virginia law school. Later, after he had been at Johns Hopkins only thirty days, he wrote to his sweetheart, "I over-taxed my eyes yesterday and am today suffering with a dull ache through my head and with throbbing orbs that refuse all use."

Nevertheless, he received his Ph.D. in political science, thus being the only president with an earned doctorate.

Ten years after leaving Johns Hopkins, his lifelong pattern of symptoms suddenly reached an acute stage while he was on the faculty at Princeton University. Indigestion and nervousness threw him upon his back on the floor, where he writhed and twisted. To his aching head and pounding stomach was added a sudden muscular ailment that deprived him of the use of his right hand, essential to the completion of the biography of George Washington upon which he was then working.

Despite his precarious health, in 1902 Woodrow Wilson was elected president of Princeton University. Within four years, however, his symptoms returned. His head seemed to pound worse than ever before, his stomach seemed to be full of pins and needles, and his right hand again became virtually useless. This time he also had severe pains in his left arm and leg. Having exhibited many of the classical symptoms of a "nervous breakdown," he woke up on a May morning in 1906 to discover that he could not see from his left eye.

As in earlier periods of complete debility, some of which lasted for many months, this attack also eventually passed. He regained his sight and the use of his right hand, and—briefly—ventured out on trips to fill speaking engagements without taking along a stomach pump.

Wilson's early months in the White House were relatively relaxed and easy; and his correspondence indicates that he enjoyed the new power he held. But the 1915 sinking of the steamer *Lusitania* by a German U-boat brought an end to his peaceful era. As the stress mounted, all of his earlier symptoms returned with new fury. At the momentous Paris conference where he suddenly surrendered upon issues he had publicly vowed to fight for, his mental turmoil was so great that he was for a time incapable of arriving at rational decisions.

Numerous other chief executives suffered from debilitating depression and similar ailments. None, however, came close to Wilson's frequent periods of helplessness.

Some analysts believe that John Adams was manic-depressive because his moods swung so wildly. Depression was commonly triggered either by a bout of illness or by anger at criticism by someone whose opinion he valued.

Thomas Jefferson suffered long periods of near helplessness from migraine headaches. John Quincy Adams freely admitted to having periods in which he experienced "uncontrollable dejection of spirits." In some of these low periods, he contemplated suicide.

Franklin Pierce's severe depressions stemmed partly from his struggles against alcoholism, which developed during a series of personal losses and tragedies. James A. Garfield went through what he called "years of darkness," or prolonged mental depression, as a young adult. William Howard Taft was often irritable and frequently depressed, but these moods were brief.

William McKinley, like Wilson, suffered a breakdown during college years, possibly from overwork. Unlike episodes in the life of the wartime leader, McKinley's early problems offered no threat to anyone. Neither did Warren G. Harding's complete mental-emotional collapse at age twenty-four. He went to a Battle Creek, Michigan, sanitarium for treatment by Dr. J. P. Kellogg. Though he later

Franklin Pierce. [BRADY STUDIO PHOTOGRAPH, NATIONAL ARCHIVES]

William McKinley (left) *at the 1899 presentation of a ceremonial sword to Admiral George Dewey.* [LIBRARY OF CONGRESS]

returned for brief periods of rest, he was never regarded as having lost control of himself.

One chief executive, usually ranked at the top or close to the top when the lasting influence of U.S. presidents is pondered, once wrote to an intimate friend:

> I am now the most miserable man living. If what I feel were equally distributed to the whole human family, there would be not one cheerful face on earth. Whether I shall ever be better, I cannot tell; I awfully forbode I shall not. To remain as I am is impossible; I must die or be better, it appears to me.

Abraham Lincoln's self-analysis is more revealing than the label that physicians of the day attached to his periods of depression: hypochondria. Some Lincoln scholars hold that his often quoted jokes and jibes were used to cover up the dark side he did not wish the public to see.

Viewed in the light of modern findings about effects of long-continued high-level stress, it is not strange that the man who presided over the Civil War frequently suffered from severe depression. Yet the total humanity of the man was never more clearly revealed than in February 1864.

When the White House stables caught fire, several carriage horses died in the smoke and flames, along with a carefully groomed and well-fed pony that had been the favorite of William Wallace ("Willie") Lincoln. The loss of Willie's pony, two years after the death of Lincoln's twelve-year-old son threw the commander-in-chief of U.S. armed forces into what biographers pass over as "a state of depression that held him many days."

Like ordinary citizens, presidents experience high and low moments in their mental health. They can be utterly devastated and laid low by difficulties, whether personal or global, yet also rise above them to moments of glory.

CHAPTER
11

Strange Dreams
and Ominous Nightmares

Strange dreams and ominous nightmares have on occasion appeared to residents of the White House, as they do to citizens in humbler homes. Because of the importance of the dreamers, their nighttime phantasies take on special significance.

Perhaps the strangest White House dream came to Abraham Lincoln in early April 1865. By this stage of the Civil War, Lincoln had received and filed at least eighty threat letters in an envelope labeled "assassination." Although he kept them, he insisted that they did not cause him worry. With this background, he had an "amazingly real" dream "of the most startling import." It was recorded in detail by Ward H. Lamon, his Illinois law partner who worked at his side during the White House years.

Because a recent dream haunted him, the president began talking with Mrs. Lincoln and Lamon one evening. It had come to him a few evenings earlier, and he could no longer keep quiet about it.

After staying up very late, the president quickly fell asleep and began to dream. Everything was deathly still, but he heard the sounds of many persons sobbing. Walking from room to room in the White House, the president finally found the grieving people in the East Room.

"Before me was a catafalque," Lincoln later told his wife and friend. Many "were weeping pitifully." He asked a soldier, "Who is dead in the White House."

The soldier answered, "The President. He was killed by an assassin!"

A loud burst of grief from the crowd caused Lincoln—the dreamer—to wake up. "I slept no more that night; and although it was only a dream, I have been strangely annoyed by it ever since," he said.

Mrs. Lincoln said she wished he had not told the dream; she did not believe in such things. But a few days later, on April 14, Good Friday

Ford's New Theatre, where Abraham Lincoln was shot.

on the calendar, the Lincolns attended a play at Ford's Theatre. The rest is history.

Tradition holds that a much earlier Lincoln experience was not so lightly dismissed by his wife. It came to him after his nomination, but before his election to the presidency. Weary after a hard day in the courtroom, Lincoln lay down in his Springfield, Illinois, bedroom.

In the never-never land between full wakefulness and sound sleep, he reared his head from the pillow and thought he saw himself in the mirror, but with two images of his own face. It puzzled him that the second image was pale, much like the face of a dead man.

When he spoke about the vision at breakfast, Mary Todd Lincoln's face became troubled. A deep believer in the supernatural, she meditated briefly before telling her husband, "It means that you will win the election and will be elected for a second term. But I fear that the pale face warns that you may not survive your second four years in the White House."

Julia Tyler, who was never charged with having dabbled in the occult as was Mary Todd Lincoln, nevertheless took dreams very seriously.

In a terrible nightmare she saw ex-president John Tyler dying in Richmond, Virginia, where he had gone as a delegate to the Confederate Congress.

She hurried to Richmond and found him quite well, but two days later he died suddenly. Because he was supporting the rebel cause, his death was ignored in the nation's capital where he was once revered.

John Quincy Adams' wife Louisa never hinted that she knew of her husband's dream life. As an adolescent in Paris, the future president had become enamored with an actress but never got up the courage to tell her of his ardor. However, he dreamed of her for many years.

"Of all the ungratified longings that I ever suffered," the president once admitted, "that of being acquainted with her, merely to tell her how much I adored her, was the most intense."

Lyndon B. Johnson experienced a number of intensely frightening dreams that were repeated many times over.

As a boy, he had dreamed of paralysis. As president, he dreamed he was sitting in a White House chair incapable of moving. It was made worse by his being able to hear subordinates bickering over the division of power.

That recurrent dream haunted Johnson every time it came, until he got out of bed, took a flashlight, and trained its beam on a portrait of Woodrow Wilson. Somehow, he found peace by looking at Wilson's face and touching the portrait with his fingers.

Lyndon B. Johnson.

On other nights, Johnson dreamed of swimming in a river but never getting close to either shore.

At age fifteen he had a vivid dream in which he saw himself locked up in a cage. Years later, a White House dream showed him sitting at his desk, fastened to his chair with a heavy chain. Then after a myocardial infarction in 1955, total inability to move haunted his White House dreams night after night. Johnson found himself, unable to move, in a big chair that sat in the middle of an open plain. Stampeding cattle were headed directly toward him, but he could do nothing except cry—uselessly—for help.

His conversations and notes fail to indicate that he glimpsed any connection between that recurring nightmare and the military stampede that constituted America's undeclared Vietnam War.

Much earlier, James A. Garfield also experienced recurring nightmares. Their details differed from those of Lyndon Johnson, but a central theme was similar. Over and over Garfield dreamed of being lost in a primeval forest—stark naked.

Another presidential dreamer, Woodrow Wilson, knew the background of his nightmares. As President of Princeton University, he fought long and hard with Dean Andrew F. West. When their bitter struggle seemed to end with West's defeat, Wilson went to Bermuda for a vacation. While there, he began having nightmares about the Princeton tug of war.

Eventually Dean West came out on top; his defeat had been only temporary. "Wilson felt destroyed," a biographer wrote. This incident was a factor leading him to give up academic life to enter the political arena.

But Wilson could not escape Andrew F. West by making that change in vocation. Again and again, the Princeton dean appeared to him in his dreams. While doughboys were fighting Germans in World War I, the president was fighting West in his dreams. These dreams continued to haunt him, even in his final illness.

Real life struggles lay behind the recurring dreams of Lyndon Johnson and Woodrow Wilson. Though less dramatic than his vision of assassination, a recurrent dream of Abraham Lincoln defies explanation.

He revealed it in a Cabinet meeting of April 14, 1865, at which Gen. Ulysses S. Grant was present. Secretary of the Navy Gideon Welles was so impressed that he made notes and included the president's comments in his own diary.

Someone asked if there was any news from Sherman, and Grant replied that he expected to hear something any hour. Lincoln spoke up to say that news would come soon, and it would be good, because "he had last night the usual dream which he had preceding nearly every great and important event of the War."

Welles pressed him for details about that recurrent dream.

Lincoln recalled it always related to water, and he was always in a ship that "was moving with great rapidity toward an indefinite shore."

He had had the same dream, said the weary chief executive, before the battles of Fort Sumter, Fort Donelson, Stones River, Vicksburg, Wilmington, Antietam, Gettysburg, and others. Thus he was sure it again meant "great good news soon"—probably from Sherman.

Voicing skepticism, General Grant ventured that such a dream might, indeed, mean that news was on the way, but it wouldn't necessarily be good.

"Great events did, indeed follow," that very evening, Gideon Welles wrote. But Grant's foreboding was right. The news was of the assassination by John Wilkes Booth.

12

Secrets of the Stars

Many Americans laughed when they saw the May 16, 1988, cover of *Time* magazine. Others expressed disbelief and shock. A few were outraged.

At the White House, members of the president's staff initially tried to deny that there was any truth to the magazine's cover story: "Astrology in the White House." Soon they admitted there might be a little truth to the story that an unidentified astrologer had been consulted by Nancy Reagan. However, they hastened to stress that no policy decisions were ever influenced by the professional reader of horoscopes.

"Truth of the matter is that former [White House] chief of staff Donald Regan deliberately took pot shots at the First Lady," one off-the-record comment from an aide of the president began.

The furor began with the publication of former White House chief of staff Donald Regan's memoir, *For the Record*. The book contained numerous tidbits about astrology. He called reliance upon this "black art" perhaps "the most closely guarded secret of the Reagan White House."

Members of the news media pounced upon the story and began digging. Soon the San Francisco *Chronicle* surmised that the astrologer was Joan Quigley. *Time* reporters then learned that she was introduced to Nancy Reagan by television talk show host Merv Griffin.

Although she had been at the White House only once, for a state dinner, Quigley revealed that she and the First Lady often conversed by telephone. The wife of the president had wanted advice concerning the timing of the president's travels and such events as the signing of the 1987 U.S.–Soviet nuclear weapons treaty.

"No policy or decision in my mind has ever been influenced by astrology," the president rather lamely insisted to reporters on May 3, 1988.

That is not the story that Donald Regan told. According to him, numerous White House decisions were made, or announced, after receiving a go-ahead from the San Francisco astrologer. No one knows

Nancy Reagan consulted an astrologer for assistance in timing important ceremonies and events.

the exact truth of the matter; even what the president and his ex-aide meant by "decisions" is unclear.

This was not the first time that stories have surfaced of otherworldly consultations in the White House. According to an earlier unofficial advisor to a chief executive, during the Civil War President Lincoln attended numerous seances. Many of them were reputedly led by Nettie Colburn, a trance medium so small and slender that some persons thought her to be a child.

Her account of experiences in Washington, entitled *Was Abraham Lincoln a Spiritualist?*, was published in Philadelphia in 1891. According to it, Nettie came to wartime Washington to visit her brother, a wounded soldier in a hospital near the capital.

An initial contact with Mary Todd Lincoln, wife of the president, led to seances at the White House at which Lincoln was present. At least, that's the tale told by the medium who was given a federal job on recommendation of Mrs. Lincoln. Nettie vowed that she held seances in the White House several times.

In one of her trances, Nettie said she gave Lincoln a detailed message from Daniel Webster. As a result, Lincoln stopped hesitating and issued the long delayed Emancipation Proclamation.

Sir Arthur Conan Doyle studied the case carefully and came to the conclusion that in this instance "spirit intervention proved to be of importance in the world's history."

Abraham Lincoln, February 9, 1861 (C. S. GERMAN, PHOTOGRAPH, NATIONAL ARCHIVES)

A later message, which also led to decisive action by the president, urged him to boost soldiers' morale by visiting military camps. That he actually paid such visits at the risk of his life is a matter of record. Whether or not his chief motive for making these visits stemmed from advice received in seances is not known. Little beyond the word of Nettie Colburn supports such a view. However, Lincoln's enemies denounced him in print as "a practicing spiritualist." A physician, Dr. Edward J. Kempf, called him "the victim of organic and emotional neurosis."

This much is certain: Long a devout reader of the Bible, Abraham Lincoln was convinced that visions and voices can reveal hidden truth. He secured, and is believed to have read, a number of books on spiritualism; and he once confided to an intimate that he always had a strong tendency toward mysticism.

What Lincoln himself termed a tendency toward mysticism was powerfully reinforced by tragedy. First, in February 1850, his three-year-old son Edward Baker ("Eddie") died after what his father described as "52 days of sickness."

Then in February 1862, eleven-year-old William Wallace ("Willie") became seriously ill in the White House. Born just nine months after the death of Eddie, of all the Lincoln boys, he was most like his father.

Initially thought to have an infection or to have suffered from exposure, blue-eyed Willie was eventually diagnosed as suffering from "bilious fever." It now appears more likely that he had a severe attack of malaria. To make matters worse, Willie's younger brother Thomas ("Tad") soon developed what seemed to be the same malady.

Willie died on February 20, and his body, embalmed by a new process, lay in state for several days in the Green Room of the White House. By the time funeral ceremonies were conducted in the East Room on February 24, Tad was somewhat better, but he was not out of danger for another two weeks.

Even though Tad got well and the oldest son, Robert, was safe at Harvard University, the loss of their third son in the same month as their second was devastating to both mother and father. Mary Todd Lincoln was confined to her room for a month and was unable to function for three months. Long afterward, she wore a black straw bonnet topped with a black crape bow signifying her mourning for Willie.

Abraham Lincoln was often in tears. He placed a band of black crape around his hat in memory of Willie and was still wearing it when he gave the Gettysburg Address in November 1863.

Once her convulsions of weeping began to subside, Mary Todd Lincoln, who never again went into the room where Willie died or the room in which his body lay in state, began consulting psychics. She was desperate for contact with the spirit of the dead boy.

Her husband, who had received numerous overtures from spiritualists, responded to none of them until after Willie's death. It was at this point of emotional crisis that Nettie Colburn, the young trance medium, was introduced to the first lady and soon afterward to the president.

According to Nettie, Lincoln received messages from Napoleon Bonaparte, William Wilberforce, and the Marquis de LaFayette. She was also the medium through whom advice was transmitted from George Washington and Benjamin Franklin.

Lincoln himself never wrote of these explorations into the mystic realm, and few biographers mention the events described by Nettie Colburn. Those who do usually conclude that the president was drawn into spiritualism by the death of Willie.

No such traumatic event can account for the long and absorbing interest of another first lady in astrology and fortunetelling. Florence King De Wolfe Harding, a strong-willed woman regarded as gullible by some of her intimates, turned to mediums for advice before and during her White House days.

Secret Service agent Harry Barker, who smuggled the first lady's consultants into and out of the White House, inserted notes from a reading into her household account book in February 1923.

Florence (Mrs. Warren G.) Harding received warnings from an astrologer.

"The President," warned the message transmitted by an astrologer, "is coming under some very powerful influence and needs to safeguard his health. . . .

"The opposition of the Moon to the Sun and Saturn in his horoscope shows that he cannot depend upon his friends. He would be suspicious of the ones he *should* trust and *trust* those he *should* be suspicious of."

That dire warning, which went unheeded by the president, was delivered just six months before his sudden death and less than thirty days before Secretary of the Interior Albert B. Fall of New Mexico resigned at the beginning of the revelations about the Teapot Dome Affair, the oil-lease scandal that remained Washington's largest before Watergate and the Iran-contra affair.

There is no authoritative evidence that crucial national or international questions ever have been settled by any president on the basis of advice from an astrologer or a medium. But, like many ordinary persons, at least three chief executives—all influenced by their wives—seem to have taken the occult seriously enough to listen to "advisors" not on the federal payroll.

CHAPTER

13

What the World's Most Powerful Men Have Thought of Their Job

"**B**eing President of the United States," said Harry Truman, "is like riding a tiger. A man has to keep on riding, or be swallowed!"

Thomas Jefferson, the third chief executive, once described the presidency as "a splendid misery." Said he, "To myself, personally, it brings nothing but unceasing drudgery and daily loss of friends."

George Washington, always cautious in speech, admitted that "so much is unexpected, so many untoward circumstances may intervene, that I feel an insuperable diffidence in my own abilities."

Theodore Roosevelt, whose winning campaign was credited in part to the fact that six other candidates effectively split votes that did not go to Republicans in 1904, tried to be philosophical. "It is a dreadful thing to come into the Presidency this way," he wrote, "but it would be a far worse thing to be morbid about it. Here is the task, and I have got to do it to the best of my ability—and that is all there is to it."

Months later and self-described as infinitely wiser, the former Rough Rider ruefully confessed: "I do but little boxing now, because it seems rather absurd for a President to appear with a black eye or a swollen nose or a cut lip."

Leaving the White House, Teddy Roosevelt sent a farewell note to William Howard Taft, his successor; "Ha ha! *You* are making up your Cabinet. *I* in a lighthearted way have spent the morning testing the rifles for my African trip. Life has compensations."

When it came Taft's turn to yield the presidential mansion to Woodrow Wilson, he said, "I'm glad to be going—this is the lonesomest place in the world."

In the previous century, John Quincy Adams had summed up his administration in a single sentence: "The four most miserable years of

Harry Truman compared life in the White House with the wild animal act at the circus.

my life were my four years in the Presidency."

Andrew Jackson, his successor, was more direct in his speech. "I can say with truth," he confided to intimates once he had taken the oath of office, "that mine is a situation of dignified slavery."

"Though it is true that I occupy a very high position," said James K. Polk, "I do so because I am the hardest working man in the country."

Having given Abraham Lincoln a brief tour of the White House, according to custom, James Buchanan turned to his successor and exclaimed, "If you are as happy, my dear sir, on entering this house as I am at leaving it and returning home, you are the happiest man in the entire nation!"

From my boyhood up, it was my ambition to be President. Now I am President of one part of this divided country, at least; but look at me! I wish I had never been born! It is a white elephant on my hands, and hard to manage. With a fire in my front and rear; having to contend with the jealousies of the military commanders, and not receiving that cordial co-operation and support from Congress that reasonably could be expected, with an active and formidable enemy in the field threatening the very life-blood of the government,—my position is anything but a bed of roses.

—Abraham Lincoln

Abraham Lincoln was at his best as a speaker when he abandoned the precise rules that govern usage and resorted to the vernacular. In a relaxed moment he responded to a query about the office he held by declaring, "I am like the man who was tarred and feathered and ridden out of town on a rail. When they asked him how he felt about it, he said that if it were not for the honor of the thing, he would rather have walked."

Reminding critics that he did not ask for the job but had tried to do his duty in it, Ulysses S. Grant lashed out at the press and the public by saying, "I have been the subject of abuse and slander scarcely ever equaled in political history."

Rutherford B. Hayes skillfully played upon distinctions between slaves and freedmen in his assessment of the office. "The escape from bondage into freedom is grateful indeed to my feelings," he said as his term drew to an end. "Even with my constitutional cheerfulness, the burden of office has not been light. Now I am glad to be a *freedman*."

> *My day is frittered away by the personal seeking of people, when it ought to be given to the great problems which concern the whole country. Four years of this kind of intellectual dissipation may cripple me for the remainder of my life.*
>
> *What might not a vigorous thinker do, if he could be allowed to use the opportunities of a Presidential term in vital, useful activity! Some Civil Service Reform will come by necessity after the wearisome years of wasted Presidents have paved the way for it.*
>
> —James A. Garfield

William Howard Taft saw the presidency as the loneliest job in the world. [LIBRARY OF CONGRESS]

During his first term in the White House, Grover Cleveland declared that "the office of President has not, to me personally, a single allurement."

Two elections later, back in the office, the man who may have wished that his opponent, Benjamin Harrison, had won re-election moaned. "I believe I shall buy or rent a house near here, where I can go and be away from this cursed constant grind."

Reflecting upon his career, ex-president John Adams wrote to a friend, "If I were to go over my life again, I would be a shoemaker rather than an American statesman."

Thomas Jefferson made notes about a 1793 cabinet meeting in which George Washington was in a rage. According to Jefferson, the Father of His Country informed his top aides that "*by god* he had rather be in his grave than in his present situation."

"My God!" James Garfield echoed decades later. "What is there in this place that a man should ever want to get in it?"

Woodrow Wilson didn't use strong language; he simply tried to analyze the position he held. "The office of President," he concluded, "requires the constitution of an athlete, the patience of a mother—and the endurance of an early Christian."

At another time Wilson concluded that "I never dreamed such loneliness and desolation of heart possible."

"A few hair shirts are part of the wardrobe of every man," Herbert Hoover later said. "The President differs from other men in that he has a much more extensive wardrobe."

"I knew this job would be too much for me," admitted Warren G. Harding in a moment of candor.

Harding also came to realize, "I am not worried about my enemies. It is my friends who are giving me trouble."

He also lamented, "This White House is a prison. I can't get away from the men who dog my footsteps. I am in jail."

"I'll be damned if I am not getting tired of this," confessed William Howard Taft. "It seems to be the profession of a President simply to hear other people talk."

Harry Truman, who confessed that he often repeated pet ideas and obsessive themes, thundered, "I have said it time and again, and I will keep on saying it, that I would rather have a Medal of Honor than be President of the United States."

James A. Garfield saw his term in office as "four years of intellectual dissipation."

John Quincy Adams called the office he held "perpetual motion and crazing cares." Cleveland described it as "this cursed constant grind," and Martin Van Buren termed it "toilsome and anxious probation."

However, some saw compensations in the job. "I have long ago used up my time," Dwight D. Eisenhower once told a sympathetic audience, "but you know, there is one thing about being the President—it is hard to tell him to sit down."

John F. Kennedy tried to be philosophical about things he couldn't change. "I know that when things don't go well they like to blame the President," he said, "but that is one of the things Presidents get paid for."

Unable to be with his dying father, Calvin Coolidge—who would become noted for brevity of speech—summed up the office in just five words: "It costs to be President."

14

Mental and Physical Health Have Been "Issues" in Many Presidential Campaigns

Mental or physical health has been an issue in at least a dozen presidential elections. Some charges were made openly, buttressed by cartoons and derisive songs. More were made by implication and were spread chiefly by word of mouth.

In 1836 Whigs wouldn't have openly dared to allege that Martin Van Buren had homosexual tendencies. Nice people didn't talk about such a subject. So Van Buren's opponents blasted the Democrat as "effeminate."

A broadside issued in Philadelphia thundered the charge without using the label:

> *Like some of the notorious Tory governors of Colonial times, Van Buren laces himself up in corsets. Wearing his elegant snuff-colored coat with velvet collar and orange cravat with lace tips, he presents an altogether exquisite appearance. WHAT THIS COUNTRY NEEDS IS A MAN!*

The insinuations about Van Buren gained their credence because he had been a widower for seventeen years when he made a bid for the presidency. In those days when a frontiersman who lost his wife was likely to re-marry within thirty days of the funeral.

Though Whigs lost the top spot in the 1836 campaign, their gambit put "a man's man" into the vice presidency. Kentucky-born Richard M. Johnson, the only vice president ever to be elected by the Senate, was an eccentric and careless dresser with a long military career. He also had two illegitimate children. When the electoral college couldn't agree on a man for the number two spot that year, the contest went to the Senate. On February 8, 1837, Johnson was chosen partly

Cartoonists and political foes were not at all subtle in their suggestions that dimunitive Martin Van Buren was homosexual.

because he was judged to be lustily normal—a good balance for the "effeminate" chief executive.

Relatively few voters of the last century considered use of alcohol a major moral issue, but a man who couldn't hold his liquor didn't have the stamina citizens wanted in a chief executive. At least four contenders for the presidency were accused of staggering from saloons. Though this made them seem "soft in the head," three of them won, anyway.

The 1840 Whig candidate, William Henry Harrison, was blasted by Democrats as practically living on hard cider. Democrats turned this into an asset that helped to bring him 234 out of 304 electoral votes.

Henry Clay of Kentucky did not fare so well. Although he was prone to get tipsy when depressed, his opponents said little about this issue in the election of 1832. However, in 1844 when it seemed he really was headed for the White House, his rivals mocked him as "getting tanked every night and sitting around dreaming of himself as King Henry I." Since Democrat James K. Polk beat Clay by only sixty-five electoral votes, no political analyst has been able to determine exactly how his drinking affected the outcome of the race.

Andrew Johnson, Lincoln's running mate in 1864, was blasted as "being so weak he threw up after a few glasses of brandy." Actually a moderate drinker under most circumstances, the false accusation did not prevent Johnson from winning.

U. S. Grant received more criticism over alcohol than any other man who has served in the nation's top office. By mentioning the matter in public, Horace Greeley, his Democratic opponent, violated an unwritten law, the "gentleman's understanding"—that such issues were left to supporters and newsmen.

Greeley's backers distributed many handbills at rallies including cartoons showing Grant as weaker than his bottle. A few such derisive sketches were published in magazines. Although there were good grounds for wondering whether the bottle might again get the upper hand over Grant, as it had early in his career, voters largely ignored the issue and put their trust in the man who had won Civil War battles after his losing bout with alcohol.

Earlier, Lincoln had been the target of one of the most scurrilous campaigns up to that time. With the Union bogged down in war, Democrats nominated Gen. George B. McClellan and touted him as being "robust, active, physically vigorous."

Lincoln was derided as "being subject to long periods of depression," "too frail in body to bear up under heavy burdens of the days," and "prone to melancholy." Only the allegation of physical frailty had no foundation in fact.

It was during this campaign that stories were circulated alleging that Lincoln had seriously considered suicide after the death of Ann Rutledge, the sweetheart of his early manhood. "Sick in the head, sick in the heart, and makes me sick in my stomach," was the description many opponents used as Lincoln pondered whether or not to run for a second term.

When the electoral votes were counted, rock-hard McClellan received 21 votes against 212 for his "sick" opponent.

In 1880 Republican vice presidential nominee Chester Arthur was tagged with the effeminate label. In spite of his height—six feet—Arthur fostered the charge by dressing like a fop. To make things worse, his Democratic opponents circulated a charge (that was true), "He doesn't even put on his own clothes; he likes to be *groomed by his valet.*"

Grover Cleveland, always a moderate but never a heavy drinker, was pictured as having serious problems with the bottle during his 1888 bid for a second term. His Republican opponent, Benjamin Harrison, who exploited the issue, received nearly 100,000 fewer votes than Cleveland, but defeated him by 58 to 42 percent in the electoral college.

Down, but far from out, Cleveland tried again four years later. Again he was the target of attack on "moral issues," as the Republicans called them. As if that was not enough, followers of Populist candidate James B. Weaver created a new version of the "sick" charge.

Despite his size, stalwart Chester A. Arthur was ridiculed as "effiminate."

They charged that "Mr. Tubby won't live to serve his term. He's so fat his heart is likely to quit any minute."

Cleveland, who had trimmed off fifty pounds to cut his weight to a mere 250, trimmed Weaver by 255 electoral votes. He became the only man ever to win nonconsecutive terms as chief executive.

Mrs. Ida McKinley, rather than her husband, William, was the target of self-appointed guardians of "full and total health in the White House" in 1896. She suffered from severe nervous disorders that may have been linked with a form of epilepsy. "Such a woman ought not to be mistress of the White House," Democrats charged. "Vote for the great William J. Bryan—solid as an oak post and not encumbered by any weakness." Despite Mrs. McKinley's long-established pattern of nervous seizures, "Post-oak Bryan" went down to defeat.

Before the campaign of 1908, old cartoons that depicted Cleveland as obese were pulled out, refurbished, and re-titled for William Howard Taft. Taft's best friends conceded—in private—that even though he stood six feet, two inches tall, 340 pounds was not a healthy weight. Nevertheless, Republican physicians competed with one another in issuing statements about lack of correlation between weight and heart attacks. Democrats compiled statistics that claimed to show exactly how much life expectancy was reduced by every extra ten pounds. In the election voters put their weight behind Big Bill Taft, and he won a resounding victory over "healthy" William Jennings Bryan.

Woodrow Wilson's health was a major issue in the campaign of 1916. Although he took pains to avoid photographers except when rested and relaxed, many news photos betrayed the strain under which he worked. *Nervous, irritable,* and *exhausted* were three of the labels most frequently (and accurately) applied to him by Republicans, who

Dwight D. Eisenhower's heart attack—never concealed from the public—did not keep him from the campaign trail or the White House.

came very close to edging him out of the second term he cherished.

Polio victim Franklin D. Roosevelt appeared to be a sitting duck for his rivals in the campaign of 1932. They found it unnecessary to say anything about his illness—it was enough to congratulate him publicly on "the great progress made toward full recovery." Strong and vigorous, Herbert Hoover was skillfully portrayed as being "strong enough to step forward in manly fashion to lead the nation in its march up the road to economic recovery." But polio-stricken Roosevelt received twenty-three million popular votes to stalwart Hoover's sixteen million and won in the electoral college by a margin of nine to one.

Dwight D. Eisenhower's 1955 heart attack may have cost him some popular votes in the election of 1956, but in the electoral college "the man with a malady"—as opponents labeled him—took 442 votes to Adlai Stevenson's 89.

Political foes considered trying to make Ronald Reagan's age a factor in the 1984 campaign but decided that his immense popularity made that issue irrelevant.

Regardless of how robust a presidential candidate may be, opponents sometimes try to tag him with a physical, emotional, or mental weakness. Maladies attributed to "sick" candidates have ranged from real, though exaggerated, conditions to imaginary. Judging from the record, once inside the polling booth voters pay little or no attention to the real or fancied state of a candidate's health.

15

Off-trail Glimpses and Intimate Insights

Ulysses S. Grant spent years on battlefields where he grew accustomed to seeing men killed and wounded by the thousands. But when he sat down to eat, he refused rare meat because he couldn't stand the sight of blood. Grant flatly refused to bathe in the nude and at age sixty said that no one had ever seen him naked since he was a boy.

During his White House years, William Howard Taft weighed over 300 pounds. After being stuck in a bathtub, he ordered a special tub from the J. L. Mott iron works for his personal use. When it arrived, four White House staff members crawled into it to have their photograph taken.

During the Spanish–American War of 1898, Theodore Roosevelt led the famous Rough Riders. Fearful that his weak eyes would cause him trouble in combat, he always took along at least half a dozen extra pairs of spectacles—in his pockets, his hat, and sewn into his uniform.

Thomas Jefferson was sometimes absent-minded, so much so that he once proposed establishing a system of annual elections to be held on February 29.

George Bush also got mixed up on dates. During his campaign, he made a dramatic reference to the anniversary of the attack on Pearl Harbor—on "September 7, 1941," instead of December 7, 1941.

Zachary Taylor was tardy in acknowledging that he had been nominated for the presidency. A delay of several days was brought about by Taylor's refusal to pay ten cents postage due on the formal letter notifying him of the nomination.

Many of the letters that Abraham Lincoln wrote with his own hand were stuck in his hat, then hand delivered by the chief executive. At his death, the only money in his pocket was a five-dollar Confederate note.

George Washington took his slave Hercules with him to the capital in Philadelphia. At intervals of just less than six months, he always sent Hercules back to Mount Vernon for a few weeks because Pennsylvania law gave freedom to a slave who spent six uninterrupted months in the state.

Jimmy Carter was the first chief executive to be born in a hospital. All thirty-eight of his predecessors were born at home.

While serving as vice president, Gerald Ford tried without success to memorize the first name of each of the approximately sixty Secret Service agents assigned to guard him and his family.

Franklin D. Roosevelt's famous wheelchair had a special piece of equipment attached during war years—a gas mask for use in the event of a sudden attack by the enemy.

President John Quincy Adams did not like ordinary persons to sit in his presence. To make it difficult for visitors to do so, he was careful to see that there were never enough chairs to go around.

Harry Truman was ambidextrous, able to use one hand as well as the other. That meant that he could throw the ball with either hand on opening day of baseball season. James A. Garfield was also ambidextrous. He could simultaneously write in Latin with one hand and in Greek with the other.

When they didn't want White House staff members and guests to know what they were saying, President and Mrs. Herbert Hoover conversed with one another in Chinese.

Skilled architect Thomas Jefferson made a structural addition to the White House during his tenure as president. Under his direction, workmen added to the building a hen house—complete with classical columns.

During years that Abraham Lincoln occupied the White House, milk was peddled from the back door of the mansion.

Once a tailor by trade, President Andrew Johnson let it be known that he wore only custom-made suits—tailored by himself.

President and Mrs. Benjamin Harrison, first occupants of the executive mansion to have electric lights, were terrified of the newfangled source of power. They were so afraid to touch switches that they often slept with every light glowing.

Andrew Jackson had the unique distinction of being thrown in jail at approximately age thirteen for refusing to follow the orders of British soldiers.

Chester A. Arthur, who casually admitted that he had at least eighty pairs of trousers and often changed clothes several times a day, inspected the White House carefully after he was elected president. He refused to move into the place until twenty-four wagon loads of furniture were hauled off and sold and the entire place was redecorated.

During his Civil War years, Ulysses S. Grant's orders sent uncounted thousands of men to their death in battle. But he went on record as regretting that twice in his life he killed wild animals.

On the day before James Monroe's inauguration, Congress appropriated $20,000 to furnish the White House. Monroe spent the money on new furniture from France and sold his own furniture to the government. He itemized the inventory to ¼¢—and eight years later he bought back the entire lot for exactly what he had charged for it.

On a Vermont excursion in the spring of 1791, Thomas Jefferson and James Madison went on a carriage ride together. Stopped by a rural law officer, both were arrested for riding in a carriage on Sunday.

One day in 1853 Franklin Pierce accidentally ran down an elderly Washington woman with his horse. Mrs. Nathan Lewis was not injured, but Constable Stanley Edelin arrested Pierce. (Nothing in the U.S. Constitution makes a chief executive immune from arrest.)

During his tenure as president, Ulysses S. Grant one day drove his carriage west on M Street entirely too fast. A black police officer ran from the sidewalk, grabbed the bridle of the president's animal, and put the chief executive under arrest. Grant's rig was briefly impounded; after posting a twenty dollar bond, he walked back to the executive mansion.

By blood and by marriage, Franklin D. Roosevelt was related to eleven other presidents: George Washington, John Adams, James

Madison, John Quincy Adams, Martin Van Buren, William Henry Harrison, Benjamin Harrison, Zachary Taylor, Ulysses S. Grant, William Howard Taft, and Theodore Roosevelt.

While engaged in a vigorous boxing match in 1904, Theodore Roosevelt suffered severe damage to his left eye. It deteriorated so rapidly that after 1908 he was unable to see with it. He concealed the handicap so skillfully that less than a dozen members of his family and intimate staffers were aware that he read and saw with only one eye.

As a boy, Andrew Jackson habitually slobbered and instantly fought anyone who laughed at the habit he was unable to control. He did not learn to stop this practice until nearly fully grown.

Calvin Coolidge apparently was preoccupied with his hair. He often had his head rubbed with vaseline while eating breakfast and more than once had his hair cut during a meal.

John Tyler's second marriage resulted in the birth of David Gardiner Tyler on July 12, 1846, more than fifteen years after the birth of the president's last child by his first wife, Letitia Christian, and three months after the proud father's fifty-sixth birthday. Six more little Tylers came along during the next fourteen years.

During the Civil War a single Ohio regiment—the twenty-third—enrolled two future presidents during a period of only four days. William McKinley enlisted as a private on June 23, 1861; Rutherford B. Hayes was commissioned as a major on June 27.

At age twenty-eight, Teddy Roosevelt served eight days as a volunteer deputy sheriff. He chased thieves over more than 300 miles of rugged terrain, caught all three culprits, and was paid a fee of $50.

Delivery of an 8,445-word inaugural address—the longest on record—was William Henry Harrison's only significant accomplishment as president. Shortly after having talked for an hour and forty minutes in a brisk March wind without hat or overcoat, he became ill. He died exactly one month later.

When John Adams was named U.S. minister to Great Britain, his friend Thomas Jefferson came from France to visit him. Together they went to Stratford to pay homage to Shakespeare at his birthplace. While touring the house in which the playwright was born, both men cut chips from a chair and took them away as souvenirs.

Abraham Lincoln, first chief executive to invite blacks to the White House as guests, strongly favored overseas colonization as a solution to the racial problems that plagued the North and the South. He backed the idea of sending American blacks to Liberia but also investigated both Haiti and Central America as places where they could colonize.

When George Washington was elected the first president, the nation had only eleven states. North Carolina did not ratify the Constitution and join the union until six months after the election, and Rhode Island held out for more than a year.

Ulysses S. Grant had a superstitious dread of retracing his footsteps. If he carelessly walked past his destination, instead of turning around and walking back on the same street, he would try to make a circuit that would bring him to his destination by another path.

Thomas Jefferson prided himself upon his "republican views," quite different from those of aristocratic George Washington. But when he became chief executive, he enlarged the White House staff to fourteen persons—more than 50 percent larger than the entire nine-man personnel of the U.S. Department of State.

When George Washington visited Virginia's famous Natural Bridge, he lingered long enough to carve his initials in a prominent spot.

In early manhood John F. Kennedy was so scrawny that schoolmates at Choate prep school called him "rat face." Careful ranking by instructors placed him sixty-fourth in a class of 112; yet comrades voted him "most likely to succeed."

On the night before his inauguration, Theodore Roosevelt received from Secretary of State John Hay "a priceless gift" of a ring. Roosevelt wore it for ceremonies the next day, keenly aware that the ring held hair cut from Abraham Lincoln's head on the night of his assassination.

On March 4, 1857, Franklin Pierce called his cabinet members together to say goodbye to them. For the only time in his adult life, he was unable to restrain his tears when he reached his secretary of war. With the likelihood of civil war becoming greater by the month, the outgoing president wept openly as he embraced Jefferson Davis.

When Theodore Roosevelt penned his autobiography, he included in it not one word about his wife Alice. They were married three years before her death in childbirth.

Although the Civil War was largely fought over the slavery issue, the man who won the war for the Union, Ulysses S. Grant, permitted police to ban blacks from White House grounds during his presidency.

George Washington suffered from poor vision for years, but he refused to use eyeglasses except with close relatives and intimate friends.

When Quaker-reared Dolley Madison, was expelled from the meeting to which she belonged, she rebelled by using rouge, wearing golden slippers, playing cards for money, and even dipping snuff.

Protected by "dear mamma," little Franklin D. Roosevelt was forced to wear dresses until age five, after which he graduated into kilts. He didn't begin to wear trousers until age eight.

James Buchanan, who had little clerical help and consequently often worked until midnight, liked plenty of light. For that reason he habitually used a rubber hose to link his table lamp with a gas outlet from a chandelier. Amazingly enough, he never caused an explosion or started a fire in the White House.

Calvin Coolidge, who didn't like to indulge himself, once broke with custom and went to a circus for the sole purpose of seeing a sea lion.

When Andrew Johnson assumed the presidency, his temporary office was decorated with a flag that had been ripped by a spur on the boot of John Wilkes Booth, Lincoln's murderer.

Warren G. Harding sometimes was short of cash when friends visited him for a poker game. In such situations he often used fine pieces of White House china when called upon to ante up.

The physician who delivered baby Rutherford to the widow Sophia B. Hayes charged her $3.50 for his services at the birth of the future president.

When outdoorsman Theodore Roosevelt, who said he always told the whole truth, wrote his autobiography, he did not even mention his first wife of three years, Alice.

Though he had studied law with zeal and passed his bar exam with ease, fledgling attorney Woodrow Wilson never established a good practice in Atlanta, Georgia. When asked why he left the practice of law, he responded that he had to get out of it when he watched two talented advocates squabble over a stolen chicken.

For more than 100 years, service personnel who regularly visited the White House included clockwinders. As late as World War I, their duties required them to wind approximately thirty-five to forty clocks at each visit.

Ex-president John Tyler was so down on his luck in 1850 that he was unable to pay a bill for $1.25 until he sold his corn crop for the year.

Franklin Pierce and his bride spent their honeymoon in a boarding house in the nation's capital.

Beginning at about age nine, Andrew Jackson served without pay as a public reader of news to many illiterate adults.

James Buchanan had a nervous twitch that caused his head to jerk—visibly and frequently—throughout his life.

As a college student, Woodrow Wilson had once hoped to make a career on the stage. As president, whenever he attended a vaudeville performance he liked to return to the White House and mimic the tap dancers and singers who had entertained him.

Rats and mice became such a problem during Andrew Johnson's years as chief executive that his daughter brought cats to the White House, set traps, and spread poison. Meanwhile, the president was craftily providing flour and water for the mice she hoped to catch.

George Washington first consented to have a life-size portrait painted by Charles Wilson Peale, the self-taught artist who also stuffed birds, pulled teeth, and repaired clocks. For the now famous painting, forty-year-old Washington wore the uniform he had used years earlier during the French and Indian War.

Although he didn't complain until it was too late to have anything done about it, Thomas Jefferson privately noted that the $25,000 annual salary paid to him was far too little to cover his expenditures. One of the reasons: He had a penchant for foreign wines and as master of the White House in one year spent $10,855.90 for liquid refreshments for his guests.

When Ulysses S. Grant was commanding the Union army at Vicksburg, Mississippi, a servant girl one day accidentally emptied a washbowl containing his false teeth into the river. He was unable to eat solid food until a dentist arrived to make a new set of dentures for him.

At the death of Andrew Johnson, grieving survivors respected the wishes of the ex-president and, in spite of social pressure from the community, refused to call in a minister.

Abraham Lincoln, who often complained about severe headache after reading for three or four hours, purchased eyeglasses in Bloomington, Illinois, for 37½¢. Years later, examination showed that they were at least three times more powerful than he needed.

Born in 1822, Jesse and Hannah Grant's baby son remained nameless for a full month. His mother wanted to call him Albert, but in the end she consented to name him Hiram for his grandfather and Ulysses in honor of the Greek hero. Given an appointment to the U.S. Military Academy, Grant was incorrectly listed by his congressman as Ulysses Simpson Grant. Without going through legal formalities, he adopted the new name and used it for the rest of his life.

James Monroe was unable to have inauguration ceremonies in the chamber of the House of Representatives, as custom then dictated. He had angered Speaker of the House Henry Clay, and Clay refused to have the ceremonies held there.

Before age thirteen, future president Andrew Jackson knew from personal experience what it is like to be thrown in jail. He went there for refusing to obey orders from British soldiers who had subdued and occupied the region in which he lived.

John Quincy Adams habitually arose about ninety minutes before sunrise. He would then take his customary four-mile constitutional before tackling the problems of the day.

Theodore Roosevelt exploded with indignation when his daughter Alice, age twenty-two, said she would like to ride in an automobile occasionally. "Certainly not" he told her, "the Roosevelts will remain a horse family!"

Part Three

Wives and Mothers

George Washington.

16

The Father of His Country Could Not Satisfy His Own Mother

Mary Ball Washington, mother of George, is sometimes depicted as "an American madonna." Such a portrayal overlooks the fact that in 1743 she sent her fatherless boy of eleven away from home and spent much of the rest of her life quarreling with him. As a result she got respect, but little love, from her son who was destined to become "first in war, first in peace, and first in the hearts of his countrymen."

Joseph Ball, grandfather of George Washington, came from England as a young man and sired a large family. When Mary was three her father died and left her 400 acres of land, fifteen cattle, three slaves and enough feathers to be made into a bed.

As other relatives died and left money, land, or both to her, the young woman accumulated "a very tidy estate." She rode on a silk plush saddle, but didn't marry until age twenty-three, long past the prevailing age for Virginia brides of her time.

Augustine Washington, known to his friends as Gus, was a widower with four children when he married Mary Ball in 1730. George, first of six children from the new union, made his arrival at 10:00 A.M. on February 11, 1732, according to the calendar then in use. He was born in a brick farmhouse in Westmoreland County, Virginia.

Gus Washington, who died when young George was eleven, had accumulated a substantial amount of property, which he carefully divided among his many children.

Little George got Ferry Farm and a tract of unimproved land, ten slaves, three lots in Fredericksburg, and a few miscellaneous bequests. It would be more accurate to say that he was supposed to get those items; actually, his mother took control and refused to part with them. George did not gain possession of Ferry Farm for nearly thirty years.

Then, and for the duration of his life, George Washington's dealings with his mother constituted "the most serious problem in his personal relations," according to historian–biographer James T. Flexner. Although in the new nation she was idealized as the perfect American mother, actually, says *The American Heritage Pictorial History of the Presidents*, "she was querulous and illiterate, and resented George's success because she felt that he neglected her."

A childhood playmate of the future first president remembered, "I was ten times more afraid of her than I ever was of my own parents."

Careful study of family documents reveals that George's mother tried to prevent him from doing anything that she didn't consider likely to benefit her. That is regarded as a major reason for her stubborn refusal to participate in any "big event" in George's life.

Some of George's moments of special triumph Mary Washington bypassed were: her son's appointment as adjutant general of Virginia (1752); his elevation to formal command of Virginia forces protecting the frontier against the French and Indians (1755); his seating in the Virginia House of Burgesses (1758); his seating in the First Continental Congress (1774); his elevation to rank of commander-in-chief of the colonial army (1775); and, finally, his inauguration as president of the United States (1789).

From early childhood, George Washington reacted to his mother very sharply. During his career as soldier and first president, he was constantly in conflict with her.

During the thirty years of her son's marriage to Martha Custis, Mary Ball Washington never visited Mount Vernon, perhaps because she was never invited to do so.

George Washington's letters, papers, and account books fill many printed volumes. But this voluminous material includes few references to his mother that fail to reflect impatience, bitterness, or outright anger at her.

A letter written in May 1749 to his half-brother Lawrence complains that he is unable to travel from Ferry Farm—legally owned by him, but actually controlled by his mother—because he doesn't have money to buy corn for his horse.

It was Lawrence who bought the estate destined to be a national monument. George Washington first occupied Mount Vernon as a tenant, paying his half-brother's widow annual rental of 15,000 pounds of tobacco. He didn't purchase the property until 1775.

Four years earlier, his mother had finally left Ferry Farm and moved into Fredericksburg. George rented some land from her, and "when he paid her what he owed for rent, he carefully noted in his account book the name of the witness in whose presence the payment was made."

Invariably, Washington's letters to his mother address her as "Honour'd Madam" and end with "Yr. most Dutiful and Obedt. Son." Actually, he was anything but dutiful and obedient. Had he been, the story of this nation—and of the world—might have been different.

Mrs. Washington violently resisted her son's decision to take part in the French and Indian War. When he donned his uniform over her protests, her nagging letters followed him along the frontier. Once, in 1755, he wrote from camp to say he couldn't provide her with either a "Dutch man" to oversee her plantation, or with butter, "for we are quite out of that part of the country where either are to be had, as there are few or no Inhabitants where we now lie Encamp'd, and butter cannot be had here to supply the wants of the Camp."

Late in 1755 the Virginia Assembly offered Washington the rank of colonel and the command of a regiment. He took the post in spite of "a hundred objections" from his mother, then curtly wrote her that "the eternal dishonour" of refusing such a post would give her greater uneasiness than his "going in an honourable Command."

Years later, instead of rejoicing at George's prominence in the American Revolution, Mary Washington remained stubbornly uncomplimentary about her son's leadership. She was so critical that many who knew her regarded her as a Tory, a supporter of the British cause.

While George was busy fighting the British, his mother greatly embarrassed him by asking the Virginia Assembly to give her a pension. He learned of the matter in 1781 and wrote to Virginia lawmakers: "Before I left Virginia, I answered all her calls for money, and since that period I have directed my Steward to do the same. Whence her distress arises, therefore, I do not know."

Washington did not like to engage in a face-to-face confrontation with his mother. Hence, he often used his brother John Augustine, four years his junior, as go-between. The death of the mediator in January 1787 led to a direct clash of personalities. Like many other skirmishes between Mary Washington and her famous son, trouble erupted over money.

Initially, she had written to George asking for cash. He sent her fifteen guineas and said it was all he had available. Then he reminded her of her ingratitude for the way he had looked after her needs. Actions of his mother caused him "to be viewed as a delinquent son, and considered, perhaps by the world, as unjust and undutiful."

Mary Ball Washington seems again to have hinted that she would like to come to Mount Vernon, for her son and daughter-in-law were thrown into a state of near panic. After they had talked at length, he wrote his mother a long letter.

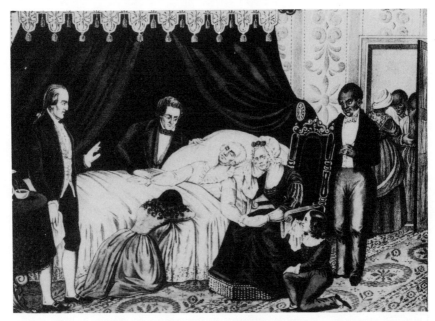

Even while on his death bed, George Washington was unable to forget his mother's ill temper and continued demands for money.

"Candor requires me to say that [my house] will never answer your purpose in any shape whatever," he began. Then he proceeded to list the many reasons she would find life at Mount Vernon wholly unsatisfactory. His own household situation, insisted Washington, would force his mother to do one of three things: "First be always dressing to appear in company; second to come into the room in dishabille; or, third, to be as it were a prisoner in your own chamber."

Since no alternative was satisfactory, his letter concluded it was simply out of the question even to think of having her under his own roof.

As death approached the iron-willed woman, she couldn't forget that, after all, George was both her first child and her oldest son. So in her last will and testament she dictated, "I give to my son, General George Washington, all my land in Accokeck Run, in the County of Stafford, and also my negro boy George. Also my best bed, bedstead, and Virginia cloth curtain, my quilted blue-and-white quilt, and my best dressing gown."

History does not record what George Washington did with the items he received as bequests. But the weight of evidence suggests that he may have handled them much as he did a letter his mother wrote him seven years earlier acknowledging that she "gott the 2 five ginnes you was soe kind to send me."

The man who led his countrymen to freedom didn't even acknowledge his mother's communication. He simply endorsed it, "From Mrs. Mary Washington 13 Mar. 1782," and put it away.

Years earlier, though, George Washington's strong-willed and illiterate mother had an impact far greater than either she or he realized at the time.

When George was fourteen, his half-brother Lawrence sent him word that Captain Green of the British Royal Navy was in need of a midshipman. A naval career offered a great many advantages, Lawrence pointed out. So George responded with eager interest, hoping soon to join His Majesty's Navy as a midshipman, the first step of a lifelong career, if just one hurdle could be crossed.

That hurdle was his mother.

Mary Washington pondered the plan, briefly seems to have come close to approval of it, then "hardened her opposition" to the idea of sending her firstborn to sea. Eventually, she flatly refused to give George permission.

Had the decision of his mother been different in 1746, the outbreak of the American Revolution might have found George Washington fighting against his countrymen as a career officer of the British Navy.

17

The Unsolved Riddle
of Nancy Hanks and Her Son

Alone among chief executives, Abraham Lincoln came from roots so obscure that little is positively known about them. Decades of persistent digging have provided a hazy sketch of his father, Thomas. But the riddle of his mother, Nancy, is almost as insoluble as it was when political rivals joked about his background in 1860.

However, Carl Sandburg found answers to some of the questions. According to his *Abraham Lincoln; the Prairie Years*, the mother of the wartime chief executive was brought to Kentucky through the Cumberland Gap by her mother, Lucy Hanks, soon after her birth in 1784.

Lucy Hanks, generally considered to have been an unmarried mother in an era when such women became social outcasts, settled near Harrodsburg, Kentucky. There she later found a husband, Henry Sparrow.

Since Hardin County then had at least one, perhaps two, other girls named Nancy Hanks, Lucy's daughter was sometimes called Nancy Sparrow. According to Sandburg, she became a woman of about 130 pounds, with dark hair and dark skin that made her gray eyes seem unusually keen. Nancy Hanks had a "somewhat accented chin and chin-bones," wrote the poet-biographer. Linked with an "outstanding forehead," they must have made her face more than casually memorable.

Strangely, Abraham Lincoln never mentioned any of these features. In his personal musing, the chief executive confided only that his mother had been born in Virginia. There is reasonably good evidence that she could not write her own name, and no contemporary description of her has survived.

William Herndon, Lincoln's long-time associate who was first his law partner, then his secretary, and finally, his biographer, was sure that the president believed himself to be—like his mother, illegitimate.

Except for vague comments that she had been born somewhere in Virginia, Lincoln's own firsthand knowledge about his mysterious mother consisted only of a fuzzy impression that when he was about nine he had whittled pegs for her coffin after she died from milk sickness—(not then known to be caused by a milch cow having eaten snake root).

Thomas Lincoln, Nancy Hanks' husband, was born in 1778 in Rockingham County, Virginia. Living much of his childhood and youth in Lincoln County, Kentucky, he became a competent carpenter, although his famous son described him as "a wandering laboring-boy."

Several facts seem to be clearly on record. Mordecai Lincoln, brother of Thomas, farmed in Washington County, Kentucky. It was to this area that Thomas went on June 10, 1806, to post at Springfield a notice of his intention to marry Nancy Hanks.

There seems to have been no clear requirement for registration of such a marriage bond, but at the courthouse in Springfield Thomas Lincoln solemnly signed papers. Two days later he and Nancy Hanks were married in a ceremony performed at Springfield by the Reverend Jesse Head of the Methodist Episcopal Church.

Birth records show that their son, named Abraham for his paternal grandfather, made his appearance on Sunday, February 12, 1809.

Given such a scarcity of hard facts concerning the background of Lincoln, it is small wonder that verbal traditions developed, proliferated, and remain alive. Passed from generation to generation by word of mouth, three tales seek to give some explanation for Abraham Lincoln's greatness by pointing to a blood line quite unlike that of a semiliterate wandering handyman.

Support of a sort for these tales comes from the fact that Thomas Lincoln survived until his son was about forty-two years old. Repeatedly informed by letter that his father was in a terminal condition, Abraham Lincoln refused to reply "because it appeared to me that I could write nothing that would do any good." Thomas Lincoln died January 17, 1851. Then a successful Illinois attorney, Lincoln did not attend the funeral of the man who claimed him as his son.

"That's because he knew that Thomas Lincoln was not his father," a multilayered body of tradition asserts.

One segment of this lore, rooted in South Carolina, is familiar to multitudes of persons born and reared in the state. Though the specific geographic locale varies from one storyteller to another, the gist of the tale is reasonably uniform.

According to it, a scruffy pair of wanderers turned up in the fall of 1807. "Couldn't find a thing to do back home," explained the fellow

Nancy Hanks gave birth to her son in a tiny log cabin now dwarfed by the protective structure built for it.

who called himself Tom and claimed to be handy with carpenter's tools. Unable to find even a temporary job, Tom left his wife, Nancy, at Easley or Pickens or Seneca—the location varies with the story-teller—and tried his luck in the Low Country.

Nancy soon got work as a tavern maid and proved she was worth every penny she was paid. She had been on the job only a few weeks before an up-and-coming lawyer, a member of the state legislature, took a special fancy to her. He took to staying over an extra night just to have more time with her.

But when Nancy asked him to feel her stomach some time about May 1808, John C. Calhoun turned all kinds of colors. He already had his eye on the U.S. Congress, and just could not afford to be saddled with scandal. So the Yale-educated political leader sent men to scout through the pine forests until they found Tom Lincoln somewhere in Walterboro, or maybe it was Barnwell.

Anyway, once the legislator found the fellow, he handed him a fist full of bills and told him to get his woman back to Kentucky in a hurry. So the man who guided the union in its fearful struggle with the

Confederate States of America is alleged to be the son of John C. Calhoun, a patrician aristocrat.

Another story, first published in book form in 1899, has an orphaned Nancy Hanks taken as a servant into the home of farmer-merchant Abraham Enloe, who lived on the rich land along the Oconoluftee River in North Carolina. Enloe took the servant girl to bed, and when she gave birth to a son the two remained in North Carolina until Enloe began to think of running for public office. Enloe then persuaded Gen. Felix Walker of Revolutionary War fame to hustle Nancy Hanks and Abraham off to Kentucky, where Tom Lincoln took her as his wife.

Numerous letters from persons who had first- or second-hand knowledge of the matter provide vivid details of the relationship. What's more, the volume devoted to *The Genesis of Lincoln* includes photographs in which Wesley Enloe—Lincoln's alleged half-brother —could easily be mistaken for the president.

Still another layer of tradition ignores the Carolinas and focuses upon events in Kentucky. Seeking better opportunity than he had found in Georgia, Revolutionary veteran Samuel Davis took his family to Mercer County, in the bluegrass region, some time in 1793.

Not many months later he moved to a 600-acre farm not far from Hopkinsville, where he built an elegant double log cabin. His new neighbors, who had already learned that some long-time friends called him Stud, joked and nudged one another. "With the brood of children he has sired, he'll need that space, and more," they said.

But such a comment failed to take into account the twenty-three-year spread in ages of the ten Davis children. By the time the youngest came along and was named Jefferson (in honor of the sitting president) Finis (to indicate that there probably would be no more), Joseph was already on his own, and his sisters were thinking of getting married.

With a huge residence on his hands, Stud Davis turned one of his biggest rooms into what was for frontier days, an elegant wayfarer's rest stop that was hired out by the day to travelers passing through the region.

Naturally he required the help of a servant girl, and most women who lived in Christian County were fully occupied on the farms of their husbands or fathers. So Samuel Davis was delighted—the story goes—when a nice looking and bright, but dirt poor, young woman wandered in from Washington County. Her brother-in-law had fallen on hard times, she explained, and she was looking for work.

Hired to work part-time on the big Davis farm, the new girl, Nancy, soon showed she was not lazy. Neither was she oblivious to the fact that men of all ages often turned to look at her as she walked past them.

Soon Nancy was with child, and some people thought the father was Stud Davis while others suggested Joseph Davis, fast becoming one of the wealthiest men in the South. Meanwhile, Nancy left for Hardin County, Kentucky, where her son was born.

If Stud was the father, the new baby was a half-brother of Stud's youngest son, Jefferson. If Joseph was the father, Abraham Lincoln was nephew to Jefferson Davis, just a little over a year his senior.

Documentation of the North Carolina story is better than that for Sandburg's account, while the Kentucky story rests on oral tradition alone. Yet even those who insist that no Davis ever came near Nancy Hanks in a carnal way are forced to acknowledge the striking physical resemblance between Jefferson Davis and Abraham Lincoln, born within one hundred miles and twenty months of one another.

These bits of folklore could be attributed to southern hatred of the leader of the union soldiers that rode roughshod over the region, were it not that without exception, they point to a biological father several rungs higher up the socio-economic ladder than Thomas Lincoln. So the parentage of an obscure child whose birthplace later became a national shrine evokes many questions for which there are no good answers. Hence it remains an open invitation to the spinning of tales whose believability is measured, not by textbook standards, but by the readiness of listeners to nod assent.

18

Courting Women and Wealth

As a high school student in greater Chicago, future first lady Hillary Rodham was nicknamed "Sister Frigidaire" by chums convinced she would spend her adult life as a nun. Rodham's high-school acquaintances surely would have been stunned had they known she later would get her law degree, marry, become a mother, name her daughter after the 1969 Joni Mitchell song "Chelsea Morning," and become our nation's first lady with an obvious savvy for national politics.

Rodham's life of surprises and outstanding achievements continued well beyond high school, marriage, and motherhood. At forty-one, she was named by the *National Law Journal* as one of the nation's one hundred most powerful lawyers while working as a senior litigating partner of the thirty-five-member Rose law firm in Little Rock, Arkansas. Of course, by then, she also was married to the state's youthful governor. This dual role carried with it political protocol that says a governor's wife attaches her husband's last name to her own. Alas, Hillary Rodham Clinton.

Not only did the Clintons share a name, they also shared a growing wealth—with Hillary bringing home most of the bacon (surely not to be confused with baking cookies in the kitchen). After Bill Clinton in 1991 announced his candidacy for the presidency, investigative reporters began digging into the couple's finances. Researchers subsequently uncovered a 1991 joint income of $234,428. Hillary accounted for about $180,000 of that through her legal work ($109,000), service on three corporate boards ($65,000), and speaking engagements ($5,500). By comparison, husband Bill pulled down $43,500 ($35,000 in salary, $3,000 from a special Arkansas fund, and $5,500 from speeches). Their joint income from other sources, including investments, came to about $11,000. For the first time in American history, a future first lady was earning an income triple that of her husband's. With a combined net worth of $697,000, the Clintons fell into the top 3 percent of U.S. couples; assets owned outright by the future president totaled only $83,000, or 12 percent of their total.

Not all of the Clintons' financial endeavors have been positive. When Hillary tried her hand at S&P stock-index futures in 1987, she lost $2,532 and quickly pulled out. However, that loss was minuscule compared to the problems still facing the Clintons in late 1995. At the time, an ongoing investigation into the Clintons' involvement with a 230-acre land development deal known as "Whitewater" threatened the Clintons with possible criminal charges.

It all started when Hillary plunked down a $20,000 down payment to buy into a $202,000 plot in the Ozark Mountains of Arkansas. The land, controlled by the Whitewater Development Company, was to be subdivided and sold to people as vacation home sites. Whitewater developer James McDouglas reportedly sold Hillary and Bill one-half interest in the development for a modest $68,380. To subsidize the initial investment, Hillary borrowed from the Union Bank of Little Rock, Arkansas, with the idea that she and Bill would become not only Whitewater partners but also vacation resort property owners. The get-rich-quick scheme eventually turned sour. Since Hillary and her husband regarded themselves as "passive investors," it was initially reported that they couldn't lose more than $69,000 on the deal. That "passive" verdict was scrapped when the Whitewater Development Company was charged with participating in irregular dealings that reportedly involved Bill's gubernatorial campaign funds.

As substantial as Hillary Rodham Clinton's earnings were, her net worth seems like a pittance compared to the real-estate fortune controlled two hundred years earlier by the future Mrs. George Washington. Martha "Patsy" Jones at eighteen married her godfather, Daniel P. Custis. Nineteen years older than Martha, Daniel lived only eight years after their marriage. He died in 1757 without a will, meaning his widow inherited land and other assets that made her one of Virginia's wealthiest people.

When he was twenty-six years old, George Washington spent about thirty-six hours on the Custis plantation. This was in March 1758. According to historian Douglas Southall Freeman, "As he [Washington] looked at the lovely Martha and across the broad, rich fields of level land, he resolved to come again."

Within a week, Washington returned to the plantation for a brief visit before riding off to attend to some important business. The courtship was quickly heating up. He soon ordered from London enough superfine blue cotton velvet to tailor a complete outfit for a tall man. This purchase suggested that he and Martha had become engaged during that second brief meeting. Upon the marriage of George and Martha in January 1759, her fortune became his. When he said, "I do," the militia officer's assets were increased by twenty thousand acres plus twenty-

Artist's conception of widow Martha Custis and her children when George Washington met them for the first time.

three thousand British pounds, two homes, and two hundred slaves. George never legally adopted Martha's children but said he "tried to treat them as if they were his own." Initially living on Martha's Williamsburg estate, the Washingtons later moved to the Mount Vernon plantation he inherited from his half-brother.

Abigail Smith didn't have a dime before marrying, but a thorough self-education had made her one of the most polished women of her era. Nine years Abigail's senior, John Adams had known his wife-to-be during years in which he mentioned her only as "a sickly child." When he discovered how much the seventeen-year-old knew about philosophy and poetry, the small-time country lawyer launched a successful two-year courtship.

Thirty-six years after marrying John, Abigail went with him when the nation's capital was moved from Philadelphia to Washington. As the first of many wives to preside over White House functions, Abigail Adams often apologized to guests about the mansion's chilly rooms. There were plenty of fine old trees growing close by, she explained, but no one in the new capital seemed interested in cutting firewood.

As first lady successor to Martha Washington, Abigail scrapped the "Lady" reference in her title and was called Mrs. Presidentress, an awkward-sounding moniker that never caught on.

A widow at twenty-three, Martha Skelton was practically penniless; everything her husband owned was inherited by their small son. That forced her to go home to Papa, a prosperous attorney and landowner. Her only apparent assets, at least as measured by eighteenth-century standards that today would be deemed sexist or politically incorrect, were her physical attractiveness and a talent for singing and playing the harpsichord. Delighted to find such an attractive woman, Thomas Jefferson persuaded Martha they ought to form a duet for life.

In ten years of marriage, Martha Jefferson had seven pregnancies. She died, at thirty-three, on September 6, 1782, probably a victim of child-bed fever. Only two of her seven children lived to maturity. Jefferson never remarried.

Soon to become notorious as America's first high-ranking traitor, Aaron Burr regularly pulled up a chair alongside the dining table at Mary Payne's boarding house. Philadelphia, then the nation's capital, had few good places to eat. Besides, Payne's pretty widowed daughter, Dolley Todd, waited tables there for her mother. It was there that Burr introduced Dolley to up-and-coming James Madison. There was an obvious mutual attraction. Although Madison was seventeen years older than Dolley, the congressman was so smitten that he took the young beauty for his wife four months later.

When British troops tried to burn the newly erected presidential mansion in 1814, a resourceful and courageous Dolley Madison grabbed a Gilbert Stuart painting of George Washington from its frame, filled an apron with silver, and bolted from the house with flames licking behind her. She obviously was no longer a near-destitute widow; instead, she had become someone who took determined measures in the president's absence.

A Virginia congressman named James Monroe was smitten with "a raving beauty" while the nation's business was still being conducted in New York. To him, the sky-blue eyes and raven-black tresses of a seventeen-year-old made it unimportant that her dad was dead broke. Having remained true to King George III during the American Revolution, Elizabeth Kortright's bankrupt father couldn't provide her with even a token dowry.

Monroe waved the dowry question aside, married Elizabeth, and soon took her with him to Paris. Caught up in a swirl of festivities, the wife of the American minister didn't then dream that she would one day succeed Dolley Madison as chatelaine of the White House. By the time this daughter of a British Loyalist had become first lady, an unidentified chronic illness made it impossible for her to be her husband's official hostess. One year after leaving the Executive Mansion, she suffered a violent seizure that resulted in her falling into an open fire. Her death at forty-four was never explained by doctors.

With a divorce pending, twenty-four-year-old Rachel Robards was down on her luck. Life in the Nashville, Tennessee, boarding house operated by her mother was humdrum until tall, lean Andy Jackson arrived in town. For the man who became an orphan at fourteen, it was love at first sight in spite of the fact that he had no idea where he would find the money to support a wife.

Fledgling lawyer Jackson, a known risk taker, had earlier inherited 350 pounds. With this small fortune, he went to Charleston, South Carolina, to partake of the high life and some gambling. After losing all his money, Jackson studied law, was admitted to the bar, and in 1788 was appointed solicitor general for the region that is now Tennessee by Judge John McNair of the Cumberland superior court. Soon after moving to Nashville and lodging at Mrs. Donelson's Boarding House, he married Rachel, believing that her divorce was final.

Two years later the couple learned to their dismay that the divorce had not become final when they married, so they had another ceremony. Political foes brought up the marriage scandal and it was a presidential campaign issue in 1828. Only once did Jackson kill a man in a duel; in 1806 he shot Charles Dickinson for having maligned the character of his Rachel.

Peggy Smith of Calvert County, Maryland, received much in the way of fine clothes and jewelry from her wealthy father. During a visit to her sister in Kentucky, she met and married Lt. Zachary Taylor who had nothing in the way of personal assets except his small military salary.

Nearly four decades later this army wife became alarmed when she saw that folks meant business about drafting her husband as a presidential candidate. While Zachary and his opponents jockeyed for position, Peggy spent much of the time on her knees. She prayed fervently but to no avail that he would lose the election so they wouldn't be subjected to White House pressures that in 1848 were already proverbial.

Robert Todd of Lexington, Kentucky, always saw to it that his daughter Mary had nothing but the best. She attended a private school where pupils mastered music, became elegant ballroom dancers, and conversed only in French. It's little wonder then that relatives and friends were appalled when she married a gawky country lawyer almost entirely self-educated, who didn't dare put his big feet on a ballroom floor and who misspelled common words.

When her husband, Abraham Lincoln, became the sixteenth president, she went far over the budget in refurbishing the White House, then brushed aside her husband's rebuke. During the years in which Abraham Lincoln's salary remained at $25,000, Mary Todd Lincoln often headed to New York and other cities for power-buying sprees. Her closets were eventually crammed with gowns and shoes she never wore. During a single four-month period she stuffed White House shelves with three hundred pairs of gloves.

As an eighteen-year-old, Rosalynn Smith worked in a beauty parlor to supplement her mother's income as a postal clerk and seamstress. She married an ensign in the U.S. Navy and said that as Mrs. Jimmy Carter she'd "happily live forever" on his barely livable salary.

Eighteen months before Rosalynn and Jimmy tied the knot, nineteen-year-old Barbara Pierce had become a navy wife. This was despite the fact that the salary of a lieutenant (junior grade) would bring a colossal change in Barbara's standard of living. Her father, publisher of *Redbook* and *McCall's* magazines, was determined that Barbara would never be in need. She knew his views, but Mrs. George Herbert Walker Bush looked to her husband and not to her father for things she couldn't live without.

Barbara Bush is especially fond of her signature three-strand pearl necklace. [THE WHITE HOUSE]

19

Wife Opposed to Women's Suffrage Wielded the Power of the Presidency for Weeks

I*studied every paper sent from the different Secretaries or Senators, and tried to digest and present in tabloid form the things that, despite my vigilance, had to go to the President. I, myself, never made a single decision regarding the disposition of public affairs. The only decision of mine was what was important and what was not, and the very important decision of when to present matters to my husband.*

Mrs. Edith Bolling Galt Wilson's explanation of her role during her husband's critical illness was disarmingly simple—on the surface. Fifteen years younger than the twenty-eighth president and seven years a widow at the time of their 1915 marriage, she literally—not figuratively—took over the nation on October 2, 1919.

That was the day on which President Woodrow Wilson suffered a stroke after having had a nervous breakdown on September 26 while on a speaking tour. Edith Wilson put her husband into seclusion, then stood guard at the door. No person entered without her permission; no document or report was handed to the chief executive without her approval, often after having been condensed to her liking.

At first, only White House insiders knew what was taking place. Even leading members of Congress and heads of federal agencies were told that the president was briefly indisposed. However, news of his serious illness slowly trickled out to the general public.

"The president became physically exhausted as a result of two long and grueling voyages to Europe in the interest of world peace," according to a statement issued by his personal physician, Admiral Cary T. Grayson.

Grayson's statement, which referred to the Paris Peace Conference of 1918 and the Treaty of Versailles in June 1919, was not released to

Widowed Edith Bolling Galt became the second Mrs. Woodrow Wilson.

the press until October 18, 1919. By then, it was widely known that Wilson was sick. But since details of his condition were kept secret, speculation abounded.

When Vice President Thomas R. Marshall tried to visit the president, he was turned away from the White House. No details were given him of the chief executive's stroke that had paralyzed his left side.

Another insider who unsuccessfully sought access to Wilson was his former intimate, Col. Edward M. House. When he published his memoirs, House minced no words in placing blame upon the shoulders of Mrs. Wilson.

Ellen Louise Axson, the president's first wife, died on August 4, 1914, and he married Edith Bolling Galt little more than a year later. During their courtship and early months as man and wife, the couple were featured in many newspaper and magazine stories as "the nation's sweethearts."

Colonel House saw things differently. "The president was enchanted by the second Mrs. Wilson and became constantly more dependent upon her," he said. "Inevitably, this meant that his personal relation with others changed."

House discovered how great the change was when he tried to communicate with his stricken friend. "Mrs. Wilson absolutely barred the door," he told reporters for the Cleveland *Plain Dealer*. "She and she alone decided what messages would be given to her husband. Responding to urgent matters of state, she sometimes produced illegible scrawls which she identified as messages from the president, and which she proceeded to interpret."

Dr. Grayson, whose wife was an intimate friend of the second Mrs. Wilson, issued strict orders. "The president must be shielded from all visitors, regardless of their rank or importance."

An official memorandum from Grayson to the press on Thursday, October 2, reported, "The President is a very sick man. After consultation in which all agreed as to his condition, it was determined that absolute rest is essential for some time."

For practical purposes, this unofficial plan to shield the stricken president put his wife in charge of the nation's business.

As she herself recalled the period, "The physicians said that if I could convey the messages of Cabinet members and others to the President, he would escape the nervous drain." He was considered to be so weak that "Even little courteous personal conversations would consume the President's strength." As a result, his wife embarked upon the program that she termed "my stewardship."

Others took a different view. Sen. Albert Fall of New Mexico protested to the Foreign Relations Committee, "We have petticoat government! Mrs. Wilson is President!"

Secretary of State Robert Laning, considered third in line for the presidency, took matters into his own hands and called a Cabinet meeting. Angered at the assumption of power, Edith Wilson demanded his resignation—in the president's name—and got it. Then, in the name of her stricken husband, she put Bainbridge Colby into the post in spite of the fact that he had no experience at all in foreign affairs.

Editors of the Chicago *Tribune* are believed to have been first to speak of this era as "Mrs. Wilson's Regency." Widely used in the nation's press, the term quickly spawned variants. The Nashville *Tennessean* described Mrs. Wilson as "the nation's first Presidentess." An editorial in the Boston *Globe* suggested that Mrs. Wilson should change her title from first lady to "Acting First Man."

Vice president Marshall was bombarded from every direction. Many congressional leaders urged him to declare himself president. Foreign heads of state paid courtesy calls upon Marshall, since they were barred from contact with Wilson. He received the Prince of Wales and gave a formal dinner for King Albert of Belgium. Marshall, incidentally, paid for that dinner out of his own salary of $12,000 a year. He was never reimbursed.

Despite mounting pressure for him to seize the reins of government, Marshall refused to act without a formal resolution by Congress and written approval by both Mrs. Wilson and Admiral Grayson. "I could throw this country into civil war by seizing the White House, but I won't," Marshall told his wife.

Political historian Michael Dorman is one of many who agreed.

"Today there is little question that Wilson—for at least a month—was disabled under the terms of the Constitution." As there was no legislation governing an orderly pattern of succession to the presidency, nothing was done.

Repeatedly, during the crucial month when Wilson's life hung in the balance, national leaders asked one another, "What on earth can we do to get the government out of Mrs. Wilson's hands?"

That vital question hung over Washington like a pall for more than a year, while the president slowly regained strength. No one in the capital doubted that Mrs. Wilson was the decisive personality in the intricate web of events.

"Woodrow Wilson was first my beloved husband whose life I was trying to save . ... and after that, he was the President of the United States," she said in denying that she had "overwhelming ambition to act as president." But her announced procedure of screening and digesting papers, deciding what would be presented to her husband and what would not, had the effect of placing top policy decisions in her hands.

Many messages sent by national leaders were not even acknowledged. Advisors trying to see the president on urgent matters of national importance had the door shut in their faces. Congressional bills became law without presidential action, and representatives of other nations were forced to deal with Wilson's subordinates.

Vice President Marshall listened to rumors, read the newspapers, and tried to keep calm. His worst moment came in Atlanta, where he was addressing the Order of Moose on November 23. After a page interrupted him with an urgent message, he announced to the stunned audience, "I cannot continue my speech. I must leave at once to take up my duties as Chief Executive of this great nation."

A long-distance telephone call that proved to be a cruel hoax—the perpetrator was never discovered—brought the tortured vice president as close to the White House as he ever got.

Dolly Gann, sister of Kansas Republican Sen. Charles Curtiss, did not call herself a feminist because that title was not yet in vogue. But she was one of the few persons in the Western world who went on public record as defending the tactics of Edith Wilson. "All the more credit to her!" she said, when she learned that the president's wife was refusing to permit him to see copies of legislation that he would normally have signed or vetoed. "I am glad that there was a woman in the White House who knew how to take the reins and use authority when it was passed upon her."

Strangely, Dolly Gann seems not to have known that Mrs. Wilson was opposed to women's suffrage. Yet she insisted upon wielding the power of the presidency!

CHAPTER

20

Wives Have Freely Broken
with Precedent

"**W**e simply cannot sit idly by and see the children disappointed next year," Lucy Hayes told her husband during the spring of 1878. He nodded agreement. No explanation was necessary; it was the talk of Washington that, after years and years in which hundreds of boys and girls rolled dyed Easter eggs down the steep western incline of Capitol Hill each Easter Monday, lawmakers had taken a firm stance. A statute that passed both houses of Congress stipulated that the last such egg rolling would take place that year, with Capitol grounds and terraces not to be used "as play grounds or otherwise" in the future.

At his wife's insistence, Hayes considered vetoing the legislation but argued that it was hardly worth doing more damage to already strained relations with lawmakers. So the first lady gave advance warning that—security or no security—the grounds of the White House would be opened to the children the following year.

Known as "the stolen election," the bitter contest of 1876 had put Hayes in the White House despite the fact that his rival captured many more popular votes. Tension was so high that, for the first time, the oath of office was taken in the White House during a private ceremony. So many assassination threats had already been received that the new chief executive put a stop to public concerts on the White House lawn. Access to the mansion and grounds was severely curtailed. Except during visiting hours of 2:00 P.M. to 10:00 P.M., guards were stationed at the external gates. During visiting hours, anyone who wished could come through the two north gates, but the entrance hall to the White House was made a guard station at which persons who wished to enter were forced to produce identification.

Washington police barred children from the lawn of the Capitol on Easter Monday, 1879, but Lucy Hayes had anticipated this development and had persuaded her husband to relax security at the executive mansion. Scores of the children trooped to the lawn of the mansion. "In rolling down their eggs," said the Washington *Star*, "the girls— some of them of pretty good size—were without regard to the extent of striped stockings displayed. They laughed, yelled, and played all morning."

It was this break with precedent and breach of established security that led to the annual Easter egg rolling at the White House, long one of the most publicized events associated with nonceremonial functions at the mansion.

Caroline Harrison, who met future President Benjamin Harrison in an Ohio village when she was fifteen and he was fourteen years old, started another holiday custom. During her husband's term in office (1889-1893) she put up Christmas trees in the White House. They had been introduced into England by Queen Victoria's German-born husband and were just beginning to become part of the American Christmas tradition. Her innovation has remained ever since. Grace Coolidge went a step further in 1923 by persuading her husband to press a switch to light the first national Christmas tree on the lawn of the mansion.

It was Lucy Hayes of Easter egg fame to whom the title of "first lady" was first applied. Writing in the *Independent* magazine, Mary Clemmer Ames used it in describing the inauguration of Rutherford B. Hayes. When Mrs. Hayes did not object, the title was picked up by other writers. Today it is in universal usage, often capitalized in media that do not capitalize the title *president* when it does not precede a name or is used in unofficial fashion.

Wide acceptance of the title is usually credited to a 1911 play entitled *The First Lady in the Land,* a production in which Dolley Madison, the wife of James Madison, was the central character. Though she never knew about her role in shaping a title similar to these bestowed upon royalty, Dolley Madison was joyfully aware of another innovation. She was the first wife of a president to serve ice cream in the executive mansion.

Tennessee-born Sarah Polk was the first president's wife to stage a traditional Thanksgiving dinner at the White House.

Abigail Fillmore considered the mansion to be cold and bare when she entered it in 1850. After being escorted through it, she told her husband she could hardly believe what she had seen: The president's house lacked books. So at her insistence, Congress passed an appropriation providing $5,000 for installing shelves and filling them with the books that made up the first library in the president's house.

Lucy Hayes, the first "first lady," was herself another "first." At age sixteen she entered Ohio Wesleyan University and graduated with

When Abigail (Mrs. Millard) Fillmore found the White House "cold and bare," she persuaded Congress to spend 5,000 dollars for the mansion's first library—Henry B. Hall engraving, 1871.

honors three years later, thereby becoming the first president's wife to have a college diploma.

To Nellie Taft fell the honor of being the first wife of a president to ride alongside her husband on Pennsylvania Avenue during inauguration festivities. Until then, it had been customary for the outgoing chief executive to occupy the seat of honor next to his successor. Members of the Congressional Committee on Arrangements argued that it was not proper for a woman to take such a part in a formal inaugural ride, but William Howard Taft's indomitable wife rode anyway and set a lasting precedent.

Julia Grant, wife of Ulysses S. Grant, was the first wife of a president to grant interviews to members of the press; and Edith Roosevelt, Theodore Roosevelt's wife, wrote the first memoirs by a White House hostess. When the book was completed, she set a price tag of $125,000 upon it and waited for a horde of would-be publishers to descend upon her. Unfortunately, no publisher met her asking price.

Another Roosevelt, the wife of Franklin Delano, was the first White House hostess to hold a formal press conference. She actually met reporters in New York before taking over the executive mansion. Then she invited the press to the Red Room for an hour with her on the Monday after her husband took office. Only women reporters were admitted to these early special sessions, however. Eleanor Roosevelt always insisted that the chief reason she launched the practice was to give women reporters access to news at the top, because they were barred from presidential press conferences.

Later in Roosevelt's four terms of office, Eleanor Roosevelt wrote her own syndicated newspaper column, "My Day." Traveling extensively around the country, she was called by the president "my eyes and ears" as she reported to him what she had seen and heard.

Lady Bird Johnson pioneered in a different milieu by actively campaigning on her husband's behalf. She started in his 1948 race for the U.S. Senate against popular Gov. Coke Stevenson, when Lyndon Johnson confessed that he "didn't have a prayer unless Lady Bird can turn voters on and out."

She did exactly that, campaigning throughout the Democratic primary as strenuously as her husband. When the 988,000 ballots were counted, political experts credited Mrs. Johnson with having brought about a big upset. Her husband won by a margin of eighty-seven votes, credited to the hard work and personal charm of Lady Bird.

Helen Taft was the power behind the first public project created by a first lady. Unhappy over the appearance of a paved road that ran through Potomac Park, she led a movement to convert it into an elegant drive. Complete with a bandstand that offered concerts two afternoons a week, Potomac Drive was formally opened on April 15, 1909. Soon it became "the most fashionable place in the capital on spring and autumn afternoons."

With the new driveway a smashing success, William Howard Taft's wife might have rested on her laurels. Instead, she continued the beautification that had become her personal project. In a daring move, she contacted Mrs. Theodora Ozaki, wife of the mayor of Tokyo, Japan. That led to extensive personal correspondence followed by diplomatic maneuvering. The result was that in 1911 Mayor Ozaki presented the first shipment of Japanese cherry trees for which the nation's capital is now famous.

John Tyler's beautiful second wife, Julia, reveled in her role as White House hostess. As a tribute to her husband who was more than thirty years her senior, she persuaded the U.S. Marine Band to play "Hail to the Chief" when Tyler made his appearance on occasions of state. Instead of fading away, that custom has become stronger as the decades have passed since the 1840s.

Another innovation by the lovely young first lady had long-range implications for advertising and business. Julia Tyler is generally credited with being the first American woman to lend her name and face to a commercial "testimonial." She did it, not as the wife of a president but as a beauty who today could be a fashion model.

Abigail Fillmore, a talented and dedicated teacher, was the first wife of a future president to hold a job after marriage. As mistress of the White House, she blazed another trail by demanding that the first stove be installed in the mansion that had previously been heated only by fireplaces.

Frances Cleveland was the first widow of a president to remarry. Five years after Cleveland's death in 1908 she became Mrs. Thomas J. Preston, wife of a Princeton University professor of archaeology.

CHAPTER
21

Wives Have Said No and Made It Stick

More frequently than might be expected, the wife of a president has had the final word by saying no to a proposal or to established precedent. Such verdicts by first ladies have affected matters ranging from entertainment to affairs of state.

Martha Washington rejected plans that would have made her the focus of public attention during her husband's first inauguration. She refused to attend the ceremony or the inaugural ball that followed.

More important, she refused to turn over to scholars or to the public letters that had passed between her and her husband. To make sure that her verdict stuck, she burned much of their correspondence.

Sarah Childress Polk banned White House dancing, long a highlight of the Washington social calendar. Playing cards were also banished. She even said no to a proposal to replace candlelit chandeliers with the new gas burning kind.

Lucy Ware Webb Hayes, described as being "opposed to all worldly vices and frivolities," put her foot down on the subject of alcohol. Although Rutherford B. Hayes admitted he hadn't been a total abstainer when elected president, even wine was never served after his first official function, a dinner for two Russian grand dukes.

Critics called the president's wife "Lemonade Lucy," and Secretary of State William M. Evarts quipped that at her entertainments "water flowed like champagne." As a matter of fact, at state dinners a decanter of water *was* put beside each plate.

Lemonade Lucy was neither the first nor the last mistress of the White House to ban alcohol. Lucretia Garfield would not serve wine at table, and one of Rosalynn Carter's first decisions was to eliminate hard liquor from the mansion's functions.

In addition to banning alcohol, Lucy Hayes ordered billiards out of the White House. John Quincy Adams had been partial to this form of

"Lemonade Lucy" (Mrs. Rutherford B.) Hayes played with children in a conservatory originally converted into a promenade for the purpose of keeping guests too busy to miss alcohol. [HAYES PRESIDENTIAL CENTER]

recreation; and during the presidency of Ulysses S. Grant his wife, Julia, had been agreeable to calling a large room the Billiard Room. Under Lucy Hayes, it became "an intimate parlor for afternoon teas."

Even though Nellie Taft said no when the president said he thought he ought to accept an invitation to play golf with John D. Rockefeller, she wouldn't have considered giving a state dinner without serving champagne. When the first family planned to attend a costume ball, Nellie Taft humiliated the president by "summarily rejecting" his suggestions for a costume. He retaliated by nicknaming her the "Council of War." When the party was held, he showed up in an attire of "voluminous proportions" that had been approved by his wife.

Nellie Taft's decisions extended beyond golf and costume balls. She refused to keep the uniformed guards at the White House door and replaced them with black footmen in livery.

Bess Truman, who knew perfectly well that precedent is all-important in the nation's capital, announced that she would break with it by refusing to hold the press conferences that Eleanor Roosevelt had begun. In spite of fervent pleas from members of the women's press corps, Mrs. Truman retorted that she had not been born in Independence, Missouri, for nothing!

Mary Todd Lincoln got much criticism when she put a stop to state dinners, pleading economy. She also called a halt to summer concerts by the Marine Band on the south lawn of the executive mansion but gave no specific reason for doing so.

Eliza Johnson, wife of Andrew Johnson, the only chief executive to face impeachment, would not take part in entertainments at which she was expected to be hostess.

Zachary Taylor's wife, Peggy, turned down most official duties. For the customary chores of White House hostess, she assigned her twenty-five-year-old daughter, Betty.

When Zachary Taylor set out for Washington, making a triumphal tour before his inauguration, his wife stayed home. She refused to leave Baton Rouge because of "the discomforts of travel at that season."

Friends of William Henry Harrison celebrated his election-night victory. But his wife, Anna, refused to have anything to do with family jubilation. Flatly disagreeing with her husband, she said that she wished his friends "had left him where he was, happy and contented in retirement," instead of pushing him into a successful contest for the presidency.

Many Americans wanted to modify the spelling of the name of James Madison's charming wife. Biographers insisted upon calling her Dorothea or Dorothy. She stubbornly refused to yield to such pressure and stuck to Dolley.

Eleanor Roosevelt went beyond Nellie Taft's refusal to have armed guards at the White House door. She said no to accompaniment by the Secret Service agent assigned to protect her. Hence she buzzed about the nation by plane, accompanied only by her secretary.

Have more recent mistresses of the White House been uniformly compliant? Not on your life!

Patricia Nixon's actions were a way of saying no to unwritten rules of etiquette. Ignoring them, she let herself be seen smoking a cigarette in a restaurant while dining there with members of the first family.

When Betty Ford went to New York to tape a television show, she found NBC studios blocked by a picket line. Refusing to be stopped, she crossed it for a show organized by *Ladies' Home Journal* magazine. After all, why should a person being honored as one of ten Women of the Year (1976) be stopped by a labor union's demonstrations?

In 1977 the General Services Administration ruled against use of a chartered plane for a planned trip of the president's wife to Philadelphia. Rosalynn Carter defied the verdict and went ahead in the plane, at a cost of $3,585.

CHAPTER
22

Love Makes the World Go 'Round!

"**R**egardless of what you have done or have not done, you face trouble," Hollywood director Mervyn LeRoy is reported to have told distressed actress Nancy Davis. "Anyone whose name gets on the mailing list of one of those real left-wing organizations is going to be challenged, sooner or later. Why don't you get some help from the Screen Actors Guild?"

Scheduled to appear in the upcoming movie *It's a Big Country* and fearful of losing her role, the petite actress took LeRoy's advice and turned to guild president Ronald Reagan. He met her for dinner to try to explain how she must have been confused with another Nancy Davis.

Reagan, busy with his own movies and with work of the Screen Actors Guild, had planned to smooth over a vexatious problem and leave his guest early. Smarting from wounds of the 1948 divorce proceedings that severed his marriage with Jane Wyman, Reagan had thrown himself into his work. However, something about Nancy Davis made their meeting more than casual. Reagan canceled his plans for the evening and after dinner took Nancy to Ciro's to see Sophie Tucker perform. Soon they were spending time with one another regularly; a simple wedding, with actor William Holden as best man, followed on March 4, 1952.

Elizabeth Anne Bloomer, age thirty, was in the early stages of postdivorce adjustment when she agreed to a friend's urging to go on a date with a handsome football player. From their first meeting, Jerry Ford liked what he saw, and they married within a year. During their brief honeymoon, they drove to Ann Arbor, Michigan, to see a Michigan–Northwestern football game.

Other first encounters between future first ladies and their mates have run the gamut of human experience, age, and circumstances.

118

Ronald Reagan and his petite, vivacious wife Nancy.

Claudia Alta Taylor, age twenty-one, was lauded in childhood as being "as pretty as a ladybird." Widely known by the nickname so conferred, she was at the home of a friend in Austin, Texas, when the lanky secretary of a congressman dropped in.

Lyndon B. Johnson invited Lady Bird to breakfast the next day; she listened with such enthusiastic interest that he decided to make a day of it with her. Before night, he proposed marriage and she accepted. During the wedding ceremony, Lyndon pressed upon the finger of his bride a $2.50 ring purchased at Sears, Roebuck, and Company.

Louisa Johnson, daughter of an American merchant who took refuge in France during the American Revolution, was just four years old when she met an American boy of twelve. Traveling through Europe with his father, John Quincy Adams barely remembered the girl when he encountered her by chance in London a few years later. He initially showed interest in Louisa's older sister Nancy, but later he and the girl he first met when she was four were married.

Abigail Power was a teacher by the time she was twenty years old. Her oldest pupil at New Hope (New York) Academy was Millard Fillmore, age nineteen. Hour after hour of hard study led the student gradually to see his teacher in a new light. Soon she became the wife of the one-time illiterate apprentice who was destined to become the thirteenth president.

Lady Bird and Lyndon B. Johnson during their White House years.

Twenty-year-old Mary Todd's first encounter with the man she eventually married took place at a Springfield, Illinois, dance when she was there on a visit to her sister. Within a few months the Kentucky-born belle was engaged to up-and-coming attorney Abraham Lincoln, whom she married after nearly two years of hesitation.

Age sixteen when she married the new tailor in town, Andrew Johnson, in Greeneville, Tennessee, Eliza McCardle was thus the youngest bride of a future president. Her impact on subsequent American history is strong, for she taught her new husband to write and to solve simple problems in mathematics. When he was apprenticed to a tailor at age fourteen, the shop foreman had taught him to read.

Julia Boggs Dent of St. Louis was no beauty. Her face was plain, and her crossed eyes caused her to squint. That is why she was not greatly interested when her brother wrote that he planned to bring home with him from West Point military academy a friend from Ohio. Ulysses S. Grant, age twenty-six, was instantly attracted to his friend's sister, four years his junior. While out for a buggy ride, he made a hasty proposal of marriage that led to an engagement opposed by both sets of parents. Jesse R. Grant and his wife refused to attend the wedding because the parents of the bride were owners of a number of slaves.

Lucretia Rudolph of Hiram, Ohio, remained a student unusually long. At age twenty-six she was at Geauga Seminary in nearby Chester.

There she met a fellow student whom she liked so much that when he transferred to nearby Eclectic Institute, she followed. Their first meeting, which took place when she was seventeen, was followed nine years later by marriage, making "Crete" the wife of future president James A. Garfield.

Caroline ("Carrie") Lavinia Scott was fifteen when her father introduced her to Benjamin Harrison, age fourteen. They frequently studied together in the evening, became secretly engaged, and postponed their wedding until he was twenty and studying law in Cincinnati.

Ida Saxton met her future husband, Bill McKinley, at a picnic in 1867. They didn't become seriously interested in one another until she returned from a European tour and took a job as cashier in her father's bank, a post then almost always reserved for men. They married in Canton, Ohio, in 1871.

Alice Hathaway Lee was seventeen and locally noted for both her good looks and her brains when she dropped in to visit next-door neighbors. There Richard Saltonstall, home from Harvard, introduced her to a friend who had come with him. Eighteen months later, the banker's daughter became Mrs. Theodore Roosevelt. She lived, though, for only three years after they married.

Edith Kermit Carow, who became Roosevelt's second wife, was never able to recall when they were first together. This much she knew: Corinne Roosevelt, sister of Teddy, was her very best girlhood friend, and her future husband was her earliest male playmate. At their 1885 wedding, the widower-bridegroom startled friends and family by wearing orange gloves for the ceremony.

A bobsledding party brought Helen ("Nellie") Herron into contact with William Howard Taft. They met in Cincinnati when she was eighteen, soon became keenly interested in one another, but waited three years to marry.

Ellen Louise Axson first saw Woodrow Wilson in 1883 at the home of a cousin. When their marriage of twenty years ended by her death from Bright's disease, her disconsolate husband openly expressed hope he would be assassinated so he could rejoin her in the spirit world.
But then another of his cousins, Helen Bones, who had replaced Ellen as White House hostess, introduced him to the widow Edith Bolling Galt, in April 1915, and Mrs. Galt became Mrs. Woodrow Wilson.

At age seventeen Eleanor Roosevelt first met Franklin D. Roosevelt, a fifth cousin. Then a social worker in New York City, she insisted that

In the most talked-about White House wedding of the century, President Grover Cleveland took his one-time ward as his bride.

the Harvard student should go with her on her rounds. He proposed marriage a few months later, and she accepted. After announcing her complete dislike for the upcoming marriage, Franklin's mother took him on a long cruise in the hope that he would forget Eleanor.

Elizabeth ("Bess") Wallace is believed to be the only future first lady who met her husband-to-be at Sunday school. It happened in Independence, Missouri, where both were born and reared. She was five years old and Harry Truman was six, so it was nearly twenty years before the Sunday school friends became lovers.

Thelma Catherine ("Pat") Ryan didn't make the grade as a professional actress, but she continued to appear onstage in amateur productions. When word got around that the pretty young teacher would play in *The Dark Tower*, up-and-coming attorney Richard Nixon suddenly became stage-struck. He auditioned for and won a role playing opposite Pat and proposed to her on the night he learned he had been given the part.

Of all women destined to become mistress of the White House, Grace Anna Goodhue claimed to have had the most unusual first encounter with a future husband. As she often told the story, while teaching at an institute for the deaf she volunteered to water the school's flowers.

Lifting her head from the watering pot one day, she happened to glance through the open window of a nearby boarding house. There she saw a boarder standing in front of a mirror, ready to shave, wearing only long underwear and a hat.

"I burst out laughing; I couldn't help myself," she recalled. "He heard me and turned to look at me. When he learned who I was, he managed to arrange a formal introduction—and that is how I became Mrs. Calvin Coolidge!"

CHAPTER
23

Off-trail Glimpses at Wives

Eliza McArdle Johnson spent nearly four years in the White House but made only one public appearance. She broke her seclusion at the time a party was given for her grandchildren.

Lou Henry Hoover had what teachers called "a natural aptitude for languages." Without formal training, she became proficient in Chinese during her travels with her engineer husband.

Using the name *Mrs. Clarke,* widowed Mary Todd Lincoln arranged for New York broker W. H. Brady to sell some of her jewelry and fine clothing. When brokers discovered the identity of "Mrs. Clarke," she was falsely accused of having stolen White House possessions. Buyers were not interested; so Brady returned most of her goods to her unsold, along with a bill for $800.

On one of her many long jaunts, Eleanor Roosevelt persuaded the pilot of her plane to let her take over the controls, which was strictly against the rules but something she had been yearning to do for many years.

Grace Coolidge asked permission of federal officials during her third year in the White House to leave "something permanent for the mansion." When they refused to let her purchase and contribute a fine piece of furniture, she crocheted a bedspread. For years it was placed on the Lincoln bed on state occasions.

Ida McKinley never fully recovered from the birth of her daughter Ida; the trauma of childbirth left her an epileptic. Nevertheless, she stoutly insisted upon performing her expected role at official functions. Her husband almost always arranged for her to be seated at his side, so that when she became briefly unconscious he could casually drape a handkerchief over her face until she recovered.

Martha Washington's famous Friday night parties were top social events in Philadelphia when that city was the nation's capital. They

Eleanor Roosevelt, of whom aids said "She had a whim of iron," demanded—and got—control of an airplane while in flight.

always ended before 9:00 PM, however, because Martha refused to stay up past that hour.

Louisa Adams, wife of John Quincy, encouraged her husband to plant a great variety of trees and shrubs on White House grounds. Then she experimented with them, trying to find a plant suited to Washington's climate on which silk worms would thrive.

Grace Coolidge fretted that her husband never seemed to have time to play baseball with their sons. When efforts to get Calvin involved failed, she went out on the White House lawn to pitch, catch, and bat with her boys.

Jane Pierce was devastated when their eleven-year old son, Bennie, was killed in a railway accident just sixty days before his father's inauguration. Pondering the tragedy, she concluded that it was a divine act whose purpose was to rid the president-elect of all distractions as he took over the reins of government. Benny's mother refused to enter into usual White House activities and spent much of her time writing letters to her dead son.

Rachel Robards married Andrew Jackson twice. Her first vows were spoken to him in 1791, at a time when she thought that her marriage to Lewis Robards had been dissolved. Why attorney Jackson never checked up on the matter is an unsolved mystery. When they found they were not legally man and wife, Andrew and Rachel went through a 1794 ceremony—after she was positive she had been granted a divorce from Robards.

Edith Bolling Galt Wilson, second wife of the wartime president, was furious that anyone dared to question her husband's judgment in asking for a declaration of war against Germany. To demonstrate her patriotism she gave up riding in gasoline-burning vehicles and learned to ride a bicycle in White House corridors. She decided to save the manpower ordinarily used in keeping the lawns of the mansion; so she secured a flock of sheep and put them out to graze. When clipped, their ninety-eight pounds of wool were sold at auction, yielding nearly $100,000 for the war effort.

Margaret Tyler was furious when official Washington ignored the death of her husband, who had served the Confederacy after his term as president. "They could have remembered his leadership in the House of Representatives and U.S. Senate and turned their heads in order not to look at his Confederate stand," she said. Then she refused to let artisans make a death mask of the sort then commonly made of famous persons and refused to have his body embalmed before burial.

When Frances Folsom was eleven, her father was killed and Grover Cleveland became the court-appointed administrator of his estate and the young girl's informal guardian. Ten years later, in a White House ceremony Frances became the first bride of an incumbent president.

Julia Grant, who suffered from crossed eyes, listened patiently when Washington physicians explained that a simple operation would uncross them. "No," she told her advisors, "I don't want surgery of any kind. My husband likes me the way I am, and I respect him too much to make a change."

Ellen Arthur made no great objection when her husband, Chester, voluntered his services to the Union army during the Civil War. However, during the many months in which he served in the New York militia, she secretly corresponded with Virginia relatives who were in

William McKinley almost casually draped a napkin or handkerchief over his wife's face when she passed out at dinners or other official functions.

Confederate uniform and offered them her full encouragement for their cause.

Edith Bolling Wilson was proud she could trace her ancestry to the Indian princess Pocahontas. To publicize her Indian heritage, she gave Indian names to most of the many U.S. merchant vessels she christened.

Mary Todd Lincoln, whose husband was largely self-taught, spent nearly four years at an exclusive girls' school in Lexington, Kentucky. During those formative years, she and her schoolmates were allowed to converse only in French.

Julia Tyler, who long wore a forehead jewel from which ropes of pearls hung, pondered what to do at her husband's death. She decided that a suitable "mourning jewel" would be a piece of coal, cut by a jeweler and carefully polished.

Preparing to leave the White House in 1909, Edith Kermit Roosevelt ordered that the numerous family pets buried in the garden of the mansion should be exhumed for reburial at the Sagamore Hill estate.

Although the White House had been electrified years earlier, Frances Cleveland insisted that the only light used in the Red Room be a kerosene oil lamp on the center table.

Caroline Harrison was ecstatic when her husband, Benjamin, became master of the White House. She insisted on giving the entire mansion a thorough inspection, something that had not been done in many years. Everything went well until a huge attic was opened and found to be infested with rats. Undaunted, the first lady looked the place over carefully, accompanied by an armed attendant who used a pistol to shoot rats that came too near them.

Grace Coolidge, who preferred the company of her husband to that of guests, was fond of dancing with him. On one occasion when they thought that all visitors had left the mansion, she was spotted "solemnly dancing with her husband a minuet—with exaggerated bows and curtsies."

Sarah Polk, a devout Presbyterian, refused to take part in anything resembling festivity on Sunday. While she was traveling with the president-elect on an Ohio River steamer, they docked at a town where residents had prepared a musical tribute. It was futile; so long as the village band was making music, she refused to set foot outside her cabin to greet supporters and admirers.

CHAPTER
24

Mothers and Sons

Sarah ("Sallie") Delano Roosevelt, daughter of a merchant who made a fortune in the China trade, hardly knew what it meant to be told no in girlhood. She spent her father's money with a free hand, traveled extensively, and then married a widower old enough to be her father.

When her son Franklin was born, she told friends that since the boy's father was infirm, she'd "simply have to take over and act like a father." She insisted upon being addressed as "Dear Mama" and seldom let the growing boy out of her sight. If he resented her tyranny, he never admitted it.

When Franklin went to Harvard, Dear Mama dutifully rented a house in Boston to remain near him. She violently objected to her son's plan to marry a distant cousin and relented only when the couple agreed to set the date at the convenience of Uncle Ted, then the president of the United States.

Once Franklin and Eleanor were married, Dear Mama really took over. She selected the house in which they would live, chose its furniture, and hired a staff of servants. When their children began to come along, Sarah Roosevelt decided that her grandchildren needed more room. So she bought two lots on New York City's East 65th Street. On one of them she built a house for Franklin and his family; next door she built a near-duplicate for herself. Just to make sure she could always enter next door, she designed a system of connecting doors that would permit her to come and go between the two houses as she pleased.

Eleanor Roosevelt took what her mother-in-law dished out. In her recollections, *My Story*, she confessed that because of her huband's mother "I was not developing any individual taste or initiative. I was simply absorbing the personalities of those about me and letting their tastes and interests dominate me."

When F.D.R. was stricken with polio, his mother demanded that he give up his public career and retire to the quiet life of a country squire. His refusal to do so was the first time he disobeyed Dear Mama.

To her dying day, Franklin D. Roosevelt addressed his mother as "Dear Mama."

Quietly encouraged by Eleanor, he embarked upon a program of physical therapy to which his mother regularly voiced objections. By the time he was nominated for the presidency, she relented enough to become the first American woman to cast a vote aimed at putting her son in the White House.

Atittudes and actions of other mothers of presidents—and the views of their sons about them—have covered a wide spectrum.

Hannah Milhous Nixon, a devout Quaker, had just one ambition for Richard: She wanted him to become a Quaker missionary.

Lillian Carter, a registered nurse and Peace Corps volunteer at age seventy, didn't try to influence the course of her son Jimmy's life, and she instilled in him a love of reading and of learning. She was in India using the Marathi language to dispense birth control information, when she had to take a leave of absence to be present at her son's inauguration as president.

Rebekah Baines Johnson tried to guide her son with a firm hand. Married to a man whom everyone called a failure, she was determined that Lyndon would "make something of himself." That is why she taught him to read at age two and had him reading the poems of Longfellow when he was three. Over and over, she told the child that when he grew up, he would have to make a name of which she could be proud. In later life Johnson called his mother "the strongest person I ever knew."

Rose Kennedy was termed by her son John Fitzgerald "the glue that held the family together." Harry Truman summed up his feelings about his mother in a single exuberant word: "Wonderful!"

Sophia Hayes wanted her son to be a minister; against her wishes, Rutherford studied law. Huldah Hoover didn't try to force her son

Herbert into religious service; she was too busy with her work as a Quaker minister to pick his vocation. Queried in later life about her, the president frowned and tried to remember. "She was a sweet-faced woman who for two years managed to keep our little family of four together," he finally said.

Anna Pierce made a more lasting impression upon her son Franklin. He called her "strong in many points and weak in a few others" but didn't explain that her weak points included alcoholism and mental depression. Her son also was tormented by these "weak points" that became familiar to him during childhood.

Phoebe Harding was the only mother of a president to be a practicing physician. Long before malpractice suits became common, she was the target of accusations by an angry patient. A child she had been treating died suddenly while using a prescribed medication that included morphine. That brought about an 1897 charge of malpractice, settled only when a fellow physician testified that "cholera infantum," not morphine, caused the death of the baby.

Mary ("Polly") Johnson was thrown on her own resources at the death of her husband. She eked out a meager living by taking in work as a weaver and spinner and managed to pick up a few extra dollars by binding out her son Andrew as an apprentice to a tailor.

Elizabeth ("Betty") Jackson also lost her husband early. She was so busy trying to maintain the household she had little time for Andrew and his two brothers. All his life, though, the president insisted that he vividly remembered the last words she spoke to him before her death, when he was fourteen. "She told me never to lie, or steal, or quarrel—so long as my manhood was not in jeopardy," he said. Not knowing that her boy would later become an attorney, she also warned him, he said, against resorting to the courts for redress against slander. "Settle them cases, yourself," the duelist who became president quoted her as having urged.

Nancy McKinley's son remembered no solemn warnings passed along during boyhood. But he never forgot that on the evening he learned he had been elected to the presidency, his mother knelt by his bed and prayed, "O God, keep my boy humble!" Her health began to fail soon after her son was inaugurated; so William McKinley paid for installation of a special telegraph wire between the White House and her home in Canton, Ohio.

Martha Ellen Young, who married John Truman and gave birth to a son whom they named Harry without bothering to confer a middle name, spent her girlhood in deeply divided Jackson County, Missouri. Because her father was accused of having Confederate leanings, he and members of his family were herded into an improvised prison camp.

Martha Truman never forgave the Union soldiers in blue for what

Warren G. Harding was the only president who could turn to his mother when he needed the services of a physician.

they did during the Civil War and managed to instill into her son a deep distrust of the federal bureaucracy. At the same time, however, she bought with hard-earned money a blackboard for little Harry. It had on it brief biographies of all U.S. presidents, causing the boy, he later said, "to think President before I could write my name clearly."

If Martha Jefferson had a significant impact of any kind upon her son Thomas, he carefully avoided reference to it. His voluminous personal diary includes just one reference to her: "March 31st—My mother died about 8 o'clock this morning in the 57th year of her age."

John Quincy Adams's mother, Abigail, was one of the most remarkable women of her era. Too sick to go to school during girlhood, she taught herself at home and became one of the best-educated women of the period. She instilled into her son a lifelong love of learning that, he said, was a matter of first magnitude in shaping his life.

Influence upon her son, the future president, was not Abigail's only memorable accomplishment. At age nineteen she married a young country lawyer, then jumped behind him on his horse to ride off to the cottage he had inherited from his father. As the wife of John Adams, she was the first woman to be mistress of the Washington, D.C., executive mansion we now call the White House. No other woman has been both the wife of a president and the mother of a president.

Part Four

The Imperial Presidency

George Washington angrily refused to become King George I.

25

Having Defeated the British, George Washington Refused to Become King

The defeat of Lord Cornwallis at Yorktown in October 1781 left Americans victorious, but in deep trouble. There was no central government, simply a loose confederation of former colonies. In Philadelphia the situation was desperate, for the Continental Congress in session was unable even to collect customs duties.

Historian James T. Flexner calls the lawmaking body of the nation that was coming into being "as helpless as a turtle that had been turned over on its back." There was no real central authority; each former colony continued to operate independently.

Military grievances were numerous, widespread, and deep-seated. Many men had not been paid for months and there was no certainty that they ever would collect what was owed to them since many now-independent colonies were deeply in dept.

Former Continental Congressman William Duer of New York surveyed the future and saw "a prospect of obscurity if not of actual want" for men who had fought through the Revolution as officers.

Although there was widespread talk about forming a strong republic, no machinery existed for choosing a head of such a nation. Every European nation then was ruled by a sovereign, not an elected official, and most Americans had spent their lives in the British tradition, where a monarchy was taken for granted.

Hence the period just after the Revolution was perhaps the most dangerous hour of what was to become the United States of America. As yet, there was no nation and no guidelines for forming one.

However, ideas were quickly being formed about what kind of head the new nation should have. Col. Lewis Nicola, a former officer held in high esteem by General Washington, sent his commander-in-chief a seven-page document. It pointed out that veterans had little hope of being properly rewarded by the Continental Congress. Hence 65-year-old Nicola, who had found backing among both military leaders and civilians, offered a way out of the political and economic quagmire.

His "scheme" for obtaining the just dues of the army—his primary objective—was simple. America, he believed, should be organized as a monarchy, with the commander-in-chief of military forces serving as king. Washington, he suggested, should take the title of George I.

It was a popular, but not original, idea. Baroness Riedesel, wife of a captured Hessian general, complained about being kept awake all night by singing Americans shouting, "God save great Washington! God damn the King!" That song indicated that many persons had already accepted, in principle, the substitution of George Washington for England's King George III.

Alexander Hamilton had gone on record as supporting the idea of "a limited monarchy." Baron von Steuben, a revered veteran of the Revolution, wanted a king for the nation he had helped to liberate.

Bands of patriots in New York City had earlier made known their desire to put George Washington upon a throne. General Benjamin Tupper, an outspoken advocate of a king, had warned that a republic could easily fall apart, while a monarchy would be stable.

In this climate, George Washington took quick and decisive action. On May 22, 1782, the day he received Nicola's proposal, he sent a formal reply. He considered his response so important that when it was sealed, fellow officers signed their names to a statement that it had been sent. This was the only time during the entire Revolution that Washington insisted upon written witnesses of this sort.

He told Nicola that he read the proposal "with a mixture of great surprise and astonishment." No event of the long war, he said, brought him more pain than learning "of there being such ideas existing in the Army as you have expressed."

He scolded Nicola for having communicated these ideas and said he viewed the entire proposal with abhorrence. What's more, he promised that he would keep the entire matter confidential. He wanted no one to hear of it who was not already a part of the plan.

"Let me conjure you then," he told his subordinate, "if you have any regard for your Country, concern for yourself or posterity, or respect for me, to banish these thoughts from your Mind, and never communicate, as from yourself, or any one else, a sentiment of like Nature."

Long ago, historian Benjamin J. Lossing pointed out that "the annals of the nations cannot present a parallel" to George Washington's refusal to let followers and admirers make him a king. His quick response put a stop to any military plan to stage a coup.

Yet the man destined to become an elected president instead of a king was keenly aware that the liberated colonies were "on the road to

Along the route that Washington took to his first inauguration, people insisted upon making preparations "suitable for a monarch."

dictatorship." In the chaos of new-found liberty, multitudes were eager to follow anyone who seemed to offer strength and stability.

Years after Washington's refusal to become a king, there still was strong support for estabishment of an American monarchy. Such views were not limited to veterans and ordinary citizens; they were held by top elected delegates to conventions and congresses. Washington himself confessed that "even respectable characters speak of a monarchial form of Government without horror."

As late as 1788 memories of the Nicola offer were still alive, although Washington said he'd "quite forgotten about it" by then and could not "recall it to mind without much difficulty."

Even those who drafted the document that welded once-separate colonies into a coherent nation leaned in favor of a powerful chief executive. For a time it appeared that this person would be formally addressed as Excellency; the title of president of the United States was adopted only after long and heated debate.

During the two centuries in which the Constitution has been in force, the powers of the chief executive have been defined and solidified many times. Frequently, as a result of an audacious move by a daring leader, but also as an effect of what many analysts term "institutional hardening," the never-ceasing power struggle between Congress and the president has more often than not been lost by lawmakers.

Hence, additional tales in this section deal with dramatic and longlasting events whose net effect has been to give the president of the United States vastly more power than that now exercised by such monarchs as those who hold titular authority over Great Britain and Japan. If George Washington could analyze the office he helped to create, he would find it hard to believe what has taken place.

26

The First President Also Was the First to Flex His Muscles

Indignantly refusing even to consider the idea of becoming King George I, George Washington had no competitor when the nation chose its first chief executive. President Washington spent eight years in the capitals—New York and Philadelphia—and exercised his constitutional authority to the limit. In addition, he managed to do some highly significant things for which he had no legal authority.

In the spring of 1794, the chief executive signed an act of Congress that placed a new excise tax upon liquor. Money from that fresh source was badly needed to reduce the national debt.

However, especially in four counties of western Pennsylvania, sturdy Scotch-Irish farmers did not look kindly upon edicts from the new capital. For decades they had been converting their rye into whisky and selling it untaxed. That excise tax upon domestic distilled liquors was an affront; they did not intend to see it collected.

Therefore, when officers were sent to enforce the new law, resistance swelled to the level of riots, and then of armed rebellion, against the federal government. Meanwhile, citizens of neighboring sections of Virginia had joined in the violent protest.

With Congress not in session, President Washington called upon Governor Mifflin of Pennsylvania to put down the disturbances. Mifflin haughtily refused. So George Washington issued a proclamation demanding that the insurgents obey the new law. Simultaneously, he sternly called upon the governors of Pennsylvania, New Jersey, Maryland, and Virginia to provide armed forces to number at least 13,000 men.

When the chief executive got word that men involved in the Whisky Rebellion numbered about 16,000, he called for 2,000 more soldiers to meet them in battle, if necessary.

Gen. Henry Lee of Virginia, placed in command of a portion of the federal body, marched toward the troubled region. At many points he found liberty poles erected; some had placards reading "Liberty! and no Excise!" George Washington had been burned in effigy at some population centers.

Although they had talked a strong fight, leaders of the internal rebellion capitulated when George Washington's army began pouring into their section. They were forced to accept the federal statutes, unmodified, and to swear their fidelity to the laws of the land.

Washington had led colonial forces that fought against British taxation; to him, it was a different matter entirely when his own citizens threatened to fight a tax of which he had approved. His actions, taken without congressional approval, effectively crushed the first major challenge to the authority of the federal government.

Once the Whisky Rebellion collapsed, the first president again took matters into his own hands. He issued a blanket pardon to the rebels on July 10, 1795, again without having consulted Congress except in unofficial ways. Lawmakers were highly insulted; they created such turmoil that George Washington was forced to appear before them in person to explain his actions and to ask for their approval after the fact.

Although the cost of putting down the Whisky Rebellion was estimated at $1,500,000, the president's actions with respect to it could be interpreted by his admirers as having been within the "reasonable power of the chief executive."

Not so his undercover dealings by which he managed to locate the new capital almost exactly where he wanted it. Powerful industrial and banking interests wanted the federal government to remain in what is now the Northeast. Members of the New York legislature thought they had gained a big advantage over competitors when in 1783 they offered to Congress "a separate district for the Honorable Congress": one square mile within the town limits of Kingston.

Annapolis, Maryland, made a similar offer and then New Jersey offered a blank check, a free site "anywhere in the colony."

Few persons in places of influence were unaware that George Washington had his heart set on establishing the permanent capital in his home state of Virginia. Even that location was not sufficiently precise to suit him. He would be satisfied with nothing less than a site on the Potomac River, which flowed past his own Mount Vernon estate.

Almost certainly prodded by the president, tobacco barons of Virginia made an offer that topped all earlier ones. They would cede to the federal government the town of Williamsburg and would contribute £100,000 toward building the capital.

Richard Lee led much of the southern assault, with New Yorkers his strongest and most vocal opponents. They seemed to be approaching stalemate when George Washington, says oral tradition, had an inspiration.

It was well known that Alexander Hamilton had advanced fiscal measures that seemed to be extreme, so far out that they had little chance of passage. But Hamilton was admired and revered throughout the Northeast. What if the Secretary of the Treasury could be persuaded to put his personal influence behind a southern site for the capital, in exchange for votes that would ensure enactment of fiscal measures he proposed?

It was this undercover swap that simultaneously ended what threatened to become two deadlocked sets of proposals. Hamilton parlayed in New York and New Jersey; in return, many southern leaders came out in favor of his fiscal proposals.

Maryland and Virginia each ceded ten square miles to the federal government. George Washington then negotiated with nineteen proprietors, who sold land for public buildings at $125 per acre. As proclaimed in 1791, the District of Columbia was a square made up of sixty-four square miles in Maryland thirty-four square miles in Virginia.

When the site of the capital city was selected on the banks of the Potomac River, precisely as the president wished, his fervent admirers insisted that it be named Washington City in his honor. He is said to have assented to this proposal "with decorum and due modesty."

Having effectively demonstrated that when the president of the United States flexes his muscles things are likely to happen, he turned his attention to intensely personal matters. During his years of leadership he had generated what, for the time, was an immense quantity of documents.

Except for personal letters written when he was not on the nation's payroll or its expense account, all of these papers had been produced at the expense of taxpayers. Logically, they were the property of the federal government.

But a president who has strong ideas is not always influenced by logic. George Washington calmly took personal possession of all the papers he could amass and treated them as his own property.

Early in his administration, he had said, "Many things which appear of little importance in themselves and at the beginning may have great and durable consequences from their having been established at the commencement of a new general government." That is, precedent can become so fixed that it is more powerful than either logic or law.

It was President Washington's extralegal appropriation of documents pertaining to his leadership that set a still-standing precedent. Every succeeding president who has cared to do so has taken personal possession of papers generated during his years in the White House. All existing presidential libraries, most of which require immense amounts of money paid to the federal government by taxpayers, owe their precise character to the fact that George Washington not only wanted government documents; he seized and kept his own documents.

CHAPTER 27

Thomas Jefferson
Went Outside the Law
in America's Largest Land Deal

A transaction termed "one of the shadiest real estate deals in history" brought the United States about 828,000 square miles at a cost of about three cents an acre. Land gained in this purchase makes up most or all of present-day Louisiana, Arkansas, Missouri, Iowa, Minnesota, North Dakota, South Dakota, Nebraska, Kansas, Oklahoma, Texas, New Mexico, Colorado, Wyoming, and Montana.

Thomas Jefferson, who made the deal, was acutely conscious that he acted without constitutional authority. What's more, no principal participant in the transaction had ever seen—or ever would see—what was then called Louisiana. No one knew the boundaries or size, which were not even discussed in detail until the papers were signed.

According to present-day experts in constitutional law, the instrument of transfer "would have horrified a first-year law student." Under its terms the United States agreed to pay Napoleon I of France more money than existed in the entire nation. To be borrowed at 6 percent interest, the sum was so great that even Jefferson's agents feared that it could cause the collapse of the federal government.

Yet the deal went through and helped to elevate "Long Tom" Jefferson to the ranks of "most important and most admired presidents of the United States."

It all started soon after the turn of the nineteenth century. Early in his war with Great Britain, Napoleon realized that the conflict would cost him his key North American outpost. New Orleans would surely fall because British sea power was overwhelming. Since he was due to lose the port city and surrounding territory, why not turn the matter to advantage by selling New Orleans to the Americans?

In Paris, Pierre Du Pont heard rumors that France might be willing to make a sale to the United States. He notified Thomas Jefferson,

American commissioners who signed the pact by which Louisiana was purchased did not know how much land was involved or how they would pay for it.

who persuaded Congress to promise the sum of $2,000,000, under strict conditions. Robert R. Livingston, U.S. minister to France, was instructed in May 1802 to make inquiries about the possible purchase of Louisiana from the French.

Thomas Jefferson did not know the exact extent of the unexplored land the French held in North America, but he knew that he wanted some of it. The valuable port of New Orleans was of prime strategic importance for the new nation. Since Jefferson doubted that Napoleon would be willing to part with all of New Orleans, he instructed his agents, "If the entire port cannot be acquired, try for a good riverbank site for a dock plus warehouses—along with *some* land at the very mouth of the river." Such a targeted site would lie east of the Mississippi; Jefferson let it be known that he was willing to leave everything west of the river in French hands.

Better than anyone else, the president knew that he was walking on very thin ice in even discussing such a deal. He knew that the Constitution does not authorize the president to purchase land for the nation.

Jefferson was so agitated that he personally drew up a proposed amendment to the Constitution and pondered the wisdom of offering it for ratification *after* the purchase had been made.

Keenly aware that he was acting more like a monarch that an elected chief executive, the president felt that he had to seize the opportunity without waiting for approval of Congress or for funding.

James Monroe was named to serve as a special envoy. He sailed for France on March 8, 1803. By the time he arrived, however, Robert Livingston had already entered into negotiations with the French.

Jefferson's instructions were clear. Monroe was to try to purchase New Orleans and about 75,000 square miles of territory. For such a deal, the president's special envoy was authorized to offer up to $9,380,000.

On Easter Sunday, April 10, 1803, Napoleon reached a decision. He considered Louisiana "already lost," but he desperately wanted to keep it out of British hands. That aspect weighed more heavily with him than the money from the sale to the Americans.

Napoleon sent for Livingston and Monroe, who hoped for approval of their modest plan to buy New Orleans and the adjacent land. Instead of giving his assent to this proposal, Napoleon astonished them by offering to sell all French possessions in North America.

Livingston and Monroe were cautiously negative in their response. They knew that the suggested purchase price involved more money than existed in the entire United States. So they came back with a counterproposal.

Dickering between high-level French officials and U.S. diplomats brought agreement. For a tract of land half as large as all of Europe west of Russia, the purchasers would pay $15,000,000, but not in cash. Payment would be by means of a special issue of stock bearing 6 percent interest and not redeemable for fifteen years.

Napoleon instructed his representatives to accept what the Americans had labeled their final offer. So a formal agreement was signed on April 30, 1803.

President Jefferson tried to keep the matter secret, but he failed. When news of the deal reached the United States, opposition was loud and furious. Federalist spokesman John Cabot fumed that "the cession of Louisiana is like selling us a ship after she is surrounded by a British fleet." Fisher Ames labeled the acquisition of land by purchase as "mean and despicable"—particularly when done by Republicans. "The less of territory, the better," Ames declared. "By adding an unmeasured world beyond the Mississippi, we rush like a comet into infinite space."

Some leaders, especially in New England, were so angry that they talked of leading their states to secede from the union. Jefferson's purchase of a wilderness by a stroke of his pen was pure madness, critics cried, calculated to foster formation of three separate republics—one in the East, a second in the South, and the third in the West. Federalist Tapping Reeve of Connecticut consulted many of his colleagues, and reported that because of the purchase of Louisiana "all

Thomas Jefferson seriously considered sponsoring a constitutional amendment to approve his Louisiana purchase—after the fact.

believe we must separate, and this is the favorable moment to do so." Highly respected Timothy Pickering of Massachusetts called Jefferson a tyrant and went on record: "I do not believe in the practicability of a long-continued union."

Despite such talk from political leaders, public opinion soon began to favor the deal. In the Senate the treaty of purchase was approved by a vote of twenty-seven to seven. Members of the House of Representatives voted eighty-nine to twenty-three in favor of issuing the stock by which the purchase was made. These actions came, of course, months after the Paris agreement had been signed.

Support for the idea of a constitutional amendment to make Jefferson's actions legal gradually faded; it did not seem to matter any longer. So at New Orleans on December 20, 1803, the United States took formal possession. In addition to the coveted port city, the deal brought land from which all or part of fourteen states were formed.

What did Napoleon get, in the end?

Hope and Company of the Netherlands joined Barin Brothers of London in offering to purchase stock at a discount. With $3,750,000 set aside to satisfy claims against France by U.S. citizens and the stock discounted, Napoleon received $9,843,750 minus commisions of brokers.

Part of the "delicious irony" of the vast transaction lay in the fact that by means of it, British bankers advanced to Napoleon cash he wanted to use for his planned invasion of Britain.

Just twenty-seven years after having framed the Declaration of Independence, Thomas Jefferson used presidential power in a fashion neither he nor any other founding father had anticipated. Constitution or no Constitution, "Long Tom" had pulled off the biggest land deal in the history of the United States.

28

Two Presidents Brought Texas into the Union "Under the Rug"

Admirers of Andrew Jackson regarded him as "the finest thing ever to come out of Tennessee." Critics vied with one another in attempts to find words with which to express their fear and disgust at traits of the chief executive whose face was shown on special playing cards, with the title of "King Andrew I."

Widely revered as "Old Hickory," Jackson showed his cavalier attitude toward legal restrictions during his famous fight with the British at New Orleans. To assume complete control of the city, Jackson imposed martial law. Simultaneously, he dissolved the state legislature, put an end to free speech, and ignored a writ of habeas corpus issued by a federal judge. That last act of defiance brought him a fine of $1,000.

Much later, his fine was refunded by a grateful Congress. But in 1817 when Jackson went off to Florida to fight the Seminoles, he had no idea that events would take such a turn.

Into Florida he carried orders from President Monroe forbidding him to enter Spanish territory except when in pursuit of troops with whom he had been fighting. Instead, Jackson led his men in an invasion of Spanish Florida, where he overthrew the governor and executed British subjects Alexander Arbuthnot and Robert Ambrister, after a hasty court martial convicted them of having incited the Seminoles. Even fiery John C. Calhoun, then U.S. secretary of war, wanted to have Jackson formally reprimanded for having gone beyond his authority. That effort failed because many Americans saw that actions of Old Hickory would lead Spain to give up Florida.

As chief executive, the man who became a folk hero as a duelist fought with Congress as though on the field of honor. He successfully brought about the demise of the Second Bank of the United States, for which the U.S. Senate voted formal censure in 1834.

Therefore national leaders and ordinary citizens knew that the occu-

Because of Andrew Jackson's "high and mighty ways," political foes mocked him as "King Andrew I." [NEW YORK HISTORICAL SOCIETY]

pant of the White House paid little attention to restrictive regulations. Use and abuse of presidential power was hotly debated, partly because many were sure that Old Hickory would once more go overboard with respect to Texas.

Public opinion was right. Andrew Jackson chose March 1837 for an act sure to infuriate multitudes of citizens. What did he have to lose? He was scheduled to relinquish the White House to Martin Van Buren.

Keenly aware that his timing meant he would suffer no personal political damage, Jackson devoted part of his last day in office to a ceremony in which the independence of the Lone Star Republic was recognized by presidential proclamation.

Texans had declared their independence a year and a day earlier as the culmination of a series of climactic events. Mexico won independence from Spain in 1821 and initially encouraged Americans to settle in her Texas province. Strings were attached to the open-door policy, however. Slavery was forbidden, and all newcomers were required to become Catholics.

During ten years an estimated 20,000 Americans swarmed across the Mississippi River into Texas. Most ignored the religious requirement, and all thumbed their noses at the prohibition of slavery. Angry

Mexican authorities eventually sent armies to subdue their rebellious Texas residents.

These frontiersmen banded together, made Tennessee-born Sam Houston their commander-in-chief, and won a decisive victory at San Jacinto. Mexican troops were forced to withdraw below the Rio Grande, but the central government refused to acknowledge the independence of the province.

Almost all citizens of the region, now called the Lone Star Republic, were eager to see it become a part of the United States. But there was strong opposition to such a course of action, particularly in the Northeast. If carved into five to seven states, the territory would guarantee southern control of Congress for years or decades to come.

Because the slavery issue was already threatening to divide the United States, anti-Texas sentiment was both deep and widespread. That is the reason Andrew Jackson avoided taking action until he was ready to leave Washington and return to Nashville. Bypassing normal channels through which Congress would have had an active part in deciding whether or not to recognize Texas as an independent nation, Jackson resorted to use of a presidential proclamation.

Although the legal ground was shaky, the now-recognized independent nation carved from Mexico got busy. President Sam Houston, Jackson's protégé and close friend, worked with the Texas congress in developing plans to perfect close ties with Great Britain.

Few if any Texans ever actually wanted their nation to become a British satellite, but they needed to mold public opinion in the United States. Their ploy worked so effectively that northern business and industrial leaders, suddenly fearful of British influence, relaxed their stand against admission of Texas to the United States.

In this climate a second president may have abused the power of his office to achieve the goal sought by Jackson and Houston.

Virginia-born John Tyler asked his secretary of state, John C. Calhoun, to draw up a treaty granting statehood to Texas. Calhoun complied and to the document attached a passage extolling the virtues of slavery. Therefore when the formal treaty was presented to the U.S. Senate, it was rejected by a vote of thirty-six to sixteen.

Tyler did not protest, but bided his time. In February 1845 he was ending his administration, and he could take risks he had dodged earlier.

Bypassing established procedures, Tyler prepared a joint resolution. Eight years after Jackson's presidential proclamation had recognized Texas's independence, this paper provided for admission of the republic into the union.

Under the Constitution, a joint resolution of Congress does not re-

President Sam Houston man-
aged to win diplomatic recog-
nition of the Republic of Texas
from a number of European
nations.

quire the two-thirds vote in the Senate that is stipulated for the making of a treaty. It becomes effective when a majority in both houses approves it.

In the Senate, it was nip-and-tuck, finally passing by a vote of twenty-seven to twenty-five. A much wider margin in the House made Tyler's legislation effective. So by means of a congressional resolution drafted by a president—not by means of a treaty between independent nations—the Lone Star Republic became the twenty-eighth state late in 1845.

CHAPTER 29

Under Pressures of Civil War the Constitution Was Pushed Aside

Before going to the White House, Abraham Lincoln spent years as a successful attorney. Yet during his administration he presided over what many of the period called "the American Bastille," referring to the infamous French prison of that name.

Under Lincoln, the lawyer-president, the Constitution was repeatedly pushed aside, and for a period the nation teetered on the brink of military dictatorship. There were wholesale arbitrary arrests, often for trifling offenses. A cherished legal right, that of release from custody under a writ of habeas corpus, was suspended over and over. Prominent citizens, including elected officials, were stripped of their power and sometimes thrown into jail.

Were such actions the punishment for citizens of the Confederate States of America fighting against Union forces? Not at all. Wanton violation of constitutionally guaranteed personal rights took place in territory solidly within the Union or under military control of Union forces.

On April 27, 1861, bowing to what appeared to be military necessity, the chief executive suspended the writ of habeas corpus along the line that marked movement of troops between Washington and Philadelphia.

That was the first of numerous actions, most of them placing power in the hands of military commanders. Florida was affected by an order of May 1861. Two months later Gen. Winfield Scott was authorized to suspend the writ of habeas corpus at any point along the military line that stretched from Washington City to New York City.

"Loyal states" were specified as the target of an October 1862 directive. Nearly a year later the nation's justices were ordered not to attempt to use habeas corpus in the case of persons affected by the universally hated military draft.

Naturally there was a storm of criticism by anti-Lincoln spokesmen and by persons who saw themselves as defenders of the U.S. Constitution. But some people solidly within the ranks of the administration whose executive power grew stronger as civil war progressed were opposed to stripping citizens of their constitutional rights.

Henry W. Halleck, who was for a time general-in-chief of the army, wrote that in his opinion "treasonable acts, in the Loyal States, should be left for trial by the courts, as provided in the Act of Congress." Rogert B. Taney, Chief Justice of the U.S. Supreme Court, objected to trampling civil rights under foot. Even he was powerless, however, for directives signed by the president placed authority in the hands of military commanders.

Maryland, home of many sympathizers with the Confederate cause, was particularly hard hit. "Obstreperous" citizens were arrested and held without trial. Some members of state legislatures were among those seized. When protests were voiced, Abraham Lincoln announced that for reasons of public safety, no information could be given out concerning offenses of persons jailed.

On August 8, 1862, a directive by Secretary of War Edward M. Stanton implemented the unspoken wishes of the president. Under terms of Stanton's order, it became a prison offense to "give aid or comfort to the enemy."

Precisely what constituted such aid or comfort?

As interpreted by authorities who were moving toward the full military dictatorship that some considered essential for preservation of the

U.S. Secretary of War Edwin M. Stanton implemented unconstitutional infringements upon rights of citizens—in keeping with the president's wishes. [NATIONAL ARCHIVES]

union, it was a prison offense to attend a meeting at which subversive statements were made. To complain about the war or to "give a hurrah for Jeff Davis" could put a person behind bars.

Many who were arrested for such offenses not only never saw the inside of a courtroom, they weren't even given the privilege of a hasty hearing before a military commission. A few people with prominent connections managed to win freedom after arbitrary arrest, but the majority were held for weeks or months.

The Prisoner of State, an 1863 volume published in New York, gave a detailed report of the suppression of the Maryland legislature and arrest of some of its members. In addition it described what the publishers termed the "kidnapping" of half a dozen notables.

An 1869 volume on *The American Bastille* summarized dozens of cases. American citizens who were arrested and thrown behind bars as "prisoners of state" came from Indiana, New Jersey, Illinois, Minnesota, New York, Ohio, Maine, Maryland, Vermont, Delaware, Pennsylvania, Kentucky, and Connecticut. Even Iowa, far removed from battle, was not immune from effects of the military dictatorship. At least one "prisoner of state" was captured in faraway California.

Election to an important office was not an automatic source of protection. In addition to Maryland legislators, Mayor Brown of Baltimore was arrested. The charge? "Complicity with those in armed rebellion against the Government of the United States." That charge could mean anything an officer wished, for he was free to define "complicity."

Moving beyond constitutional bounds in a different fashion, the Lincoln administration devised a punishment without legal standing in the United States. Former U.S. Congressman Clement L. Vallandigham, a consistent source of trouble because of his demand that peace be made between warring sections, refused to be silenced. At a meeting in Columbus, Ohio, he publicly criticized the president, Gen. Ambrose Burnside, and orders that he said violated civil rights. To conclude his personal demonstration against them he called the chief executive "King Lincoln," then spat upon a copy of the military order that forbade criticism of administration policies.

Arrested and jailed, the former congressman knew that a writ of habeas corpus was unlikely to bring freedom, yet he asked for it. U.S. Circuit Court Judge Humphrey H. Leavitt refused to issue such a writ, and Vallandigham was ordered placed in close confinement for the duration of the war. New York Governor Horatio Seymour exploded. He insisted that the president should personally intervene, contending that Lincoln's response to his demand would "determine in the minds of more than one half of the people of the Loyal States,

Arrested at 2:00 A.M. and charged with treason, ex-Congressman Clement L. Vallandigham received the extra-constitutional sentence of banishment.

whether the war is waged to put down rebellion at the South, or destroy free institutions at the North."

This blunt language from New York's governor threw the celebrated case into the lap of the president. Pondering alternatives, Abraham Lincoln concluded that he could neither free the accused nor affirm the verdict of the military commission. So he resorted to punishment for which there was neither legal basis nor precedent; he decided to banish Vallandigham from Union territory.

Lambdin P. Milligan, another native of Ohio who was considered a threat to the Union, was arrested after detectives heard him speak at a Plymouth, Indiana, meeting. Charged with treason and found guilty after a series of moves and countermoves, he was ordered to be executed by hanging. President Andrew Johnson, who had succeeded slain Abraham Lincoln, approved the sentence in May 1865.

Lee had surrendered at Appomatox a month earlier; the war was over. Still, Milligan's execution date was set for Friday, May 19. That is when Gov. Oliver P. Morton of Indiana sent J. W. Pettit as a special representative to the White House. With execution delayed, on June 1 Milligan's sentence was commuted to life imprisonment at hard labor.

Appealed all the way to the U.S. Supreme Court, Milligan's sentence was set aside in April 1866. With the war over and Lincoln dead, the nation's top jurists handed down a seven-part ruling. Paragraph five of that ruling stipulated—too late to help thousands—that even when the privilege of habeas corpus is suspended, a citizen not in military service "cannot be tried, convicted, or sentenced otherwise than by the ordinary courts of law."

That ruling effectively ended the era during which the nation had been perilously close to military dictatorship. But it did nothing to address the central issue of presidential assumption of powers not stipulated in the Constitution.

Far the most dramatic and long-lasting exercise of such power on the part of the Civil War president was his world-renowned Emancipation Proclamation.

Earlier, Abraham Lincoln had gone on record as believing that the slavery issue could best be handled by sending blacks to the new African state of Liberia, or by gradual emancipation with compensation to owners of slaves. As the war progressed, it became increasingly evident that such measures would not solve the problem. At the same time, blacks in slavery were seen as potential sources of aid to the Union.

Beginning about June 1862, Lincoln worked on the draft of a presidential proclamation that would have the effect of boosting the war effort. After days of work, the president submitted a draft of his paper to members of his cabinet, who varied widely in their reactions.

Salmon P. Chase, secretary of the treasury, said he wished the language were stronger in reference to the arming of blacks. Postmaster General Montgomery Blair deprecated the policy on the grounds that it would cost the administration the fall elections. William Henry Seward, secretary of state, said that "I fear the effect of so important a step. It may be viewed as the last measure of an exhausted government, stretching forth its hands to Ethiopia, instead of Ethiopia stretching forth its hands to the government."

If anyone present at that fateful meeting pondered that the U.S. Constitution does not empower the president to liberate slaves, he kept his thoughts to himself. But on Seward's advice Lincoln agreed to wait for a major military victory to make public the document he had decided to issue, regardless of what advisors might think.

In September 1862 came the opportunity. In the bloody battle of Antietam, Union forces failed to win a decisive victory but at least managed to stop the Confederates in their drive toward Washington. Lincoln called his cabinet together again. He first read a funny chapter from the latest book by Artemus Ward, then made public a new draft of his preliminary proclamation.

"I do not wish your advice about the main matter," he said, "for that I have determined for myself. If there is anything in the expressions I use which any one of you thinks had best be changed, I shall be glad to receive the suggestions."

When released, the presidential order stipulated that if states then in rebellion did not return to their allegiance within one hundred days—by January 1, 1863—"the President will issue another proclamation whereby the slaves in those states will become forever free."

When the final Emancipation Proclamation was issued on January 1, many ardent abolitionists protested loudly. They noted that not only did it free no slaves in states loyal to the Union, but it also endorsed "the effort to colonize persons of African descent" as a means of ridding the nation of them.

Regions designated as in a state of rebellion, and therefore theoretically affected, were Arkansas, Texas, Louisiana (except 13 counties), Mississippi, Alabama, Florida, Georgia, South Carolina, North Carolina, and Virginia (except West Virginia and seven other counties).

Lincoln's edict, therefore, applied to slaves held in a region over which he had no authority. It was stipulated that slave-holding states in Union territory, and regions specifically exempted in the proclamation, should be "for the present, left precisely as if this proclamation were not issued."

Not one slave actually gained freedom on January 1, 1863, but the psychological and political effects of the Emancipation Proclamation were enormous. Both England and France had been wavering about which side to support in the U.S. Civil War. Lincoln's edict helped to swing both public opinion and official policies of these nations toward the Union cause. If anyone bothered to comment that the chief executive had no constitutional authority for his edict, that comment was lost in the hubbub of excitement over what from a distance seemed to be a giant step toward social justice.

Acting in his role as commander-in-chief of Union military forces, Abraham Lincoln issued the Emancipation Proclamation as a war measure. Nothing in the Constitution prohibited slavery; Congress had taken no action and had not been consulted. Still, the edict caught the attention of the world, and its real purpose was seldom emphasized.

Subsequent chief executives have learned from Lincoln, however. Citing exigencies of war or other national emergencies, presidents have increasingly relied upon edicts and proclamations to effect ends not readily accomplished by conventional processes. More and more, decisions by presidents have been made and implemented in secret, concealed not only from the public, but also from other elected officials.

Hence the document now generally viewed as having been framed by Lincoln in the name of freedom has had the long-range effect of reducing personal freedom of all U.S. citizens, who are increasingly subject to still-expanding powers of the "imperial presidency."

CHAPTER

30

Herbert Hoover
Sent Future Military Leaders
against Veterans

A t the time of their inauguration, only a few chief executives commanded the respect and admiration that Americans focused upon Herbert Hoover on March 4, 1929. It was widely known that he had started at the bottom, pushing ore carts in a California mine for seventy hours a week, and had made millions as a mining engineer in Burma. In the aftermath of World War I he had headed American relief efforts in stricken Europe and had been economic advisor to Woodrow Wilson before serving seven years as U.S. Secretary of Commerce. Here was a man who was self-made in the best sense of that term. Though wealthy and powerful, such a man obviously could never forget that he had once been poor and powerless.

That line of reasoning prevailed until the effects of Black Thursday, October 24, 1929, began to be felt throughout the nation. From the first, Hoover made it clear that federal attempts to offset the stock market crash would be limited to big business. He was steadfast in his opposition to any program designed to give direct federal aid to the unemployed and the homeless.

Therefore, by New Year's Day 1932 the president had become an object of derision. Throughout the nation the cold and the hungry called newspapers "Hoover blankets." Rabbits and ponies slaughtered for food were dubbed "Hoover hogs." In a symbolic gesture, many men consistently wore their trousers with empty pockets turned inside out, displaying "Hoover flags" in a futile show of anger at the occupant of the White House.

It was in this climate of national despair that Walter W. Waters of Portland, Oregon, became spokesman for and leader of a special group of disgruntled citizens: veterans of World War I who were down on their luck. Congress had earlier voted a special bonus of about $1,000

Though organized on the west coast, the Bonus Army was soon augmented by units from New York and other eastern states.

per man, but it was payable in twenty years. Hungry, desperate veterans decided that they wanted at least part of that bonus immediately.

Under Waters's leadership, men formed what they called the Bonus Expeditionary Force, or B.E.F., an obvious take-off on World War I's American Expeditionary Force. When their petitions and protests went unheard, they decided to march on Washington, D.C., to present and dramatize their demands.

When Herbert Hoover ordered members of the B.E.F. to remain at home, they ignored him. Initially small, their band gradually swelled as it moved slowly across the continent. At distant points other groups of veterans organized and began moving toward the capital, hoping to arrive at about the same time as the B.E.F.

By late June, an estimated 8,000 to 10,000 veterans had reached the outskirts of Washington. By then generally called the Bonus Army, the bands of men who had fought in World War I established a camp in mud flats across the Anacostia River from the capital. They built shacks of tar paper—which they called "Hoover Villas"—dug latrines, and organized soup kitchens.

With the U.S. Senate scheduled to vote on their demand for immediate partial payment of the promised bonus, nearly 10,000 veterans converged upon the Capitol. Their presence had no effect; lawmakers quashed the proposal that the president had promised to veto if enacted.

Some weary marchers went home, but most remained. They were

little, if any, more miserable in Anacostia Flats than they would be back home. A few lucky ones managed to set up squatters' camps in partly demolished buildings on lower Pennsylvania Avenue. Soon they were given four days to vacate these buildings.

At 9:40 A.M. on July 28, 1932, "Commander-in-chief" Walter Waters shouted to his men, "We've been double-crossed! We have ten minutes to get out, instead of four days!"

More than 200 veterans cleared a building without incident. But ten minutes later a small band of them rushed the 100 District of Columbia policemen who were standing guard. Bricks were thrown for five minutes, then the tension eased. Early that afternoon, new violence erupted.

One B.E.F. member, never identified, wanted to get his hands on U.S. Treasury agents who were directing the work of police officers. Four members of the Washington police force were attacked; two of them opened fire. William J. Haska of Chicago was killed on the spot, and wounded veteran Eric Carlson died the next day.

All police officers of the capital's forces were ordered to the scene of the melee, but 660 men were helpless against 20,000 ragged and desperate veterans. The clash of these forces launched one of the worst riots in American history.

Herbert Hoover, who had assumed personal command of anti-veteran forces, had already decided what he would do in case the conflict grew worse. Without hesitation, he sent for federal troops to

Following the orders of the president, General Douglas MacArthur led assault forces whose ranks included future president Dwight D. Eisenhower and George S. Patton.

subdue men whose numbers included many who had spent months in trenches in France.

Upon orders of the president, Gen. Douglas MacArthur directed a series of assaults aimed at driving the dissidents from Washington. His liaison officer with the D.C. police department was Maj. Dwight D. Eisenhower. Maj. George S. Patton commanded one of the units under MacArthur's command.

MacArthur, Eisenhower, and Patton had a powerful force: troops of cavalry with sabers drawn, ready to charge; six tanks; infantry units whose members had their bayonets in place and from whose belts hung cannisters of tear gas. This force, quite without parallel in America's annals, had clear-cut orders. They were to use any means necessary to drive out members of the B.E.F. who occupied Anacostia Flats and a dozen other makeshift camps.

Although each leader of the forces assigned to drive out the veterans was destined to become a top military leader, by a quirk of fate the three of them—MacArthur, Eisenhower, and Patton—were together in only one battle, that of Anacostia Flats. Once all federal buildings had been cleared of protesters, the action moved to Maryland and Anacostia Flats, focal point of a clash that many seasoned observers termed "a battle almost as violent as some during the Civil War."

Tear gas caused thousands of men to abandon cardboard boxes, tar-paper shacks, and shelters made of egg crates and rusty tin. Women who had come to be with their men and who resisted orders were shown the business end of bayonets. Frightened and crying children were prodded out of the battle line.

Troops of the attacking army then set fire to the shacks and burned Anacostia Flats to the ground. Maryland officials offered members of the Bonus Army free transportation, hoping to get them across the state line into Pennsylvania, where they could be dumped.

Already Hoover was blamed for the Great Depression; now his decision to use federal troops against men who had risked their lives for their country drew additional criticism. It was dubbed "the most emperor-like action by a twentieth-century president." Aware that he had no chance of re-election, Hoover ignored public sentiment and refused an invitation to ceremonies that brought the bonus march to a formal end.

As remnants of the defeated Bonus Expeditionary Army headed back home, Bill Haska received one benefit to which his service record entitled him, burial in Arlington National Cemetery. At the funeral services, which Herbert Hoover chose not to attend, the honor guard was made up of men from the Third Cavalry, one of the units called up by the president to fight and to win the Battle of Anacostia Flats.

31

The East Wing Staff Has Mushroomed in Near Secrecy

"**O**ne should not live to oneself," Edith Carow (Mrs. Theodore) Roosevelt said in a letter to her son Ted. "It was a temptation to me, only Father would not allow it."

Keenly conscious of others—relatives, constituents, admirers, and members of the general public—she fretted that there was seldom enough time in the day to handle personal correspondence. She was especially aware of the way the public felt about members of the president's household because some of her own letters to Mrs. McKinley were never answered.

Talking things over with her husband, Edith Roosevelt told him that she would never be able to keep up with the letters she felt obligated to write unless she had some help. Roosevelt admitted that this was a problem and took a radical step.

For more than 100 years, no wife of a president had enjoyed the assistance of a personal secretary. But Teddy Roosevelt arranged to get a war department clerk, Isabella L. Hagner, assigned as a part-time social secretary to the first lady. Soon work accumulated so much that she became a full-time aide to Mrs. Roosevelt, though still on the war department payroll.

"I cannot say that I felt entirely at ease, but I do know that I was very thrilled," Hagner later said as she recalled having launched a brand new federal operation.

If she were alive today, she would hardly believe what has gradually taken place.

During the Reagan presidency, an average of about sixteen aides worked directly for Nancy Reagan. Unofficially known as the East Wing staff, these people are listed on official rolls as employees of the Office of the First Lady.

Edith Carow (Mrs. Theodore) Roosevelt rejoiced at having a War Department clerk assigned to her—part time—to help with her correspondence.

Can an ordinary citizen find out what this network of helpers costs taxpayers? Not easily. A call to the Office of Management and Budget late in Ronald Reagan's second term was referred to Elaine Crispen, whose primary function was to serve as press secretary to the first lady.

It took a written request to get a response that said very little, except that members of a big staff work at scheduling, projects, press, social matters, and correspondence.

According to Crispen, the East Wing staffers had no information about White House operations prior to the Reagan years. They were unable to provide any information about the size of early staffs assigned to the wives of presidents or the money required to keep them functioning.

Part, but not all, of the vacuum of information can be filled by scanning issues of the Washington *Post*. According to a story in that newspaper, Mabel Hobart Brandon, head of a public relations firm, was Nancy Reagan's first social secretary. Muffie, as she is known to friends, started in 1981 at a salary of $45,000-plus per year. Linda Faulkner, who later took over the post, headed a larger staff than that of any first lady since Lou (Mrs. Herbert) Hoover began the practice.

Soon after she became mistress of the White House in 1929, Mrs. Hoover expanded her staff to three, all of whom functioned as secretaries. One of them, Polly Randolph, was on the federal payroll. Her colleagues, Ruth Festler and Mildred Hall, were paid by Mrs. Hoover. Collectively, they constituted the largest staff of a first lady up to that time.

A recent issue of the official *Federal Executive Directory* listed Nancy Reagan's staff as consisting of: chief of staff; executive assistant to chief of staff; special assistant; staff assistant; press secretary to the first lady; deputy press secretary; staff assistant; social secretary for the first lady; deputy social secretary; staff assistant; projects, scheduling and advance director; deputy directory; staff assistant; correspondence director.

Perhaps it should be noted, in passing, that the function of social secretary that Mrs. Roosevelt put first gradually drifted to the bottom of the pecking order in the staff assigned to the first lady.

Salaries are not listed in the *Directory*, and inquiries about them are treated as though it is none of a citizen's business. However, scattered through the pages of the *Post*, there are suggestive clues.

Muffie Brandon's 1981 salary was nowhere near the highest. Jennefer Hirshberg, who took over as Mrs. Reagan's press secretary in 1985, started at $53,733, $28,733 more than Abraham Lincoln was paid as president.

James Rosebush, who resigned as the first lady's chief of staff in 1986, vacated a $72,000 position. Lee Verstandig, who succeeded him, stayed just twenty-four days before announcing his resignation. By that time, in-house rivalry was intense between the staff of the president (whose title is not uniformly capitalized) and that of the first lady (whose title is almost always capitalized in many federal publications and in press releases). West Wing staff members answer directly to the president; East Wingers are responsible to the first lady.

Under Jacqueline Kennedy, her social secretary designed new press policies. Reporters were no longer allowed to talk with guests at social events arranged by the social secretary.

As late as Jimmy Carter's tenure, the first lady still had no chief of staff. Rosalynn Carter had to make-do with Mary Finch Hoyt as "secretary to the first lady and East Wing co-ordinator."

Hoyt initially supervised social secretary Gretchen Poston and six other aides. Soon, however, Mrs. Carter was said to be giving considerable personal direction to a staff that had grown to eighteen in number. As reported in the Washington *Post* in 1977, it wasn't Congress or the president, but the first lady, who took action to boost salaries of her staffers.

Rosalynn Carter raised one of her aides to $45,000 and two to $40,000. Other salaries were reported only in terms of brackets. Seven East Wing aides received "between $20,000 and $40,000." Eight got less than $20,000 annually.

It would take extensive research under the Freedom of Information Act to learn precisely how much Nancy Reagan's staff members were paid, and what it cost to operate the East Wing staff during her husband's presidency.

Sarah (Mrs. James K.) Polk worked—unpaid—as her husband's private secretary. Often they stayed at the desk together for twelve or fourteen hours a day. Thinking of her long hours on the job for her husband, unpaid secretary Sarah Polk might have some harsh words to say if she could look over today's East Wing staff and its budget.

Viewed from any perspective, the exploding growth of the first lady's staff gives insight into the degree to which the "imperial presidency" has flourished during the twentieth century.

Part Five

Trailblazers

John Quincy Adams was the first chief executive to give an interview to a woman reporter, but not by choice.

32

John Quincy Adams Reluctantly Talked to a Woman Reporter

J ohn Quincy Adams, the only chief executive who was also the son of a president, was by far the most urbane early resident of the White House. Educated at home in his youth, he read Shakespeare with ease at age ten.

When he went with his famous father to France, the boy was enrolled in the Passy Academy near Paris. There he was taught to dance and to fence, and to appreciate art and music, in addition to learning subjects commonly taught in American schools. Before returning home, he also studied at a Latin school in Amsterdam and at Leyden University.

A scholar educated in the classics, Adams was also a proficient linguist. He was at home with Greek and Latin and became fluent in both French and Dutch. He confessed, almost as though a bit ashamed, that he never did "quite master the Spanish language," although he could read it rapidly.

Back in the United States, he spent two years at Harvard University, where he became a member of the Phi Beta Kappa Society and graduated second in the class of 1787. Almost as a lark, he mastered shorthand before studying law for three years.

Adams served his country as minister to the Netherlands, minister to Prussia, minister to Russia, chief negotiator of the Treaty of Ghent by which the War of 1812 came to a formal end, minister to Great Britain, U.S. secretary of state, and as a member of both the Massachusetts and the U.S. Senate.

In an 1824 bid for the presidency, he was defeated by Andrew Jackson, who received 152,933 popular votes to his own 115,696. However, since neither man had a majority in the electoral college, the choice of chief executive devolved upon the House of Representatives. Somewhat to his surprise, Adams was elected on the first ballot.

Many people who considered themselves in the avant-garde were delighted that the White House would be occupied by so well-trav-eled, well-educated, and sophisticated a man as Adams was known to be. Although there was no formal feminist movement at that time, a few "enlightened" women who wanted a greater degree of independence were also pleased: John Quincy Adams was "their man," they believed.

Thus it was that some of Adams's staunchest admirers were startled when he refused to give an interview to a woman reporter. He must have misunderstood, a representative of a women's group told him; there was no plan to take advantage of him in what was then a novel situation.

Adams replied he had not misunderstood; although he was willing, at convenient times, to talk with men journalists, he had no intention of breaking with precedent by submitting to an interview with Mrs. Anne Royall—now, or ever.

Maryland native Anne Royall, age 55, was the widow of a Revolutionary War veteran who had been left penniless at her husband's death. Having no training in any vocation or skill, she had turned to writing to earn a living.

A fiery crusader long before there was an organized body ready to champion women's rights, she led a challenge against the powerful Bank of the United States. To bolster her own prestige and to boost causes for which she was fighting, she had decided that she must have an interview with the president. Curtly rebuffed without explanation, she resorted—says Washington tradition—to use of friends as intermediaries. When she learned through them that John Quincy Adams was firmly opposed to talking with her, or any other women journalist, Anne Royall resorted to a ruse never repeated.

Observing the president's daily routines, she noticed that he liked to swim in the Potomac very early in the morning. Bathing suits had not yet been invented, so the chief executive frequently went skinny-dipping in the 1.75-mile wide river at 5:00 A.M.

Mrs. Royall made her plans carefully and executed them on a morning in the mid-1820s. Very early she went to the bank of the river at a point south of the executive mansion. Already, she had earned the nickname "The Dreaded." Now she intended to show the most powerful man in the nation what that meant.

She watched while the president undressed, folded his clothes neatly, and thrust them into a clump of willows. When he was in water up to his arm pits, Anne Royall emerged from hiding, unfolded the garments and waved them at Adams, and then sat down on them.

The president waded within speaking distance and ordered her to return his clothes and go away.

She laughed.

When the chief executive showed bewilderment, she introduced herself and explained that she had come for an interview.

Adams reluctantly agreed to see her at the executive mansion.

This time, it was the reporter's turn to issue a blunt refusal. She had no intention of doing anything of the sort, she said. She wanted his views on a number of pressing national topics, and she wanted them now. If he did not answer her questions promptly, she warned, she would begin to scream to attract the attention of fishermen downstream.

Standing in water up to his chin, John Quincy Adams responded to Anne Royall's questions about the Bank of the United States and national fiscal policy.

In spite of this incident, John Quincy Adams, who was elected congressman after serving as president, continued his early-morning swims. He reputedly took his last nude dip in the Potomac at age seventy-nine.

CHAPTER
33

A Landmark Campaign Made the Log Cabin a Powerful Symbol

William Henry Harrison had no advance teams, no speech writers, no sound bite specialists, no television "spin doctors." Yet the sixty-eight-year-old Whig candidate for the White House was packaged and sold to voters in such fashion that his campaign is recognized as the first modern one.

It all began when a friend of Henry Clay allegedly discussed the former major general with a writer for the Baltimore *American* newspaper. Harrison was called by the nickname *Tippecanoe* after his defeat of the Shawnee Indians in the Battle of Tippecanoe in 1811. Clay ticked off the reasons why he thought Harrison was unsuited for the role of chief executive. Then, according to the newspaper account of the conversation, Clay suggested a way to derail his campaign: "Give him a barrel of Hard Cider, and settle a pension of two thousand a year on him, and my word for it, he will sit the remainder of his days in his Log Cabin, by the side of a 'seacoal' fire and study moral philosophy."

A Harrisburg, Pennsylvania, newspaper editor, Richard S. Elliott, saw the derogatory paragraph and became fighting mad. He discussed it with his friend Thomas Elder, a banker who was dedicated to the Whig cause. Elder, says oral tradition, had just finished a successful advertising campaign for his bank.

"Passion and prejudice are powerful tools," he mused. "Properly aroused and directed, they will do about as much good as principle and reason in a heated political contest." Acting upon this reasoning, the banker commissioned an artist to make a sketch that showed what he conceived to be Harrison's log cabin, with a big cider barrel next to the door and a coonskin on the wall.

People who saw printed versions of the cartoon paused, laughed, and confessed that they thought they could vote for a man such as

Supporters of William Henry Harrison published sketches said to depict the log cabin in which he was born—despite the fact that he was actually born in a three-story brick mansion.

Harrison was said to be. Within weeks, the Whig struggle for the White House had become the "log cabin and hard cider" campaign. It depicted to voters a man who lived in a simple cabin whose door was seldom shut, who drank nothing stronger than cider, and who plowed his tiny fields with his own hands.

Backers of Harrison went into action when they noted public reaction to "log cabin and hard cider." Nationwide, Whigs organized parades that featured crudely made floats of log cabins with outside latchstrings. Plenty of barrels of hard cider, of course, were available for drinking. Tiny paper replicas or metal badges of log cabins were handed out. Tunesmiths turned out one log cabin song after another. Printers turned out many "log cabin anecdotes" in broadside form, along with hard cider and log cabin almanacs for the year 1841.

One enthusiastic band of Whigs fashioned an immense ball of paper, taller than a man's head, and rolled it through the streets of Baltimore and other cities to symbolize their certainty that voters would "keep the ball a-rolling" for the man who lived in a log cabin and drank hard cider. Their effort served to win a permanent place in American speech for the phrase "Keep the ball rolling."

Henry Clay, who may not have been aware that he was linked with the meteoric rise of the new symbol, thundered that "the battle is now between the log cabin and the palaces, between hard cider and champagne."

One fact, however, was overlooked. Not even Harrison's rivals bothered to discover that he had been born on February 9, 1773, in a three-story brick mansion on the vast Harrison plantation in Charles City County, Virginia. Along with masses of ordinary voters, most members of the opposing Democratic party who backed Van Buren took it for granted that the Whig candidate actually was born in a log cabin.

Neither was serious attention given to Whig publicity about the log cabin in which Harrison and his wife were said to have lived near North Bend, Ohio. There was a grain of truth to the story; as a young army officer, Harrison really did buy a tract of land and erect on it a log cabin. Even when brand new, however, the residence was not remotely like the log cabins of the frontier. Harrison's had five separate rooms and, after less than three years, he began adding to it in every direction. By 1840 the original log cabin was but one corner of a house whose estimated value was a whopping $20,000. His "tiny farm" actually covered 2,000 acres.

Name calling was prominent in the first modern campaign for the presidency. Van Buren's followers mocked Harrison as "Granny" because of his age (sixty-eight) and as "General Mum" because he seldom spoke out on controversial topics. Whigs had their own set of labels for Harrison's opponent, the incumbent president, Martin Van Buren, but instead they capitalized upon endorsements by public figures. Not content with glowing tributes framed by prominent members of their party, they may have been the first to make political hay from names in the field of entertainment. At the urging of Harrison's campaign leaders, the "log cabin and hard cider" candidate was warmly endorsed by Chang and Eng, the original Siamese twins who had barnstormed throughout the nation under the guidance of Phineas T. Barnum.

Before it was over, the campaign of 1840 had many of the qualities of a three-ring circus. William Henry Harrison, obeying the mandates of those who guided his campaign, did not express his views on public issues. He stayed home and said little on any subject. Far better, he conceded, to let the "log cabin and hard cider" symbol do the talking.

Although Martin Van Buren was the handpicked successor of powerful Andrew Jackson, his bid for a second term was logjammed by a log cabin. Harrison collected just under 80 percent of the electoral vote in spite of the fact that his popular vote total was only about 125,000 greater than that of his opponent.

Having proved its power, the log cabin became an enduring symbol in American politics. For the record, of the first twelve presidents (Harrison was the ninth), only Andrew Jackson had been born in a log cabin. Beginning with Millard Fillmore, five consecutive presidents could legitimately claim log cabin birth: Pierce, Buchanan, Lincoln,

By deriding his political opponent, Henry Clay, who wanted to derail the candidacy of William Henry Harrison, provided the first modern campaign symbol.

and Johnson. The twentieth president, James A. Garfield, was the last born in this typical frontier home. One of the cabins, Lincoln's birthplace, is now a national monument encased in a protective building.

Once created, a political myth dies hard. Despite his birth in a brick mansion, Harrison rode to victory astride a log cabin. As a result, it became virtually mandatory for presidential candidates to belittle their financial resources and to minimize their early opportunities.

Abraham Lincoln, a successful attorney, regularly said that he came from "common stock" and proudly belonged to this breed. He once said—with great exaggeration—that his life story could be summed up in one phrase: "the short and simple annals of the poor."

Followers rallied behind him as "the rail-splitter." But the nickname, says biographer Stephen B. Oates, was not fashioned until 1860, when Lincoln was 50 years old and two of his followers carried rotted fence rails into the Illinois State Republican Convention. Looking at the crude banner proclaiming "Abraham Lincoln, the Rail Candidate for President," someone asked Lincoln whether he had actually split the rails. He said he didn't know, but he "reckoned he'd mauled better ones since becoming a man." The "rail splitter" image thus was created, and it caught the imagination of backers who correctly believed it would make Lincoln a "homespun hero."

The vote-getting power of the log cabin symbol, and its modern counterparts, is beyond scientific measurement. This much is certain, however: facts frequently have played a minor role in winning the presidency. But appeals to the idea that a candidate has travelled the long, hard road from poverty to success have often led straight to the White House.

34

John Tyler Ignored Opposition and Moved into the White House

"**S**ee what the ruckus is about, Taze," Vice President John Tyler said to his eleven-year-old son on a bright April afternoon. A rider, obviously headed toward the Taylor mansion, was waving his hat and shouting as he came nearer. Tyler, who had been playing marbles with his son Tazewell, had just lost a game of "knucks" and was on his knees—knuckles on the ground—ready to receive the light blows that came with a loss.

Tazewell ran to the gate, then came back much faster than he had gone. "It's Mr. Fletcher, Father," he reported.

John Tyler straightened up to greet the son of Secretary of State Daniel Webster. Without waiting for a salutation, the rider blurted, "Mr. President, I have been instructed by the secretary of state to deliver this dispatch to you without an instant's delay."

Tyler took a quick look at the document proffered by Fletcher Webster, then exclaimed, "O Lord! How did it happen? Is it true that Harrison is dead so soon?"

"Yes, sir, Mr. President," responded Webster. "Washington is in mourning; you are requested to go—dressed just as you are now."

That tale, one of many linked with the career of the trailblazer who was the first vice president to succeed a president who died in office, cannot be documented. Neither can a variant account, according to which Tyler was sleeping soundly in his lovely home when a courier dashed into Williamsburg, Virginia, early on the morning of April 5, 1841. According to this story, Fletcher Webster woke the vice president from his slumber and before he was fully alert blurted out the news that President William Henry Harrison had died the previous day.

Regardless of precisely what he was doing when the news arrived,

Tyler lost no time in riding to the capital. On the journey, he pondered the implications of the message to him signed by Daniel Webster. Co-signers of the document were other members of Harrison's cabinet: Secretary of the Treasury Thomas Ewing, Secretary of War John Bell, Attorney General John J. Crittenden, and Secretary of the Navy George E. Badger. Postmaster General Francis Granger is believed to have been absent from the capital when the message was penned.

"So the old warrior is dead . . ." mused John Tyler, who was perhaps the first man picked as a vice presidential candidate as a result of a political trade. Tyler allegedly got the second spot on the Whig ticket because he had promised, a year earlier, not to run against the incumbent Whig senator from Virginia. No matter how he got it, he was—at least in his own eyes—subordinate only to Harrison after the election of 1840.

A former general and veteran of many battles, President Harrison had refused to wear a hat or a coat when he mounted a white horse to ride to the Capitol to take the oath of office. Ignoring the blustery March weather, he spent 105 minutes reading his 8,578-word inaugural address, the longest on record.

Before he had attended the last of three inaugural balls, Harrison was coughing and his eyes were beginning to redden. A severe cold turned into pneumonia, and on April 4—one month to the day after the inauguration—the sixty-eight-year-old president was dead.

Slender John Tyler, six feet tall, reflected upon his legal career as he rode toward Washington. As a defense attorney in criminal cases, he had made a reputation for finding in statute books a sentence or a phrase, perhaps even a single word, upon which he could base a successful defense. On this journey he did not reflect upon the laws of Virginia, however. He pondered the meaning of the U.S. Constitution.

By the time John Tyler arrived in the capital, he had made up his mind. Lacking a constitutional provision for distribution of power at the death of a president, he, John Tyler, would assume the office, the sooner, the better.

It would not be easy, he recognized. As an admirer of Thomas Jefferson, he had made political enemies of leaders who advocated a more powerful central government. Tyler had gone so far as to spurn suggestions that his own state would benefit from distribution of funds collected at the federal level. "Virginia, sir," he proudly said, "is not in so poor a condition as to require a charitable donation from the Congress of the United States."

As a strong advocate of states' rights, he was widely criticized even by members of his own party who believed in increasing the power of the federal government. Therefore, on political issues alone, he knew

Artist's conception of Fletcher Webster's arrival at John Tyler's home with news that death had made the White House vacant.

that he would face strong opposition sure to be augmented by those who would read the Constitution carefully and conclude that it had no clear provision to guide succession to the office made vacant by the death of a chief executive.

Having considered all aspects of the complicated issue, personal as well as national, John Tyler rode into Washington determined that only he should succeed William Henry Harrison.

His political foes had other ideas. John McKeon of Pennsylvania immediately introduced into the House of Representatives a special resolution. Under its terms, the vice president would be recognized as acting president, holding that office while lawmakers decided how to choose a new, permanent president. McKeon's resolution failed to survive a voice vote, but many leaders refused to acknowledge that Tyler was, indeed, president of the United States. Some of them sent urgent messages about matters of great importance to the White House, addressed to, "Hon. John Tyler, Acting President."

Tyler refused to open letters addressed in this fashion and proceeded to exercise the powers and perform the duties of the president. He paid no attention when newspapers scoffed at him as "His Accidency" and failed to be shaken when his entire inherited cabinet, with the exception of Webster who was engaged in important diplomatic negotiations, resigned in a body.

By going through the customary motions of the presidency and by remaining unflappable in spite of moves to divest him of power, John Tyler rode out the storm. When he emerged victorious, his personal triumph became a powerful precedent. From his time forward, each vacancy created by the death of a chief executive has been immediately filled by his vice president.

Until the Twenty-fifth Amendment was ratified in 1967 there was no constitutional authority for presidential disability and succession. Afterward, Richard Nixon had authority to choose someone to fill the office made vacant by Spiro Agnew's resignation in October 1973.

President Nixon is said to have wanted John Connally of Texas as his new vice president, but he wavered when objections were raised. Governor Nelson Rockefeller of New York and Governor Ronald Reagan of California were considered before he selected Gerald R. Ford. As the first vice president thus appointed, Ford assumed the presidency upon Nixon's resignation.

Both houses of Congress wrestled for years with the thorny problem of presidential succession. When a solution was finally achieved, it followed the precedent established by John Tyler in 1841. Because of him, the vice president is the first in line permanently to succeed a dead president or, for a time, to take over the powers of the office in the event a president is incapacitated.

CHAPTER
35

Crete Garfield
Took the First Fumbling Steps
toward Air Conditioning

The White House
July 2, 1881

MRS. JAMES A. GARFIELD:
  The President wishes me to say to you from him that he has been seriously hurt—how seriously he cannot yet say. He is himself and hopes you will come to him soon. He sends his love to you.

                                      —ROCKWELL
"God reigns, and the Government in Washington still lives!"

Vacationing in a seaside cottage at Elberon, New Jersey, the president's wife was recuperating from a severe attack of malaria. But the telegram from Colonel Rockwell, her husband's secretary, caused her to go into action within minutes.

Famous for her ability to face difficult situations without losing her equanimity, Lucretia Garfield—known as Crete to her husband and intimate friends—immediately began making arrangements for transportation to the capital. Arrival of another set of telegrams informed her that a special train would take her to the bedside of the president. By then she knew he had been shot, but she had no details.

Accompanied by his sons, Harry and James, Garfield had left the White House soon after 9:00 A.M. They were bound for Williamstown, Massachusetts, where the chief executive, who had been in office four months, was to deliver the commencement address at his alma mater, Williams College.

In the waiting room of the Baltimore and Potomac Railroad, Secretary of State James G. Blaine signaled that he wanted a word with the

174

Lucretia ("Crete") Garfield had the happy inspiration of trying to make her husband more comfortable by lowering the temperature, even slightly—John Sartain engraving.

president. While they talked, Officer Patrick Kearney of the District of Columbia Police Department—charged with safeguarding the head of state—noticed a man who acted suspiciously.

With Kearney watching, thirty-nine-year-old Charles J. Guiteau edged close to the president. Suddenly he pulled out a .44 British Bulldog revolver—an expensive model that Guiteau considered suitable for display in a museum—and fired two shots.

Garfield dropped to the floor, bleeding profusely. It took nearly half an hour for District of Columbia Health Officer Smith Townsend to reach the scene. He made a quick examination, determined that one bullet had barely grazed the president's arm, but shook his head soberly when he reported that the second had entered his back and might have perforated his liver.

At Dr. Townsend's orders, aides gave the stricken chief executive enough brandy to enable him to stand the pain when they took him in their arms and moved him upstairs, where someone found a mattress on which he was stretched.

About seventy-five minutes after the president was shot, an ambulance arrived. As it moved slowly through the streets toward the White House, a swelling crowd of curious people ran after it on foot. By that time, Garfield was sufficiently recovered to give an occasional wave of the hand to onlookers.

About three hours after having been put to bed in his own room, the president was awakened from light sleep by the sobbing of his fifteen-year-old son Jimmy. "Hope for the best, son," he urged. Remembering happy family hours aboard small ships, he told his son that "I know the hull is a little damaged, but the wheelhouse is all right."

Lucretia Garfield, frail from illness and unable to restrain her sobs, reached her husband's bedside about 7:00 P.M. She nodded understanding when doctors gestured for her to leave after less than a quarter of an hour. "He could be gone within thirty minutes," one of them sadly informed her.

That verdict was based upon the assumption that the liver had been shattered, a diagnosis soon found to be erroneous. Incredibly, by Sunday morning, July 3, the president seemed to be breathing almost normally. His temperature hovered just under 100°—so hopes of his wife and of the nation began to soar.

Then the famous—or infamous—July heat wave long associated with the nation's capital struck with a vengeance. Temperatures soared well above that of the stricken president's body, and stayed there much of the day. Soon the nights, too, became unbearable.

Recalling his boyhood days in Cuyahoga County, Ohio, and the log cabin that was his childhood home, Garfield repeatedly said that he found the solid walls of the White House stifling. "If it would even cool off a little at night, as it always did in my father's log cabin, I believe I would begin to improve," he told his wife.

A native of the same Ohio County in which her husband was born, Crete Garfield began to talk with him about old times there. They remembered with pleasure their days in the Geauga Seminary in Chester and the teacher who had taught both of them. They discussed the way farming had changed since their childhood and laughed as they recalled having once taken part in cutting ice from a pond with huge saws, then helping to store it for use in the warm months.

"Ice!" Crete Garfield reputedly cried, interrupting their reverie. "That's it! Ice!"

Mrs. Garfield rushed from the bedroom and called instructions to aides. "Go out and buy every pound of ice you can find! Hurry! This stifling air is killing the president!"

Tubs and buckets, hastily arranged as close to the wounded man's bed as possible, were filled with ice. Garfield smiled his gratitude and seemed to rest easier.

Within hours, U.S. Army engineers began building special water tight "troughs" to hold entire blocks of ice. Mrs. Garfield, the children, members of the household staff, and eager volunteers took turns waving palmetto fans to circulate the air cooled by melting ice.

At a time when the term "air conditioning" had not yet been coined, the crude system sparked by the first lady's inspiration made the White House the nation's first structure in which the temperature was artificially lowered by even a degree or two.

Several inventors came forward with devices they had perfected;

most proved of no help. But R. S. Jennings of Baltimore was sure his invention would help restore the president to health. Instead of blocks of ice, he relied upon ice water, with which big sheets of cheesecloth were kept wet. A crude but workable electric blower took the place of fans waved by hand. It did reduce the temperature of the sick room, but also made it so humid that Garfield could hardly breathe.

John Wesley Powell, director of the Geological Survey, tried to improve upon the Jennings device. Already it had been calculated that air cooled by melting ice, at the rate of about 100 pounds per hour, would alter the temperature of the sickroom. In order to reduce the input of moist air, Powell inserted between the huge "ice trough" and the president's room a device that held big blocks of ice, which trapped much of the moisture.

After seventy-two hours of around-the-clock work, this improved version of the system went into action. It employed three tons of ice and a system of tin tubes and ducts with which to drain off melting water.

On July 12, 1881, the world's first "air conditioning machine" went into action. An aide joyfully recorded that air entering the sick room was, for the first time, "truly cool, as well as dry, and ample in supply."

With the cost of using the system mounting rapidly, subscription offices were opened in several major cities. Members of the general public contributed generously toward the cost of providing the 500,000 pounds of ice eventually used in the White House that hot, humid July.

Nevertheless, the president grew weaker as the days passed. He was eventually sent to the seacoast by special train and died after serving only 199 days, 79 of which were in continuous pain from Guiteau's bullet.

Military engineers, who had helped to perfect the cumbersome but workable system to make James Garfield more comfortable, prepared a formal summary of their work and its results.

"Work at the Executive Mansion has demonstrated," they wrote, "that it is now possible to place the temperature and humidity of definite quantities of air at any point that may be desired."

Air conditioning had been born in a desperate effort to save the life of a president.

36

A Master of Words, John F. Kennedy Was Also a War Hero Who Narrowly Escaped Death

"**C**ollect as many notes and working papers as you can locate," attorney Clark Clifford instructed John F. Kennedy. "Make sure that Drew Pearson has an opportunity to see these things, personally. If he does not change his position then, it will be time to consider legal action."

Political commentator Pearson seems to have taken enough time with the documents to reach a different conclusion from that which he had publicly announced earlier. He formally retracted allegations that the senator from Massachusetts was not the real author of best-selling *Profiles in Courage*. Once Pearson made his retraction, talk of a $50 million lawsuit against him and the American Broadcasting Company was dropped.

His personal notes suggest that some time in 1954 John F. Kennedy conceived the idea of writing a magazine article about bravery in the political arena. Concentrating upon U.S. senators, he began to compile lists of men who had shown conspicuous valor. That led to discarding the idea of a magazine article in favor of producing a small book. He thought it might be called *Patterns of Political Courage*.

As the book began to take shape, with the aid of research assistants and stenographers, Senator Kennedy looked about for a publisher. Cass Canfield of Harper and Brothers made a few suggestions, then drew up a contract that included a $500 advance.

These Brave Men, These Great Men, and *The Patriots* were considered as titles and discarded. With the book now designed to depict courageous senators who did what they believed to be right rather than doing as constituents wished, Kennedy's project became *Profiles in Courage*.

A youthful John F. Kennedy reads the war news.

Theodore C. Sorenson of Nebraska, Kennedy's number two legislative aide, helped to put the author's material in final shape. It was the work of Sorenson and other aides that prompted the celebrated journalist Drew Pearson to charge that Kennedy had not actually written the book that carried his name.

Judges who worked under the direction of the Pulitzer Prize committee had already made up their minds before Pearson issued his apologetic retraction. When their list of winners in the field of letters for 1957 was issued, it placed John F. Kennedy in the company of Eugene O'Neill.

Long before *Profiles in Courage* won a Pulitzer Prize, it was a national best seller. Selections were published in *Harper's, Collier's, Reader's Digest,* the *New York Times Magazine,* and other media. Television rights were sold to the "Kraft Theater." Hebrew, Persian, and Japanese versions were issued in rapid-fire order.

Kennedy reputedly "whooped like a high school basketball player after having helped to win a state championship" on the day he received a telegram saying that sales of the book had passed 100,000 copies. Better than almost anyone else in the political arena, he realized that *Profiles* would mean a giant step upward.

His expectations were well founded. His book put him into the chair of a special committee established to identify and honor five senators of the past. Wide publicity about the senators who were honored boosted Kennedy's political fortunes, already riding high.

Years earlier, the man who was White House bound had discovered that his skill in the use of words meant much more than a name on the title page of a book.

As a senior at Harvard University, his political science major required him to write a thesis. Pondering alternatives, Kennedy decided on a bold step. Instead of depending on library research as was customary, he would write his own views on a major issue and would depend largely upon personal experience.

Late in 1939 the British liner *Athenia* had been torpedoed in the North Atlantic. Jack's father, who was then ambassador to Great Britain, had dispatched the youth to take charge of American passengers on the ship who had survived the blast. His mission delayed his return to Harvard and convinced him that Great Britain's complacency had led to the infamous Munich Pact that may have persuaded Adolf Hitler to expand his dreams of conquest.

"England's Foreign Policy Since 1731" seemed a sufficiently sedate and academic title for a thesis of about seventy pages. But as the paper began to take shape with the help of stenographers and typists hired by the affluent Harvard senior, his strong personal views caused it to be transformed into "Appeasement at Munich."

Strongly affected by his personal experiences on the Continent and in England, the paper more than doubled in length, to 150 pages. Winston Churchill, asserted the author, was clearly prophetic. Americans should survey Europe through the eyes of Churchill and prepare themselves for war, if necessary.

Kennedy's thesis was lauded by faculty members who gave it the second highest grade possible, *magna cum laude*. Jack had gleefully forwarded the third carbon to his father in London. There, Joseph Kennedy showed it to veteran newsman Arthur Krock.

Instantly intrigued with the basic argument of the paper, Krock snorted that it had no business "collecting dust at Harvard's Widener Library." Instead, said Krock, it should be edited for general readers and published as soon as possible. "I'll even arrange for my own literary agent, Gertrude Algase, to handle it," he offered.

Jack Kennedy worked rapidly with Krock to get his academic paper ready for a wider audience. Winston Churchill's *While England Slept* led Krock to suggest the title that was adopted: *Why England Slept.*

Wilfred Funk, Inc., received the edited manuscript in the spring of 1940 and copies were off the presses in July. Jack Kennedy, age twenty-three, was now a scholar-turned-author.

The Nazi invasion of Denmark, Norway, and the Low Countries in April 1940 had coincided neatly for *Why England Slept* to be labeled as "profoundly prophetic" by American readers.

Aided by a preface by *Time-Life* publisher Henry R. Luce, the piece of work that had begun life as a college thesis became a Book-of-the-Month Club selection.

When Jack's book was published in England during the blitz, it created a sensation. Taking a second and even more careful look at it, the *New York Times* termed it a volume "of such painstaking scholarship, such mature understanding and fair-mindedness, such penetrating and timely conclusions that it is a notable textbook for our times."

The two books by John F. Kennedy helped to create for him a "natural constituency" when he challenged Senator Hubert Humphrey of Minnesota for the Democratic nomination for the presidency. A third book, not by him but about him, was also a significant factor in the 1960 campaign. Robert J. Donovan, chief of the Washington Bureau of the New York *Herald Tribune,* wrote it not as a political instrument, but as a gripping record of American heroism in World War II.

Long before writing *Why England Slept,* Jack Kennedy had suffered frequent excruciating back pain from football injuries, which caused medical examiners to turn him down when he applied first to the navy and then to the army for active duty.

An intensive program of treatment and physical therapy brought Kennedy into such condition that upon re-application to the Navy, he was accepted and awarded a commission. A desk job in Washington proved stifling; soon he managed to be re-assigned to a torpedo boat training station.

In April 1943 Lieutenant John F. Kennedy was placed in command of the torpedo boat *PT 109.* Based on the island of Rendova, south of New Georgia in the Pacific, Kennedy spent a few weeks trying to slow the flow of Japanese provisions to an advance base.

With two other officers and ten enlisted men, he was on patrol near the Solomon Islands very early on the morning of August 2, 1943. Suddenly the Japanese destroyer *Amigari* appeared out of the darkness; with Kennedy at the wheel, the torpedo boat was slashed in half and her skipper's back was reinjured.

Watertight bulkheads in the bow kept the hull of the craft afloat and provided a refuge of a sort to Kennedy and five of his men. Five others—some of them badly burned—were in the water. It took nearly three hours to get the survivors to the torpedo boat.

By daybreak it was clear that the position of the Americans was desperate. Floating helplessly, they knew their only hope of survival was to reach distant tiny islands. Still, the Americans waited for hours in hope of rescue by comrades.

John F. Kennedy with PT-109 crew members Paul Fay (left) *and Lenny Thom* (right).

With hopes fading, at 2:00 P.M. Lieutenant Kennedy ordered the evacuation of the floating hulk. The most badly burned crewman, McMahon, would die unless someone engaged in heroic measures to save him. Kennedy converted a kapok shirt into a towline, slipped into the water face down while comrades placed McMahon above him, and took the towline in his teeth. Then Kennedy towed McMahon for four hours, before staggering ashore at tiny Plum Pudding Island.

Their refuge proved to have too few coconut trees to provide cover and was soon found to be far off the course of American vessels patrolling the region.

Three days later, the Americans moved to somewhat larger Cross Island, which was exposed to Japanese planes but somewhat closer to American lines. By now most of the eleven survivors were violently ill from drinking coconut juice, and Kennedy's malaria was getting worse.

When a small group of Solomon Islands natives appeared, Kennedy used sign language that he hoped communicated, telling them to take a message to the nearest white man's post. He was not sure they understood until a large Melanesian appeared with a message that began, "On His Majesty's Service. . . ."

Natives had paddled their dugout thirty-eight miles to a post manned by Australians. Covered with palm branches to conceal himself from the Japanese, Kennedy made the long trip in the canoe and arranged for the rescue of his men.

"I had so many close calls during six or seven days that I quit counting them," he later told his father. Back in the states, Kennedy stopped in New York to take in night clubs and Broadway shows. One evening he went to the theater with John and Frances Hersey, who persuaded him to tell them a bit about his experiences in the South Pacific. That encounter led Hersey to write a vivid account entitled "Survival" that appeared in the *New Yorker* magazine.

Hersey's dramatic story inspired Robert J. Donovan to interview all survivors and to write the best-selling book *PT-109*. By arrangement with Kennedy, publishers paid $2,500 to each crew member of the torpedo boat or to their survivors. Also, the $2,000 paid by the *Reader's Digest* to reprint Hersey's story went to the Navy Relief Fund.

A then-popular television series, "Navy Log," prepared and aired a film version of Jack Kennedy's wartime exploits. Then, as public interest gradually subsided, it appeared that the story would be forgotten. However, John F. Kennedy decided to seek the Democratic nomination for the presidency in 1960. His family influence was great enough to preempt a scheduled program to bring the *PT-109* segment from "Navy Log" back for a rerun.

Campaign workers made the most of Kennedy's heroism and stressed that his chief rival, Hubert Humphrey, had been a wartime stay-at-home. Great numbers of reprints of the *Reader's Digest* article were used as campaign literature. How large a boost the candidate gained from reminding the public of his exploits in the South Pacific, no analyst can say, but when Democrats convened to select a nominee, John F. Kennedy swept to victory on the first ballot.

In the ensuing battle with Republican Richard M. Nixon, Kennedy's supporters stressed his back injuries and malaria to depict him as "one of the few presidential candidates to suffer physical agony while under enemy fire."

Swept into the White House, John F. Kennedy once more demonstrated his mastery of language by becoming the first chief executive to make full, effective use of television. In almost Churchillian fashion, he framed biting, singing sentences that became familiar throughout the world.

In private, the president sometimes admitted that he realized he was a superb communicator. Nearly always, though, he qualified that admission by saying that the most effective message he ever framed was scratched by a sheath knife on the inside of a coconut shell. Handed to strangers who spoke no English, the desperate message, labeled simply "Nauro," read:

NATIVE KNOWS POSIT
HE CAN PILOT 11 ALIVE NEED
SMALL BOAT
                    KENNEDY

That wartime communication from a self-effacing hero not only brought dramatic rescue; it helped propel the writer into the nation's highest office.

37

George Bush Was the Navy's Youngest Pilot

O n September 2, 1944, a Grumman Avenger torpedo bomber was flying cover for U.S. naval forces converging upon a Japanese-held island. Pilot George Bush, who became the Navy's youngest flier soon after he enlisted on his eighteenth birthday, was at the controls. While approaching the target island, he felt "a sudden jolt, not very severe." Within minutes, though, the cockpit filled with heavy smoke.

Fighting for oxygen, George Bush kept his plane on course and managed to deliver four bombs. By then, his plane was blazing, clearly crippled beyond the possibility of returning to the carrier.

Repeatedly questioned about this traumatic experience during the presidential campaign of 1988, Vice President Bush answered few questions. His memory of having the plane go down with two of his mates, after he had bailed out, was still so vivid that he preferred to say little about the experience.

After bailing out of his doomed bomber, he hit the water very hard. Members of a submarine crew picked him up and got him to emergency medical care. He was so badly battered that it took several months to regain his strength, but then he requested and got reassignment to combat.

The U.S. Navy's youngest pilot flew fifty-eight missions—a total of about 1,228 hours—and somehow survived four crashes. His heroism brought him the Distinguished Flying Cross, which he mentions only in response to direct questions, and then very briefly.

At least thirty earlier chief executives had military experience, but Bush blazed a trail by becoming the first combat pilot to be elected president.

Only three presidents have had long professional military careers and top-level military training. Zachary Taylor started out as a first lieutenant, paid $30 a month with twelve dollars subsistence in 1808. By 1838 he was a brigadier general called Old Rough and Ready by his men. His distinguished leadership during the Mexican War propelled him into the White House.

Ulysses S. Grant graduated from the U.S. Military Academy at West Point, muffed his chances at promotion, and took off his uniform—only to put it back on when the Civil War broke out.

Dwight D. Eisenhower graduated from West Point in 1915 and received World War I promotions that made him a lieutenant colonel. During World War II, he became a five-star general.

While Jimmy Carter graduated from Annapolis and had seven years of submarine duty, he had no combat experience.

In addition to George Bush, twenty-six other chief executives were civilian-soldiers who had little or no military training before putting on their uniforms. Except for airplane pilot Bush, all of them served on land or on the sea, from a few weeks to several years of combat.

George Washington began his military career, not as a buck private in the rear rank, but as a major in the Virginia militia—with no training or experience. He learned military tactics by fighting the French and their Indian allies, then years later became head of the poorly trained and undisciplined Continental Army. When victorious General Washington was unanimously chosen to serve as the first president, his unique experience led the founding fathers to attach the title and authority of commander-in-chief of armed forces to the presidency.

Three of Washington's successors had no military experience. James Monroe, the fifth chief executive, spent two years in the Continental Army during the American Revolution. He suffered a severe wound in the battle of Trenton at Christmas 1776 and rose in rank from lieutenant to major.

As an adolescent prisoner of war during the Revolution, Andrew Jackson was slashed with a sword for refusing to clean a British officer's boots. The incident fueled a lifelong hatred of the British that helped to motivate him for his smashing victory at New Orleans in 1815.

On the trip home to Nashville up the Natchez Trace, one of his soldiers characterized him as "tough as hickory." The nickname "Old Hickory" stuck through subsequent military campaigns against Indians and political campaigns that indelibly stamped Jacksonian democracy upon American history.

William Henry Harrison joined the army in 1791 as an ensign. He fought in the Indian wars of the northwest, then left military service after six years. Back in uniform during the War of 1812 as a major general of Kentucky militia, the future president won quick promotion. He was at the head of forces that defeated the British and Indians in the Battle of the Thames, during which the noted warrior Tecumseh was killed.

Television ads in George Bush's presidential campaign frequently identified him as "the Navy's youngest pilot," but the candidate himself never discussed his combat experience.

His successor, John Tyler, was briefly a captain of militia during the War of 1812. His unit, the Charles City Rifles, saw no combat, but for his brief service the future chief executive was given a bonus of 160 acres of land in Iowa.

James K. Polk, who preceded professional soldier Zachary Taylor, had no military experience at all. Neither did Taylor's successor, Millard Fillmore.

Like Tyler, James Buchanan wore a uniform during the War of 1812, but he never heard the whine of British bullets.

Abraham Lincoln's preparation for his role as commander-in-chief of Union forces during the Civil War—no empty title, but one which described his actual day-to-day activity as top commander—consisted of about eighty days' service during the Black Hawk War. Initially a captain of volunteers, then a private in a company of rangers, Lincoln saw no combat. He joked that the only blood shed for his country was lost to mosquitoes. As the most influential single person in the Civil War, Lincoln saw at least 1,100,000 Americans shed their blood, while 623,000 of them died in the struggle guided by the Black Hawk War veteran.

Andrew Johnson, who succeeded to the presidency upon Lincoln's assassination, had served as military governor of Tennessee. He had no actual military experience.

Rutherford B. Hayes joined the Twenty-third Ohio Volunteers in June 1861 as major. He fought in at least fifty engagements, was wounded several times, and became a major general. Four days before Hayes enlisted, eighteen-year-old William McKinley joined the same regiment. He began as a private and rose to the rank of brevet major. McKinley fought bravely in several battles, but did not receive a scratch.

Also a Civil War veteran, James Garfield started as a lieutenant colonel and became a major general. His most daring battlefield exploits were at Chickamauga in September 1863. Chester A. Arthur spent more than four Civil War years in uniform as judge advocate and quartermaster general in the New York state militia. He won renown for his knowledge of U.S. Army regulations, but never came close to combat.

Grover Cleveland, another president who never wore a military uniform, bought his way out of Civil War service. No stigma was attached to this commonplace practice, although political foes later tried to make capital out of it.

Theodore Roosevelt commanded the First U.S. Volunteer Cavalry Regiment during the Spanish-American War. In the Battle of San Juan Hill, his unit captured Kettle Hill. During World War I, he badly wanted to recruit a special volunteer force and lead it to Europe, but Woodrow Wilson refused to give the necessary permission.

Following Teddy Roosevelt's presidency, the nation had its longest-ever unbroken period of leadership by men with no military background or experience: Taft, Wilson, Harding, Coolidge, Hoover, and Franklin D. Roosevelt.

Harry Truman, a captain of an artillery unit during World War I, fought through the Vosges Mountains and the Meuse-Argonne offensive. Though promoted to major, he was neither decorated nor wounded.

John F. Kennedy, the first chief executive who saw significant sea duty in time of war, spent four years in the U.S. Navy. He started as an ensign and was awarded the Navy and Marine Corps medal for heroism.

Lyndon B. Johnson spent a year as a lieutenant commander in the navy while retaining his seat in the House of Representatives.

Richard Nixon served in the navy for four years. Much of the time he was in charge of combat air transport, but he did not experience combat with the Japanese.

Gerald Ford also spent four years in the navy on the light aircraft carrier U.S.S. *Monterey*, which took part in at least ten major South Pacific battles.

Ronald Reagan spent three years in the air force during World War II, but poor eyesight kept him from flying in combat.

No analyst has ever attempted to determine precisely how much—or how little—the military experience of the chief executives has contributed to their roles as commanders-in-chief. But the election of George Bush clearly marked a watershed. Future chief executives with military experience are far more likely to have tasted aerial warfare than the kind of ground action that prevailed up to and through the era of Teddy Roosevelt and his Rough Riders.

CHAPTER

38

To Shake Hands
or Not to Shake Hands

During the first twelve years of the nation's existence, chief executives frequently received guests, but did not shake hands with them. Instead, when presented to the president a citizen simply bowed and his host bowed, too.

During an Independence Day gathering, Thomas Jefferson decided to dramatize his strong Republican views. By no means a believer in democracy as conceived today, the man from Monticello had more faith in the common citizen than did the Federalist John Adams or his nonpartisan predecessor George Washington. So at the July 4 celebrations, the third president started the practice of shaking hands with constituents, lawmakers, and members of the general public.

Earlier, opponents of Federalists had charged them with trying to set up a hereditary privileged class. That was well short of the monarchy that Washington had indignantly repudiated, but it was far from a democracy. Political opponents adopted the name *Republican* to make it clear that they stood for "a pure republic with no shred of monarchy attached to it."

Just two weeks after becoming the first president, Washington told aides that he was willing to receive "visits of compliment" twice a week, on Tuesdays and Fridays. Tuesdays were for men only. Friday affairs were tea parties over which Martha presided and to which both men and women came.

For these festive occasions, the Father of his Country dressed in the prevailing fashion of the aristocracy on both sides of the Atlantic. He wore black velvet knee breeches and in one yellow-gloved hand he held a hat ornamented with a black cockade. Typically, the white leather scabbard of his dress sword protruded from under his black coat.

On ceremonial occasions, all chairs were removed from the room in which Washington stood, to prevent any guest from taking a seat. Always, the president's silver knee buckles and shoe buckles were freshly

Thomas Jefferson broke with precedent by shaking hands with visitors, while dressed like a middle-level British landholder, with hair unpowdered.

shined. According to more than one critic, the president's dignified bow was always made "while his hands were so disposed as to indicate that the salutation was not to be accompanied with shaking of hands."

Described as "standing uneasily when the door was thrown open," Washington bowed so stiffly that some guests criticized his movements. He was said to have "remained rather aloof" even on such festive occasions as Christmas.

Washington never occupied the White House. When the capital was moved to the newly created District of Columbia, it was his successor who first opened to the public what was then called the Executive Mansion.

John Adams, a staunch Federalist, had a liking for velvet pants and silk stockings. Although dress styles had changed from Washington's time, he followed Washington's lead and restricted his "intercourse with guests" to exchanging bows.

Jefferson did away with formal receptions. Refusing to powder his hair, he dressed like the English country gentry. Sometimes he put on an old brown coat, corduroy breeches, and carpet slippers without heels. His attire was deliberately chosen "to set an example of Republican simplicity."

In a gesture that must have set many Washington tongues wagging Jefferson did not bow to his July 4 guests but enthusiastically shook hands with more than one hundred of them.

William Henry Harrison may have been the first chief executive to suffer from excessive handshaking. At his 1841 inauguration, Washington newspapers noted that there would be no handshaking as a part of the inaugural ceremonies because the president had a sore hand and arm, a legacy of the campaign.

By the time the last White House reception was held by the James K. Polks, it had become traditional that every guest would have an opportunity to press the hand of the president and his wife, if she was in the room. When the retiring chief executive went to his room just after midnight, he paused to make an entry in his diary, "Shook hands with well-wishers continuously for more than three hours."

Five years later, in 1853, Millard Fillmore expanded the handshaking ritual to include notable guests. Novelist Washington Irving, though elated at being singled out at the reception that was still called "the president's levee," was less than enthusiastic about what took place. "I had to shake hands with man, woman and child who beset me on all sides, until I felt as if it was becoming rather absurd," he reported later.

Like William Henry Harrison, Abraham Lincoln is known to have suffered from shaking hands. When the time came for the all-important ceremonial signing of the Emancipation Proclamation, the president's secretary recalled, "Lincoln took a pen, dipped it in ink, moved his hand to the place for the signature, held it a moment and dropped the pen. After a little hesitation he again took up the pen and went through the same movement as before."

His hesitancy, aides said, was purely physical, not uncertainty about the wisdom of his action. He had been shaking hands since 9:00 A.M. so continuously that his right arm "was almost paralyzed." In a rare personal comment, Lincoln later in the day told Congressman Schuyler Colfax that he feared his signature of the morning was somewhat tremulous and uneven. "I regret it," he reputedly said, "but I was powerless to do better. Three hours' hand-shaking is not calculated to improve a man's chirography."

From the time of his first levee, the man whom political opponents called "the rail-splitter" had tried to make physical contact with every person who attended. It was in social functions that he developed a pattern of using both hands and arms simultaneously, customarily extending his right hand to men, his left to women.

Two years after having had muscular spasms at the signing of the Emancipation Proclamation, Lincoln was the central figure at "the largest reception of the season." It began at 8:00 P.M., and an aide reported that, "the president shook hands with more than 6,000 persons this evening."

By the time of the Cleveland administration, that feat was no longer

Grover Cleveland's aides claimed that he once shook hands with 8,000 persons during a single evening.

astonishing. At a Chicago rally during the campaign, he insisted that he shook 6,000 hands on a single occasion, with no after effects. By 1886, White House reports boosted the estimate of hands shaken at public receptions to at least 8,000. Not to be outdone, Mrs. Cleveland gave a Blue Room reception for 5,000 guests and insisted that she shook hands with each of them, at the rate of forty to fifty per minute for more than two hours.

What may have been an all-time record was set at another of the first lady's receptions. With average attendance by the public having jumped to 6,000—three times the number involved in a "card" reception for which invitations were required—a beautifully sunny day brought out 9,000 visitors. Mrs. Cleveland dutifully shook their hands as they passed through the Blue Room, but she had to have both arms massaged when soreness from her right arm created "a sympathetic ache" in her left.

Handshaking took a new turn on the afternoon of September 6, 1901. Visiting the Pan-American Exposition at Buffalo, New York, William McKinley patiently greeted a long line of people who had come to the Temple of Music in order to wish him well.

Leon F. Czolgosz, a Detroit native of Polish background, slowly worked his way toward the chief executive. As McKinley stretched out his hand, Czolgosz fired two shots from a .32 Iver Johnson revolver that was concealed in a bandage wrapped around his right hand. One bullet seems to have been stopped by a button, but the second hit the president in the abdomen. It passed through his stomach, nicked his left kidney, and stopped in his pancreas.

Strangely, the death of McKinley had no immediate impact upon

As William McKinley reached to shake hands with a stranger, Leon Czolgosz fired two shots from a revolver concealed in a bandage wrapped about his hand.

what had become a long-established custom. As president, Theodore Roosevelt shook hands with all the enthusiasm he exhibited in other activities. On New Year's Day 1907, he pressed the hands of 8,100 callers—by actual count.

Warren G. Harding was never the center of enough attention to come close to Roosevelt's record. Most of his handshaking was done informally, rather than on public occasions. Conducting a front porch campaign for the presidency from his home in Marion, Ohio, he greeted a small but continuous stream of well wishers. To his secretary the president-to-be confided, "Shaking hands is the most pleasant thing I do."

Franklin D. Roosevelt held receptions and dinners to which thousands of guests came, but the president found it difficult to stand to shake more than about 1,000 hands as he had to be locked into his leg braces. Consequently he called upon the first lady to substitute for him when he became weary. Eleanor Roosevelt thought nothing of shaking 1,500 hands during a single session, she said, and more than once had as many as five separate social functions in a single day.

Those days are gone forever. The need for increased security now limits such White House mob scenes as formerly took place. While Thomas Jefferson probably would fume at finding himself unable to get anywhere close to the president, should he be alive today and manage to get past the many guards protecting chief executives today, the changed demands upon the first family and the mood of the world have made such protection necessary.

CHAPTER
39

Many a Pet Has Lived in the White House

"**M**r. Jefferson received me almost as though he were the owner of a haberdashery or some other small business," Brockholst Livingston of New York reported many times after accepting a presidential appointment to the U.S. Supreme Court.

"When I came for my interview, at the president's invitation, there were no formalities," said the jurist. "A maid ushered me into the room where he was busy signing documents. To my astonishment, a bird was perched upon his shoulder as casually as though sheltered in an oak tree.

"When Mr. Jefferson noticed my astonishment, he turned and introduced himself. Then he said, 'Do not be disturbed by Curious. I needed something to love, and when I found a little mockingbird, I tamed it and became its friend.'"

Curious not only spent many hours on the president's shoulder, the bird habitually took food from Jefferson's lips. During its first few days in the executive mansion, the mockingbird fluttered about as though investigating—leading to bestowal of its name. After becoming thoroughly at home in the new surroundings, Curious learned to follow Jefferson when he went up or down the stairs, hopping after him step by step.

Since there is no record that George Washington or John Adams took more than casual interest in tame animals or birds, Curious rates a special niche as the first pet to whom the occupant of the president's house paid serious attention. Margaret Bayard Smith, who wrote a detailed description of the *First Forty Years of Washington Society*, insisted that Thomas Jefferson "could not live without something to love—and how he did love this bird!"

Perhaps because the third president set the precedent, birds were often given the run of the White House in later years. Dolley Madison was inordinately fond of her parrot, so much so that when she fled from the mansion because the British were coming, she saved nothing

Lou (Mrs. Herbert) Hoover enlarged the White House Rose Gardens and converted a hallway into an immense aviary for her canaries.

except a few pieces of silver, a bundle of official documents, a portrait of George Washington, and her beloved bird.

Lou Hoover found the White House depressing when she took charge of it. So she converted one end of an extremely long hallway into an aviary. Blocked off with palms and equipped with bamboo furniture, it featured an immense cage in which nearly two dozen canaries flitted about, filling the air with their musical notes. Later, the first lady installed other bird cages among the palms. Sitting on tall standards, they too soon had feathered inhabitants whose calls became familiar to frequent visitors to the mansion.

The most unusual—if not the most melodic—feathered pet to find a haven in the White House won a special place in the heart of Tad (Thomas) Lincoln. When the boy was about ten years old, admirers of the president sent a big turkey gobbler as a gift. Named Jack, the bird was designated for the table at Thanksgiving dinner.

Tad, however, successfully begged that Jack be given a reprieve, at least until Christmas. When the special day came near, the boy again pleaded for clemency. He made such a commotion that his father temporarily adjourned a cabinet meeting to see what was the matter. Upon learning the cause of the disturbance, Abraham Lincoln solemnly penned a document that he termed a stay of execution. Waving the paper gleefully, Tad ran to the kitchen to inform the cook that he would have to find something else for Christmas dinner.

Other pets of the Lincoln era included a goat that casually pulled a little wagon, ponies, kittens, and rabbits. Usually there were several dogs underfoot but only one of them—Jib—won a place in chronicles of the period. Jib liked to jump into the president's lap when the family sat down to eat. Like Jefferson's mockingbird, Jib expected and got tasty morsels slipped to him by the chief executive.

John Quincy Adams took considerable pride in the silkworms he personally raised, and Andrew Johnson bred white mice. Numerous cows were at the White House from time to time, but only one of them, Taft's Pauline Wayne, was a true pet rather than a convenient source of milk and butter.

The most varied and colorful pet era came during the tenure of Theodore Roosevelt, whose six children ranged in age from four to seventeen when he took office. Quentin, the baby of the family, was idolized by his older brothers, Archibald and Kermit. Quentin, in turn, was ready to give everything he had to them.

When Archie came down with measles and said he was lonesome to see his calico pony, Algonquin, Quentin helped Kermit smuggle the animal into an elevator and lead him to Archie's bedroom. They thought they had gotten away with their prank until Algonquin reared and pounded the floor with his hoofs. Quentin had forgotten that the pony would be frightened by the sight of a kangaroo rat that Archie permitted to run freely about the room when not in his master's pocket.

Dogs and cats abounded in the Roosevelt household, which at one time also included a black bear, a one-legged rooster, and at least three garden snakes.

Notwithstanding snakes, a bear, and a kangaroo rat, the all-time favorite kind of pet of presidents and their families is the dog.

Perpetually the Rough Rider in public, Teddy Roosevelt was actually an old softie who permitted his six children to bring their pets into the White House. [LIBRARY OF CONGRESS]

Warren G. Harding so enjoyed his trained Airedale, Laddie Boy, who sat stiffly upright on chairs upon command, that he more than once brought the dog to perform at cabinet meetings. Franklin D. Roosevelt's Scottie, Fala, became known around the world during his long administration. However, Fala did not create as big a flap as Old Blaze, the dog owned by Roosevelt's son Elliott. During World War II, Blaze once bumped a serviceman from his purchased seat on an airplane.

Roosevelt's successor, Harry Truman, had a less celebrated animal named Mike, an Irish setter of which the president was inordinately fond.

John F. Kennedy, though said to be allergic to dog hair, never seemed to tire of petting his favorite, Charlie. And when it was learned

Lyndon B. Johnson displayed the beagle Him to Dwight D. Eisenhower.

that Pushinka, pregnant daughter of the Soviet space dog Khrushchev was being given to the Kennedys, Jackie Kennedy herself took charge of the arrangements. Instead of asking a servant to prepare for the arrival of the famous animal, the first lady cut strips of paper and made beds that she declared to be "just right for newborn puppies."

Her husband later helped teach Pushinka to climb a ladder to the tree house built for his daughter Caroline. When the Russian dog reached the top, Kennedy—flanked by photographers—was standing by to pet and praise her. "These photos ought to be worth at least six million votes," the president told newsmen who photographed him reaching for the Russian dog.

Lyndon B. Johnson created a different kind of news when he picked up his beagles Him and Her by the ears. Animal lovers throughout the nation protested the president's treatment of the beagles, but said little about his constant attention to them and to Edgar, a gift from F.B.I. director J. Edgar Hoover. Lady Bird said the president spoiled Bianca as well as Yuki, a little mongrel for whom he bought tiny boots to wear in the rain.

Richard Nixon's small cocker spaniel will always be mentioned by name in history books. As Dwight Eisenhower's vice presidential running mate in 1952, Nixon was accused of dipping into a secret slush fund. Eisenhower's friends urged him to force Nixon to withdraw from the campaign. To save what seemed to be a lost career, Nixon went on national television to vindicate himself. In an emotional conclusion, he admitted to one gift which he vowed to keep, the cocker spaniel Checkers that had been given to his small daughters. The "Checkers Speech" produced a public groundswell, Eisenhower reconsidered, and the Eisenhower-Nixon ticket easily won the election.

Barbara Bush, wife of the forty-first president, George Bush, is a dog lover. Her English springer spaniel, Millie, "literally comes between us at night," the president complains. "She wedges right up between our heads, and Bar likes it." In 1984, Mrs. Bush wrote a book, C. Fred's Story, a wry look at Washington life as told by "the first dog," to promote her literacy project.

40

A Wild Pitch Launched a Lasting Sports Ritual

Charles Evans Hughes, a longtime associate of William Howard Taft, was one of the few persons who never bit his tongue in talking with the president. "You're entirely too heavy," he told the chief executive one day in 1910. "You know it, and everyone else knows it. But you're not nearly so flabby as the cartoonists think. Why don't you show them that you still have plenty of muscle?"

Taft, who weighed about 330 pounds, was interested. From the gleam in Hughes's eyes, he was sure that the future chief justice had a specific proposal in mind. So he waited expectantly.

"Get involved in a sport," Hughes urged. "Any sport. How about baseball?"

Although the idea was intriguing, reality soon overpowered fantasy. Taft ruefully confessed that he "wasn't up to anything more than a ceremonial appearance, maybe."

That conversation had long-range effects that neither man anticipated. It led to the decision to give reporters and photographers a chance to see the six-foot, two-inch chief executive with the huge handlebar mustache in action—of a sort. After a series of negotiations, it was arranged that, for the first time, the president would open the baseball season.

On April 14, 1910, Griffith Stadium was crowded with fans, mostly Washingtonians, who were eager to see their team whip the visiting Philadelphia Athletics. Advance press coverage had brought out a capacity crowd to watch the president take part in what was rapidly becoming the great American pastime.

William Howard Taft was escorted to the mound. Instead of the ceremonial toss that many spectators anticipated, the big man made an honest try for the plate. But the first ball of the season went wild, and spectators roared. Smiling, the president went to a box and watched the game.

Twenty-nine years after William Howard Taft delivered the first presidential pitch in 1910, Herbert Hoover opened the baseball season from a box at Griffith Stadium, Washington D.C.

By the time Herbert Hoover opened the 1929 world series, the perfunctory presidential underhanded toss was from a spot high in the stadium. As a news event, the ceremony launched by Taft has lost much of its impact. Yet with details varied, it has proved surprisingly resilient. In April 1989, President George Bush opened the baseball season with a ground-level toss delivered in Balitmore.

Woodrow Wilson, the first president to have an active interest in football, made no headlines as a result of ceremonial appearances. However, devotees of the game credit him with having been a key figure in the development of the sport.

As a professor at Bryn Mawr College in Pennsylvania, earning $1,500 a year, the future president took on two unpaid extracurricular activities. He organized a debating society and coached the football team.

Earlier, as a Princeton University undergraduate, he had been a sidelines proponent of intercollegiate matches in the game that was then little different from rugby. When students organized a football association to aid the Princeton team, Wilson was a director and association secretary.

By the time Woodrow Wilson became president of Princeton, deaths and crippling injuries to players had given football a bad name. A single season, 1902, saw 18 gridiron deaths and at least 150 serious injuries. Working with a faculty committee, Wilson helped to formulate major changes in the rules. These led, among other things, to legalization of the forward pass. At the same time, the Intercollegiate Football Rules Committee—forerunner of the NCAA—was formed. Proud of his role in having helped to save what he termed "a very noble game," Woodrow Wilson watched two seasons of play under revised rules and conceded that "the game is a better one, but it must be made better still."

As a student at the U.S. Military Academy, Dwight D. Eisenhower was on his way to becoming a star halfback when the problem Wilson had tried to eliminate—injury in play—took him off the gridiron permanently. Ike was so disconsolate at his knee injury that he became moody and for a time considered dropping out of school.

Franklin D. Roosevelt played football at exclusive Groton prep school but failed to win a letter.

John F. Kennedy, an enthusiastic spectator, occasionally played touch football with intimate friends and members of his family. The first chief executive to rank as a football star was Gerald R. Ford, whose desire to study law led him to turn down offers from both the Green Bay Packers and the Detroit Lions. At the University of Michigan, Ford not only made the Wolverines his first year, he was named "outstanding freshman." Three years and three varsity letters later, he was chosen as the team's most valuable player and was center in the 1935 All-Star game. That season's performance led to the offers of professional contracts.

William Howard Taft was the first presidential golfer, but his swings were not much better controlled than his first presidential baseball pitch. Wilson was the first serious golfer to occupy the Oval Office, but his score seldom dropped below 115. Harding and Coolidge played, but didn't like to talk about their scores.

With the presidency of Dwight D. Eisenhower, things changed. For Ike, it was a bad day if his score reached 85. His admirers in the U.S. Golf Association, perhaps fearful that his interest would wane, installed a putting green for him adjacent to the White House rose garden. Ike was such a devotee of play at Augusta, Georgia, that a special cottage there still bears his name.

Termed "a superb golfer" by his admirers, John F. Kennedy typically shot in the upper 70s. Only six years after his death, the Oval Office was occupied by another golfer, Richard M. Nixon, whose score was about 15 strokes higher. Gerald R. Ford had a handicap of 18 when he became chief executive.

Nebraska-born Ford was the first president to be skilled on the ski slopes. He had no close Oval Office rival there except Georgia-born Jimmy Carter.

George Washington was the first chief executive regularly to ride to the hounds. Among his successors, only Theodore Roosevelt participated in the bone-breaking sport with some regularity.

Many chief executives have opted for less strenuous and less dangerous sports and recreational activities. John Quincy Adams was the first president to claim skill at billiards. He installed a mahogany table

At Augusta, Georgia's world-famous golf course, the Eisenhower cottage is a permanent reminder of the passion with which the president played.

covered with green felt in the White House. James Garfield and Benjamin Harrison also were players.

Warren G. Harding was the first president to be a true devotee of poker, although some earlier chief executives had known a little about the game. Harry Truman played frequently and, although he insisted on small stakes, always kept his cards close to his chest. Lyndon B. Johnson was a mediocre player; opponents said he tended to bluff too much to win with any regularity. Richard Nixon, who played cautiously, was described by old-time poker hands as being "very, very sharp."

William McKinley played both euchre and cribbage, chiefly with his wife. Woodrow Wilson was an avid bridge player at times and when under stress was likely to play solitaire to relax.

Crippled Franklin D. Roosevelt, a polio victim, turned to stamp collecting as a hobby. Andrew Johnson played checkers; Lyndon B. Johnson liked dominoes; and chess was a diversion for James Madison, James Garfield, and Rutherford B. Hayes.

General Ulysses S. Grant was the first president to find solace in the artist's brush and easel. Although his paintings, especially those of horses, did not approach the level of great art, they were better than passable. Dwight D. Eisenhower also liked to paint.

Thomas Jefferson, the first president to give public performances on a musical instrument, was said to have "a tender touch" when he played his favorite violin. John Tyler performed on the same instrument, while Harry Truman and Richard Nixon played the piano with enthusiasm.

Theodore Roosevelt was the first chief executive to play tennis, a game also liked by Taft, Ford, and Carter.

Presidential fishing expeditions, often in icy mountain streams rather than in smoke-filled rooms where the sport was for votes, started with George Washington. Pierce, Hayes, Garfield, Arthur, Coolidge, and Hoover were ardent fishermen. Chester A. Arthur belonged to the exclusive Restigouche Salmon Club, while Herbert Hoover was a frequent fisherman in the Rapidan River rapids. And newsmen reported that Jimmy Carter was attacked by a "killer rabbit" while fishing.

Horse back riding as a presidential recreation may have started with James Madison; it reached its peak of a sort with Ronald Reagan, who looked forward to it during vacations on his California ranch.

Recreational walking began with John Quincy Adams and claimed at least as many devotees as horseback riding. Coolidge regularly walked twice a day, except in the most severe weather. Harry Truman seldom walked more than once a day, but when he set out on his early morning treks, he nearly always followed a course that measured two miles, which he covered at 128 steps per minute.

A few chief executives have gone in for kinds of recreation and sport favored by no other president. George Washington enjoyed breeding animals and took special pleasure in the exploits of his jackass Royal Gift. Andrew Jackson entered his own horses in races; he also raised and fought gamecocks.

For all-round rough-and-tumble fun, however, Theodore Roosevelt has had no peer in the White House. He played polo with the same verve and dash shown when he led the famous charge up San Juan Hill. He was an unashamed devotee of hunting and proudly posed with big game he bagged on an African expedition.

No walker for walking's sake, Teddy liked to hike, provided that terrain was rough enough to suit him. He liked to row and to skinny-dip in icy water. During his days as governor of New York, he regularly wrestled with a middleweight champion. He started boxing very early and kept it up in spite of serious injury to an eye, reluctantly abandoning the sport only when, as president, he took a few too many hard blows from sparring partners. That was when the Rough Rider who had tried practically every strenuous sport that was known in his era achieved another presidential "first and only" by mastering jiu-jitsu.

CHAPTER
41

William Howard Taft's Stanley Steamer Was Squeezed into the White House Stable

"**I**'m sorry, Mr. President," said long-time presidential aide Major Archibald Butt. "We've made all of the measurements twice. There's no way to get your steamer into the stable without moving other things out."

William Howard Taft, says Washington folklore, drew himself up to his full six-foot, two-inch height. "Archie," he demanded, "don't bring me measurements; just do as I say."

Butt, who oversaw much of the White House's operation during the early years of the twentieth century, had dealt with chief executives before. Undaunted, he retorted, "Yes, sir, Mr. President. But don't say that Mother Shipton didn't have you in mind when she wrote that 'Carriages without horses shall go, / And *accidents fill the world with woe.*'"

Ignoring the emphasis added to a widely familiar hoax that posed as fifteenth-century prophecy, Taft turned back to Major Butt. "Get rid of the carriages—all of them except the Roosevelt brougham."

Following the instructions of the chief executive, carriages in which presidents and their wives had ridden many times were rolled into storage areas and covered with canvas. That created a big empty space in the stable on 17th Street, a space large enough, in spite of what Butt originally thought, to accommodate not one, but four presidential automobiles.

Along with the president, chauffeur George H. Robinson took special pride in the biggest of the lot, a seven-passenger White Steamer purchased by Taft in the weeks just before his inauguration. Gleaming silver plate contrasted sharply with black-lacquered steel of the body, one so immense that Robinson soon found he could turn the vehicle around only by going to one of the city's traffic circles.

Taft was the first chief executive consistently to use White House automobiles instead of horses and carriages. In 1902 that innovation created far more talk throughout the country than his revival of the special war-time tax on income that had been started under Abraham Lincoln, then soon dropped. Under Taft only the income of corporations was taxed—at the rate of 2 percent of profits.

Federally owned cars used by the Tafts included a limousine and a touring car for the president, as well as a small landaulet for Mrs. Taft. During the eight years of the Wilson presidency, the same arrangement continued. Under Warren G. Harding a second limousine, plus a small car for the president's secretary, came into the White House garage.

Calvin Coolidge accepted the pattern he inherited and did not modify it. But Herbert Hoover, who was accustomed to wealth and the use of it, accumulated automobiles enthusiastically. He added two more limousines, to make up a fleet of four, plus a touring car for Secret Service agents and one car each for the three presidential secretaries.

Mrs. Hoover seldom used any of the presidential vehicles. She did not need to do so; she had the exclusive use of a landaulet, or town car, and optional use of two other cars and two baggage wagons.

Except for an occasional brief trip on a sailing vessel, the earliest chief executives used only their own muscles, or horse power, for transportation.

Accustomed to the saddle from boyhood, George Washington had no intention of being taken for an ordinary citizen on ceremonial occasions. That is why he ordered leopard skins and other elaborate gear "for suitable dress for horse on state occasions."

His hogskin saddle—draped with leopard skins only occasionally— was complete with two girths, plus "1 pair of best plated stirrip irons" and seven yards of gold cloth. His coat of arms was fastened to the saddle with "silver tuff nails, price unknown."

For his first inauguration, George Washington took his seat in a coach drawn by four horses. He was careful not to soil his white silk stockings and spread open his brown broadcloth suit with sterling silver buttons in the shape of spread-winged eagles so that the garment would not be creased by the jostling of the carriage.

Thomas Jefferson authorized the purchase of four full-blooded bays at the then-astronomical price of $1,600 so that his coach would be pulled by "the best that money could buy." But for sheer pleasure, he reveled in "the magnificent Wildair," his favorite saddle horse.

Franklin Pierce was less kindly in his thoughts of horses. In the only major Mexican War battle in which he participated, artillery startled his mount. Abruptly tossed forward, the future chief executive felt the pommel of his saddle driven into his groin. He fainted from pain, and the horse fell in such fashion that it broke its own leg and tore its rider's knee.

While Andrew Jackson was the first president to ride in a railroad train, he spent countless hours in the saddle and day after day in stage-coaches. When horses were discussed, his eyes became bright with excitement, for he owned and put at stud a beautiful bay named Trux-ton. While in his prime, Jackson's animal was never beaten in the two-mile race and, when retired from the track, he sired at least 400 fine colts. That is the reason why Jackson reputedly admitted that he made more money from one horse than from all the land and houses he ever bought for investment purposes.

William Henry Harrison scorned the use of a carriage, and so he rode in his inaugural parade on a splendid white charger. Martin Van Buren preferred the same kind of animal, but liked a different color— coal black.

Abraham Lincoln, who claimed to have arrived in Springfield, Illinois, in an ox-cart, preferred his own legs to the saddle or a carriage. However, on a New York spending spree, his fashion-minded wife paid $900 for a carriage she deemed suitable for use by the president. Lincoln rode in it only when he could not find an excuse to stay out of it, but in emergency situations he got into whatever conveyance was at hand. In October 1862 at Antietam battlefield and in a hurry to get to Bakerville, Maryland, to review troops, he commandeered a field ambulance and jolted three miles to his destination.

Grover Cleveland's presidential stable consisted of five animals; three of them, he often boasted, were "perfectly matched browns." Three additional horses were provided at government expense, enabling the chief executive and the first lady to make use of a landau, a victoria, a brougham, and a simple black buggy.

By the time Theodore Roosevelt took office, the White House stable was empty. Under an austerity budget, allowances for horses and carriages provided for the president's use were eliminated. Therefore Roosevelt brought to Washington six of his own saddle mounts and two pairs of carriage horses. Even the landau, brougham, surrey, and small open trap most frequently used by the president's daughter were personal, not government, property.

At least two four-legged veterans long had the run of White House grounds. Zachary Taylor vowed that his favorite mount, Claybank, "was smarter than most ordinary folk and all politicians." But it was his battle-tried Old Whitey who was turned loose to graze on the White House lawn. Tyler described this animal as "slightly knock-kneed and with a tail much thinned by numerous applications for 'a hair of him as a keepsake.'" John Tyler's favorite mount, the General, never smelled gunpowder in spite of his name. Like Old Whitey, he

Archie Butt often accompanied William Howard Taft for jaunts in his Stanley Steamer, which was so huge it could be turned around only in traffic circles.

did as he pleased in the vicinity of the White House. When he died, Taylor saw to it that he had proper burial and above his grave placed a monument that read: "Here lies the body of my good horse, The General. For twenty years he bore me faithfully, and in all that time he never made a blunder. Would that his master could say the same!"

Ulysses S. Grant, who had many horses shot from under him during the Civil War, loved the big animals from early childhood. His parents told friends that he got along much better with horses than with people. At Cairo, Illinois, writing to his wife after a clash with Confederates, he did not mention his own injuries, but bemoaned the death of his bay saddle mount.

As president, Grant had one of the finest stables ever assembled in the capital. One of them, a natural pacer, he fondly called Jeff Davis. Egypt, Cincinnati, and the ponies Reb and Billy Button were among the dozen or so animals then found at the White House.

For most ceremonial occasions, horsepower was useless without a suitable vehicle. George Washington started the practice of securing the best carriages that money could buy. His personal favorite—canary in color—was decorated with gilt nymphs and cupids. Such a vehicle deserved—and got—six perfectly matched animals whose hoofs were painted black and whose teeth were scoured before they were hitched to the ornate presidential carriage.

Andrew Jackson's favorite vehicle was an elegant phaeton fashioned from oak from the frigate *Constitution*. It outlasted Old Hickory by many years. Oldtimers in the capital vowed that, until Taft brought his White Steamer to town, the most eye-catching presidential vehicle was Chester A. Arthur's landau. Dark green in color and drawn by mahogany bays across whose backs were draped monogrammed blankets of dark green kersey, the carriage that was "picked out in red" was so distinctive that as soon as it came into eyesight small boys began shouting, "Here comes the president!"

Seated in casual splendor, President Arthur seldom went driving without using a lap robe of Labrador otter that was lined with dark green and had been embroidered to show the monogram "C.A.A."

Despite the precedent established by big William Howard Taft, who may have turned to automobiles because few horses were strong enough to bear his weight, the first president to ride in a self-propelled vehicle was William McKinley. His trip was no pleasure jaunt, however; when shot at Buffalo, New York, he rode to the hospital in an electric ambulance.

Woodrow Wilson was the last chief executive to ride to his inauguration in a horse-drawn carriage, and perhaps the first consistently to rely upon the power of gasoline. Wilson chose a big Pierce-Arrow touring car but, when fuel became scarce during World War I, the chief executive left his Pierce-Arrow in the garage and rode to church with his wife in a horse-drawn victoria.

Warren G. Harding, who was the first president to ride to his inauguration in an automobile in 1921, was also the first chief executive who knew how to drive.

Andrew Johnson started the practice of making presidential trips by train, but there was no official private car until the *Ferdinand Magellan* was built for the use of Franklin D. Roosevelt in 1940. In the period when trains provided the fastest way to travel long distances, a presidential train often included eighteen or twenty—sometimes even twenty-eight—cars.

William Howard Taft requisitioned two navy boats for use as presidential yachts. Theodore Roosevelt had earlier put the gunboat *Mayflower* into such special service. In the name of economy, Hoover ordered the 275-foot vessel placed in dry dock, where she burned early in 1931. Franklin D. Roosevelt used three yachts: the *Sequoia*, the *Potomac*, and the *Williamsburg*. Since all vessels put to such use belonged to the U.S. Navy, taxpayers picked up the tab for maintenance and operation of them.

Although his claim is dubious, Theodore Roosevelt liked to say that he was the first chief executive to ride in an automobile. Far more credibility is attached to his assertion that he was first to ride in a submarine and in an airplane.

Dwight D. Eisenhower was the first president to have a pilot's license and probably was first to travel extensively by helicopter.

With the systematic use of Air Force One, presidential travel gained an entirely new dimension, for presidents mirror the nation—from horseback to jet plane in just a little over 200 years.

CHAPTER
42

First Events and Achievements

Franklin Pierce was the first president to have a full-time bodyguard. A federal employee was assigned to protect him, at the request of the chief executive.

Martin Van Buren, whose term of office began on March 4, 1837, was the first president to be born an American citizen. He made his appearance at Kinderhook, New York, on December 5, 1782. All earlier chief executives were born as British subjects.

Judson Welliver, a veteran newspaper reporter, was the first person selected to write speeches for a president. He assumed this responsibility during the tenure of Warren G. Harding, who had come to know and like him during campaign trips. Even his closest friends admitted that another reason for turning to Welliver for help lay in the fact that Harding was notoriously clumsy when he tried to write his own speeches.

John Tyler, who picked a bride many years his junior, was the first president to marry while in office. Ex-president John Quincy Adams, age seventy-seven, was righteously indignant and turned to his famous diary to report that the newlyweds were the laughingstock of the capital.

The first president to lie in state in the East Room after death was William Henry Harrison. For this occasion the windows, walls, and even the doors of the big room were draped in black.

Herbert Clark Hoover, a native of West Branch, Iowa, was the first chief executive to be born west of the Mississippi River—on August 10, 1874.

Ulysses S. Grant was the first graduate of the U.S. Military Academy at West Point to occupy the White House. It was during his tenure that *Harper's Weekly* artist Thomas Nast drew the first cartoon depicting the Republican party as an elephant.

Warren G. Harding, the first president to employ a speech writer, thought poorly of his own efforts in this department.

Noted big game hunter Theodore Roosevelt was the first president to gain a special kind of immortality through an American-created toy. It all came about as a result of a bear hunt he went on in Panther Creek swamp near Yazoo City, Mississippi. He had a good shot at a bear but refused it because she had a little cub with her. Toy makers reacted by producing miniature "teddy bears," a perennial favorite in toy stores. Roosevelt also originated a commercial slogan. While dining at the Maxwell House Hotel in Nashville, Tennessee, he was served after-dinner coffee roasted by a local company named after the hotel. "It's good to the last drop," the former Rough Rider proclaimed; and that became the slogan of Maxwell House coffee.

Jimmy Carter was the first chief executive to be born in a hospital. Wise Hospital in Plains, Georgia, was later turned into a convalescent home.

Woodrow Wilson was the first president to speak to the nation by means of radio, but it was Franklin D. Roosevelt who effectively captured the medium with his still-remembered "fireside chats." Former actor Ronald Reagan was the first master of the White House to be rated as "superb" in both radio and television.

Andrew Jackson, who was the first president to ride on a railroad train, did so in 1833, riding all the way from Ellicott's Mill, Maryland, to Baltimore.

Abraham Lincoln was the first chief executive with a full beard. (Martin Van Buren had had bushy sideburns.) When nominated, Lincoln was clean shaven, but a letter from a small girl, Grace Bedell of Westfield, New York, is credited with having permanently changed his appearance. She wrote him she thought he would look nice with a beard. Later on a campaign tour, his train stopped at Westfield and

Lincoln had the eleven-year-old brought forward. He kissed her and said, "You see, I let these whiskers grow for you, Grace."

John Adams, who took the oath of office in chambers of the House of Representatives, was the first chief executive to whom the oath was administered by the Chief Justice of the U.S. Supreme Court.

Thomas Jefferson was the first head of state to prepare a written state of the union message for members of Congress. Both Washington and Adams delivered their messages orally, in person, without full manuscripts. The author of the Declaration of Independence was a superb writer but a poor orator. Therefore he decided not to appear in person but to pen his statement, announcing that no reply would be expected from lawmakers.

Theodore Roosevelt was first to use stationery embossed to read "The White House" instead of "The Executive Mansion." Until repainted after the British set fire to it in the War of 1812, the mansion was not white. When paint covered the scars of war, the new name was coined—but for the most part remained in oral rather than written or printed use until Roosevelt's time.

President and Mrs. Harding were the first to have an official entertainment fund. A few earlier chief executives managed to get the use of tax money to cover the costs of levees, receptions, and state dinners; but until the former newspaper man from Marion, Ohio, took charge, no money was appropriated specifically for such purposes.

James K. Polk was the first "dark horse" to reach the White House. At the Democratic convention of 1844, many delegates expected ex-president Martin Van Buren to win without a fight. Initially, Polk had only token support, receiving his first four votes on the eighth ballot. Eventually he topped Van Buren and all other opponents, even though when the convention began few delegates had known enough about him to consider him a possible nominee.

Old Hickory, as his soldiers called Andrew Jackson, was not only the first president to be commemorated by an equestrian statue, he was the first American to be honored in such fashion. Sculptor Clark Mills used cannon captured in the War of 1812 to cast the Jackson statue. It was unveiled on January 8, 1853, precisely thirty-eight years after Old Hickory's famous victory over the British at New Orleans.

Rutherford B. Hayes was the first chief executive to have the use of a typewriter in space that much later became known as the Oval Office. He had four salaried secretaries, one of whom persuaded him in 1880 to order from Fairbanks and Company a machine that they sold as their Improved Number Two Typewriter.

A cartoon of Andrew Jackson, the last president born as a British subject, leading Van Buren, the first born as an American subject, along the trail to the White House.

When Lyndon B. Johnson decided while in Australia to fly back to Washington via Europe, rather than to return as he had gone, he became the first president to circumnavigate the globe.

John Adams was the first chief executive to sue political foes for criminal libel. He did so under the hated Alien and Sedition Acts. Though soon repealed, while in force they led to the prosecution of twenty-five Republican editors and printers, ten of whom were convicted. No other president took comparable action until Theodore Roosevelt sued the New York *World* because of criticism about his Panama Canal activities. When the case reached the Supreme Court, a rare unanimous decision was announced—in favor of the *World*.

Andrew Johnson, who succeeded slain Abraham Lincoln, did not follow his predecessor's example by going to the War Department to send and receive telegrams. Instead, he was the first chief executive to have a telegraph room in the White House.

Rutherford B. Hayes was responsible for installation of the first White House telephone, put there on trial on May 10, 1879. Earlier, Hayes had spoken over the novel device at least once. While visiting in Providence, Rhode Island, in 1877, he talked briefly with Alexander Graham Bell by means of the system Bell had devised.

Theodore Roosevelt caused a great deal of critical comment when he made a three-day visit to the Canal Zone in Panama in 1906, thereby becoming the first chief executive to leave the United States while in

Iowa native Herbert Clark Hoover was the first chief excutive born west of the Mississippi River.

office. He was also the first to have his voice recorded. When he won the Nobel Peace Prize in 1906—the first American ever to win any Nobel prize—he used his $36,735 award to establish a trust fund whose goal was promotion of industrial peace.

John Adams, the chief executive who was first to occupy the executive mansion now called the White House, was also the first to open the president's home to the general public. Built on a scale that critics assailed as regal, a mansion of comparable size in England or Ireland would have had a staff of perhaps two dozen servants; not even one was provided for the lavish new residence in the new capital. So Adams and his wife paid for what little household help they had out of their own pockets.

Part Six

Money Matters

Modern Monticello is a monument to Thomas Jefferson's genius as an architect-builder. [THOMAS JEFFERSON MEMORIAL FOUNDATION]

43

Deeply in Debt, Thomas Jefferson Tried to Sell Monticello at Lottery

In January 1826, eighty-three-year-old Thomas Jefferson wrote to his grandson, saying, "there is not enough cash on hand to pay grocery bills at the local stores."

Having tried everything else and having failed to raise money to pay pressing bills, the master of Monticello decided to part with his beloved mansion. It would bring more, he was sure, if offered as the grand prize in a lottery rather than being sold in a typical real estate transaction. So he persuaded the Virginia legislature to pass a special bill permitting him to conduct the lottery.

Jefferson owned thousands of acres of land. In 1782, only one other man in Albermarle County, Virginia, owned more slaves than did Jefferson. But during most of his adult life the author of the Declaration of Independence showed a knack for spending more money than he made. In 1808, his last full year as president, the cost of maintaining his Washington household ran to about $8,000 more than his combined income from salary and farm lands. So when he left the White House he borrowed $8,000 on his own signature and persuaded James Madison to endorse an additional promissory note.

Jefferson was about $20,000 in debt at the time he relinquished the reins of government, but his fiscal dilemma never caused him to restrain his spending. According to Captain Edmund Bacon, long-time overseer at Monticello, during "many weeks the 26 spare horse stalls were not sufficient for the visitors' mounts. I have often sent a wagonload of hay up to the stable, and the next morning there would not be enough to make a bird's nest."

It was not unusual for as many as fifty guests to congregate at Jefferson's mansion. According to his daughter, "some of them remained for weeks or even months at a time."

Jefferson had an eye for a fine horse and a fancy rig, so he found it hard to turn down an offer of an animal or a vehicle that he liked. He spent freely for imported wine and fine cheese and didn't have the heart to hint to a guest that a lengthy stay was a financial burden.

One of Jefferson's efforts to produce ready cash has had a long lasting benefit for Americans. A small library in the Capitol was burned by the British in the War of 1812. Soon afterward, Thomas Jefferson wrote to his old friend Samuel Harrison Smith asking him to act as broker in offering the Jefferson library to Congress. "I have been fifty years making it," Jefferson wrote. Although he had made no exact inventory, he was sure he owned more than 6,000 volumes, nearly all of them being bound in leather.

After days of debate, Congress agreed to pay the former chief executive $23,950 for his beloved library. From this nucleus of books has grown the prestigious Library of Congress.

Money from that sale was too little to alleviate Jefferson's financial plight, as his debts totaled about $107,000.

By January 1826, bankruptcy was imminent, so Jefferson conceived his lottery scheme. He confided to a few trusted friends, "It will injure no one, but to me it is almost a question of life and death."

Before the lottery could be held, the legislature would have to grant a bill of authorization. Lobbying his plan, Jefferson wrote to lawmakers, "It is a common idea that games of chance are immoral. But what is chance? If we consider chance immoral, then every pursuit of human industry is immoral."

"My own debts have become considerable," he confessed in February 1826 to James Madison. "Land has lost its character of being a resource. So the idea occurred to me of selling by way of lottery."

Many Virginia legislators wanted nothing to do with Jefferson's scheme, in spite of their respect for the aging leader. Joseph Cabell, an old friend, tried to win support from Dabney Carr, Jr., but Carr balked so strongly that young Jefferson Randolph ruefully reported to his grandfather, "The policy of this state has been against lotteries as immoral, and the first view of the subject was calculated to give alarm."

A few intimate friends of the ex-president tried unsuccessfully to arrange for him an $80,000 loan, interest free, from the state of Virginia. However, finally the lower house of the legislature passed the Jefferson Lottery Bill by a margin of just four votes; in the senate, resistance collapsed a few days later. With the coveted authorization in hand, elaborate plans were made and printers ran off big batches of tickets. Two of Jefferson's old political enemies—John Randolph and John Marshall—surprised him by buying heavily. "Out of pity that the author of the Declaration of Independence has suffered public humiliation," John Randolph purchased $500 worth of tickets.

Nevertheless, even though Virginia governor John Tyler lent his prestige to sales rallies, public response was very poor. It was soon clear that the lottery would not raise enough money to pay Jefferson's debts. With only a fraction of the tickets sold, the plan was reluctantly abandoned.

Without Jefferson's knowledge, his influential friends opened "public subscriptions" for his financial relief. New Yorkers sent $8,500; $5,000 came from Philadelphia and $3,000 from Baltimore.

Yet receipts from lottery ticket sales and public subscriptions, combined, didn't come anywhere near what Jefferson owed.

Six months after the start of the lottery scheme, Thomas Jefferson died on July 4, 1826, and his beloved Monticello went under the auctioneer's hammer to satisfy creditors. Later the mansion fell into neglect for nearly a century, but was eventually rescued and restored by Jefferson devotees. Few who now visit the marvelous colonial mansion realize that the architect-builder-statesman-president who designed and long occupied it saw the failure of his lottery as "a deadly blast of all my peace of mind, during my remaining days."

44

For James Monroe, "Compensation" Was Too Little, Too Late

Known to posterity for his Monroe Doctrine that warns European powers against intervention in the Western hemisphere, James Monroe was at the end of his rope when John Quincy Adams took over the White House on March 4, 1825.

Because Mrs. Monroe was too ill to travel, the ex-president and his wife remained for three weeks as guests of the Adams family. They then left for their Oak Hill estate in Loudoun County, Virginia.

It was no pleasure jaunt, however; they traveled with heavy hearts. James Monroe owed at least $75,000 that he had no way of paying. In April, he offered his 3,500-acre plantation for sale; but no one made an offer that he considered to be reasonable. Soon he was being pressed by New York's John Jacob Astor, who asked him to pay at least part of what was owed to him.

Monroe's troubles—unlike those of Thomas Jefferson—stemmed almost entirely from his many years of public service. He had gone to France in 1794 to spend two years as U.S. minister there. After a term as governor of Virginia, he then accepted Jefferson's invitation to become a special envoy, playing a key role in the Louisiana Purchase. Four years as minister to Great Britain were followed by service as U.S. secretary of state and then by a period as secretary of war.

Monroe spent much more than he was paid while serving abroad; during his absence from America he was forced to sell a 950-acre tract of land near Charlottesville to settle neighborhood debts. During his years in cabinet posts he incurred extraordinary expenses because inspection tours and other activities essential to performance of his duties.

Born to wealth as a member of the Virginia aristocracy, he found it humiliating to turn to the federal government for help, but he saw no

Congress voted to repay James Monroe 30 thousand dollars of the more than 65 thousand he spent from his own pocket during a lifetime of service to the nation.

other way out of his dilemma. So he began a long and complicated series of efforts to get "compensation" from Congress. One of the many documents that was drawn up was entitled: "The Memoir of James Monroe, Esqr., relating to his Unsettled Claims upon the People and the Government of the United States."

He meticulously listed the things he had done in service to the nation, detailing what they had cost over his salary. So much paper was generated that in a later period it was impossible to reproduce all the documents in a thick volume called *James Monroe, Public Claimant.*

Month after month, the ex-president, whose health was beginning to fail, pressed lawmakers. He reminded them that he had started his patriotic career as a Revolutionary soldier and had been wounded in the Battle of Trenton. He ticked off major accomplishments that could not have been made had he not repeatedly dipped into his own funds. His out-of-pocket expenditures as a public servant had cost him, he showed, tens of thousands of dollars in each of several key positions.

While Congress debated and delayed, citizens of Albemarle County, Virginia, sent a formal memorial to lawmakers. They stressed that before entering fifty years of service to his country, young Monroe had been a man of ample property. But, they said, "in the retirement of his old age, he is suffering from the grievous calamities of poverty, ruined by his services to the nation."

Congressmen who were friendly to Monroe managed to get various claims before congressional committees. Committee reports were considered by both houses in several sessions. Finally, in 1829 a select committee of the House debated for three weeks. Then committee members acted favorably on a bill that directed the secretary of the treasury to pay the claimant $65,780.96.

Many lawmakers were indignant when they learned of the recommendation. They threatened to have the entire appropriation deleted from fiscal measures unless it was drastically reduced. In the end, Congress voted in the fall of 1830 to pay Monroe $30,000 "for public services, losses, and sacrifices."

When the money arrived in April, it was a classic case of "too little, too late." Monroe was able to settle some of his most pressing obligations, but soon announced with a heavy heart that he would be forced to sell Oak Grove, not at its worth, but for whatever it would bring.

His daughter Maria, who had married Samuel Gouverneur—recently named postmaster of New York City—wrote that they would make room for him in their modest home not far from the Bowery. By then, John Quincy Adams had described his predecessor as "dying in wretchedness and beggary."

Instead of being besieged with offers when he again placed Oak Grove on the market, Monroe found no indication of interest. So he left the plantation in the hands of brokers and went to live with his daughter. The trauma of the relocation was too much for his strength; about one month after receiving belated payment of a fraction of his claims he died, far from Virginia, on July 4, 1831. His death came five years to the day after the deaths of both Jefferson and Adams on Independence Day 1826. No other president, except these three, has died on July 4.

Several other presidents—notably Andrew Jackson, Ulysses S. Grant, and Warren G. Harding—have died as debtors. Jackson, like George Washington, was "land poor," holding title to vast tracts of land but having little cash. Unlike Washington, whose valuable estate more than paid all of his outstanding obligations, Jackson's western lands could not be sold immediately. So Old Hickory's known unpaid obligations, not counting household bills, ran to an estimated $26,000.

Warren G. Harding ran up what may have been the largest debt of a chief executive. Trading on the stock market under a "blind account" that did not show his name, he ran up a huge deficit. As a result he sold his Marion, Ohio, *Star* newspaper for $550,000—on paper.

A few years earlier, before entering the White House, he had offered the newspaper for sale at $140,000 and had found no takers. But now Louis H. Brush and Roy D. Moore, owners of a chain of small-town papers in Ohio, agreed to give the president notes payable in return for "occasional contributions" to the *Star* and their other papers.

Brush–Moore notes payable were far from cash, so Harding arranged for broker Samuel Ungerleider to discount them. He used part of the cash to pay some of his obligations and the rest as margin with which to purchase securities whose full price he could not produce.

Plunging heavily, the president bought more than $500,000 worth of stock on margin. Issues he favored included Bethlehem Steel, which he felt was sure to go up because of information he had from the firm's president, Charles Schwab. On the advice of another industrialist, he bought a big block of Mexican Seaboard Railroad warrants. Then he purchased stock of the Pure Oil Company, and some miscellaneous smaller lots.

In the summer of 1923 the president set out on what he called a "voyage of understanding" that was designed to take him across much of the nation. While at the Palace Hotel in San Francisco, he died suddenly on August 2. Almost at once, stories of corruption in high places began to unfold.

The death of the president, plus revelations about his corrupt administration, had a devastating effect upon his stock portfolio. Bethlehem Steel dropped 20 percent in 90 days. During the same period, Mexican Seaboard warrants lost half their value.

Having traded under the name of Walter Ferguson as well as in a separate blind account, Harding died owing his broker an estimated $200,000. The attorney for Harding's estate knew that the broker was eager to avoid publicity. As a result, he told heirs of the dead president that they need feel no responsibility for more than a fraction of the debts left behind by Harding. That meant that what may have been the largest-ever debt of a chief executive was settled by his death.

Elaborate though it was, the funeral of insolvent Harding was—for the times—small by comparison with that of deeply indebted Monroe. Alive, the man who had framed the famous doctrine about North and South America had been all but ignored by his countrymen. Dead, he was treated with pomp and ceremony. His New York City funeral was the biggest the city had ever seen.

Throughout the nation, flags were lowered to half-mast. Military and naval officers wore crepe on their left sleeves, and bells tolled in every big city and many small ones. In New York, guns fired 73 salutes at one-minute intervals.

Back in Virginia at the plantation that was still up for sale, there was an empty grave in the double vault designed by the president himself. Instead of sending Monroe to lie beside his wife in the vault at his plantation, survivors buried him in the Gouverneur vault in New York City. More than twenty-five years later his body was removed to Hollywood Cemetery in Richmond, Virginia.

CHAPTER

45

Phony White House Controversy Became Major Campaign Issue

T he cost of a presidential campaign now runs in excess of fifty million dollars, but in 1840 a trifling sum became a major campaign issue.

It started when President Martin Van Buren made what he thought was a routine request of a congressional committee. To improve the executive mansion and grounds, he asked for $3,665.

Whig Representative Charles Ogle of Pennsylvania made political hay out of the president's request. Speaking in the House of Representatives, he delivered an impassioned speech about the "financially irresponsible" president who was seeking re-election. Then the Whigs used Ogle's speech as an important campaign document in the 1840 contest.

Son of a farmer and an innkeeper, Van Buren was reared in a lower middle class family. As he moved up the political ladder, he developed increasingly expensive tastes. Once he took the oath of office as president, his actions played into the hands of critics. He rode to his inauguration in an elegant phaeton complete with liveried servants, an equippage that was especially conspicuous because the nation was already in the early stages of a financial depression that climaxed in the Panic of 1837.

Despite bank closings and the failure of thousands of small businesses, the incumbent president easily was nominated again by the Democrats for the next presidential campaign. Only two incumbent presidents—John Adams and his son John Quincy Adams—had ever been defeated for re-election.

Very early, advisors warned Van Buren that economic problems could cost him votes. Treasury Secretary Levi Woodbury begged the president to practice extreme care in his personal financial dealings.

*Martin Van Buren was often
depicted as bearing a price
tag; here he rides on the back
of Andrew Jackson.*

"Whatever else this administration does," he warned in 1839, "we must convince the rank and file of voters that the tax dollar is spent with great care." Anything that even had the appearance of profligate spending must be avoided.

It was in this climate that Van Buren decided to refurbish the White House for his next four-year term. He made a detailed list of essential alterations and repairs, then added a few suggestions about purchase of furniture and improvement of the grounds. His "want list" involved an outlay of $3,665.

Van Buren's request went to the House of Representatives when that body was sitting as a committee of the whole to act on appropriations for the year 1840. Almost as soon as the budget bill was presented, Congressman Ogle rose to amend it by striking out the clause that read, "For alterations and repairs of the President's house and furniture, for purchasing trees, shrubs, and compost, and for superintendency of the grounds, three thousand six hundred and sixty-five dollars."

Once his amendment was seconded, Ogle delivered a prepared address that would be printed in the *Congressional Record*. From that source, it could be reprinted and circulated as an official document.

Ogle called his speech "The Royal Splendors of the President's Palace." Excerpts from it show how hard he hit his political foe:

> I consider this a very important item—not as to the amount, but as to the principles involved. I resist the principle on which it is demanded as anti-democratic—as running counter to the plain, simple, and frugal notions of our republican People.
>
> Are honest citizens everywhere ready to maintain, for the private accommodation of the president, A ROYAL ESTABLISHMENT *at the cost of the nation?*
>
> Will they longer feel inclined to support their *chief servant* in a PALACE *as splended as that of the Caesars, and as richly adorned as the proudest Asiatic mansion?*
>
> You may depend upon it that something must be out of gear. The present occupant of the palace loves tassels, rosettes, and girlish finery almost as much as a real "Bank Whig" loves hard cider.
>
> I would respectfully inquire whether *silk tassels and rosettes* are considered *household furniture* in the legitimate democratic meaning of the term.
>
> Mr. Chairman, in my opinion it is time the people of the United States should know that their money goes to buy for the plain hard-handed democratic President, knives, forks, and spoons of gold—that he may dine in the style of the monarchs of Europe.
>
> I had thought that it was bad enough for the farmers, mechanics, and laborers of the country to provide hay and pasturage for Mr. Van Buren's race and carriage horses; to pay for the manure on his potato, celery, cauliflower, and asparagus beds; to pay the hire of a British gardener to topdress his strawberry vines; but, sir, to HEM his DISH RAGS, pay for his LARDING NEEDLES and LIQUOR STANDS is still worse.
>
> Aye, sir, worse, if possible than filling the apartments of the House of the American People with royal and imperial Wilton rugs, foreign cut wine coolers, French bedsteads, and one hundred dollar artificial flowers.

Ogle's diatribe thundered on and on. Van Buren, he charged, wore the perfume fancied by Queen Victoria. He slept in a Louis XV bed and used "Fanny Kemble" green glass finger cups. Unable properly to admire himself in "a plain 8 x 10 looking glass like any honest citizen of Tulpehacken valley might use," he charged, "our PRESIDENT uses gold-framed mirrors as big as a barn door to behold his plain Republican self."

Delighted Whigs elevated the speech to the major subject of attack in their campaign. Sometimes in full, but more often in fragments, "The Speech of Gold" was reprinted hundreds of times, always with the notation that it was an official document of the U.S. Congress.

One of the longest political songs ever used in a campaign, a fourteen-page epic, consisted of "questions and answers" drawn from or inspired by Ogle's address. A shorter but even more damaging song, a doggerel version of the Ogle speech, was set to a jingling tune and swept the county as a comparison between Van Buren and his opponent, William Henry Harrison:

> *Let Van Buren from his cooler of silver, drink wine,*
> *And lounge on his cushioned settee.*
> *Our man on his buckeye bench can recline;*
> *Content with hard cider is he!*
> *Our man lives in a cabin built wholly of logs,*
> *Drinks only his own cider, too;*
> *He ploughs his own ground, he feeds his own hogs,*
> *This hero of Tippecanoe!*

For many voters, the contrast between a "log cabin and hard cider" candidate and one who "lived in a palace of gold, like Caesar's," was convincing. Van Buren lost even his home state and took just 60 electoral votes to Harrison's 234.

Out of the White House, the ex-president summarized his defeat by protesting, "I was drunk down, sung down, and lied down." Then he retired to live in an elegant Italo-Grecian mansion in his native city.

Regardless of the blend of truth and falsehood in Charles Ogle's charges, his speech based upon a request for $3,665 makes that sum the biggest little amount ever to be a major factor in a presidential election.

CHAPTER
46

Abraham Lincoln Was a High-powered and Sometimes High-priced Attorney

Viewed through the mists of time, Abraham Lincoln is often seen as a small-time backwoods lawyer who barely managed to keep food on the table. In reality, he was an all-purpose attorney of great skill who took virtually any client and collected some very big fees. Lincoln argued all kinds of cases: murder, disputed wills, maritime law, foreclosures, debt, slander, patent infringement, divorce, rape, horse theft, land titles, ejectments, personal injury, and suits involving slaves.

Although he defended clients accused of murder, he also acted as a court-appointed prosecutor in murder cases and represented slaves and slaveowners in cases involving fugitive slaves.

At age 32 he won freedom for a girl in the celebrated 1841 case of *Bailey vs. Cromwell,* heard by the Illinois Supreme Court. The girl, named Nance, had been sold in a state where slavery was illegal, and therefore the sale was voided and Nance was set free. In another case, which he lost, he represented a slave owner who sued some abolitionists who had harbored runaway slaves.

Yet just six years later, having recently been elected to Congress but not yet having taken his seat, Lincoln took the opposite side in the famous Matson case. It was tried in Charleston, Illinois, near the home of the attorney's father, stepmother, and other relatives. Since Lincoln had plenty of legal business elsewhere, some analysts think he took the Matson case primarily in order to be near his family for several weeks.

These slaves had fled when their owner, Kentucky planter Robert Matson, threatened to send a slave's wife and children into the deep south to work the cotton fields. Matson hired Abraham Lincoln to sue the abolitionists for the $2,500 he said their actions had cost him.

When Lincoln lost the case and Matson lost his slaves, he refused to pay the young Illinois lawyer.

During active legal practice from 1837 to 1860, the future chief executive represented at least five railroads. In one case he represented a plaintiff seeking damages from a railroad—and himself sued another. Four of his cases in which he represented clients suing railroads went to the Illinois supreme court.

Several thousand cases took Lincoln away from home about six months out of every twelve during a period of twenty-three years. By 1850 he was earning an estimated $5,000 a year—in an era when $1,250 would purchase a splendid two-story home.

Some legal contests in which he took part involved small sums. A schoolmaster had borrowed $200 and could not or would not pay it back. Lincoln won for the lender in a suit against the man who had lent him books and taught him the art of surveying. He took to the Illinois supreme court a case involving a three-dollar dispute over "a scrub male hog."

Many of his cases involved large sums. He defended a wealthy man being sued for $10,000 because he had beaten an editor with a stick. Using humor to charm the jury, the attorney who deprecated himself as a "jack-leg" got his client off for a few hundred dollars.

After an accident in which one steamboat rammed another, Lincoln won a $3,600 verdict for a client who came to him because of his widespread reputation.

In terms of dollars involved, Lincoln's biggest case concerned ownership of shore land at the mouth of the Chicago River. Sued for $624,236.70, the Ohio and Mississippi Railroad retained Lincoln, who managed to get the case all the way to the U.S. Supreme Court. When the high court ruled, his clients had to pay only $312,133.35 plus $256.54 damages.

In terms of personal triumph, he soared highest in complicated litigation that involved the biggest corporation in the state: the Illinois Central Railroad. Representing the rail line against his own former law partners, Lincoln lost the initial bout in the circuit court. Then he appealed to the state supreme court, where he won. At that point he presented his clients with a bill for $2,000 and received from them a check for $200 in payment for his services. Angered at their treatment of him, Lincoln sued the giant corporation for the balance of the bill.

Ordered by the court to pay Lincoln $4,800, the Illinois Central balked once more. So "backwoods lawyer" Lincoln secured an order for the sheriff to seize the railroad's property, action that led to prompt settlement in full.

Twice Lincoln defended that same railroad in suits asking for damages to livestock in transit. Other big clients included the Chicago

Abraham Lincoln served as counsel for the defense for a client accused of murder—Theodore Schrader Lithograph, 1865. [LIBRARY OF CONGRESS]

and Alton Railroad, the Ohio and Mississippi, the Rock Island, and the Tonica and Petersburg.

Yet as prosecutor he found time to handle the case against a man accused of raping a seven-year-old and rejoiced when the defendant drew a sentence of eighteen years.

On the other side of the fence, defense attorney Lincoln pleaded for Samuel Short, who had shot boys for raiding his watermelon patch. Lincoln won the case, but Short would not pay his fee. Thereupon the attorney went to court again, suing to collect from Short.

Abraham Lincoln appeared most often in circuit courts, but he also tried cases in federal courts. Involved in at least 200 Illinois supreme court cases, he twice appeared before the U.S. Supreme Court.

He lost the case of accused killer William Fraim, who was hanged in 1839. But he won for William Trailor and saved him from the scaffold. Trailor did not pay his legal fees and died of natural causes four years later. Lincoln promptly sued his estate and collected.

Lincoln defended John M. Manny, who was being sued by industrial giant Cyrus H. McCormick for alleged infringement of a patent. He lost that one, but he won when he sued the Great Western Railroad on behalf of brakeman Jasper Harris, who had been injured in an accident.

He even defended one man who faced thirty-five indictments for obstruction of a public highway, and in another instance he won $600 for his client when a man named Dungey was called "a negro" by his brother-in-law. He represented a McLean County bank in a suit against the city of Bloomington, Illinois. And in Springfield, he charged the gas company $500 for a title search concerning the two city lots on which its plant was located. He represented plaintiffs in suits against the Great Western Railroad, the Illinois River Railroad Company, and the St. Louis, Alton, and Chicago Railroad Company.

Memories of a lucrative law practice were on Lincoln's mind in the spring of 1865. On the afternoon of April 14, he confided to his wife that he might like to open a law office in Chicago when his term of office was completed. However, that night he went to Ford's Theater, where an assassin's bullet ended his plan.

CHAPTER
47

Ulysses S. Grant Won
His Battle with Bankruptcy

"**I** propose to fight it out on this line, if it takes all summer," ex-president Ulysses S. Grant slowly wrote, one word at a time. His message had nothing to do with memories of the siege of Petersburg or any other epochal Civil War campaign. Rather it focused on his struggle with words and was addressed to Mark Twain.

America's most popular nineteenth-century humorist, flush with cash as a result of his books selling at incredible rates, had invested some of his royalties into the publishing firm of Webster & Company. Tradition says that neophyte publisher Twain happened to catch a portion of a newspaper sheet floating through the air. He gave the scrap of paper a glance, and to his surprise saw part of a story dealing with the financial troubles of Ulysses S. Grant.

Immediately, without consulting his senior partners, Mark Twain contacted Grant and offered him $25,000 as an advance against royalties to be earned from his memoirs—not a word of which had been written.

Grant hesitated. He desperately needed the money, but he was not sure he could produce a book. It would take months to write his personal story, and he was suffering from terminal cancer.

Yet there was another reason to act on Twain's offer. On leaving the White House, the Civil War hero had put every dollar he had into a brokerage firm launched by his son in partnership with Ferdinand Ward. When Grant and Ward seemed about to go under, the ex-president borrowed heavily from William H. Vanderbilt to keep the firm afloat.

Even the Vanderbilt money was not enough, and 1884 saw the brokerage firm file for bankruptcy. Grant was not only wiped out financially, he was heavily in debt to Vanderbilt and others from whom he had borrowed.

At this point showman Phineas T. Barnum made a rescue offer. He would give General Grant a down payment of $100,000 if he could get

Ulysses S. Grant raced with death to complete his first and only book, a two-volume memoir published by Mark Twain.

the use of his war trophies for a traveling display. In addition, said Barnum, he would pay Grant part of the gate receipts.

Ulysses S. Grant pondered the Barnum offer for less than sixty seconds. "No," he said sadly, "I cannot consider such a proposal. My swords and uniforms and medals and battle flags are destined for other use." He did not explain to the showman that he had already arranged to give these to Vanderbilt as partial payment for the money he owed the financier. It was against this background that Ulysses Grant decided to write his book in a race against death.

He asked Adam Badeau to help him. Having been Grant's military secretary for a year and having already written an immense *Military History of Ulysses S. Grant*, Badeau was a logical choice for a ghostwriter.

Definitely interested when queried, Adam Badeau required what Grant did not have—$1,000 a month, payable in advance. His stipulation that he would also receive 10 percent of all profits from the book in addition to monthly payments was theoretical at this stage. No one knew whether or not there ever would be any profits.

Grant pondered, hesitated briefly, then turned down Badeau's demands. If his memoirs were to be written, he would perform the job himself.

At his country home in Mount McGregor, New York, the dying warrior began his race with the calendar and with death. At first, he dictated to a stenographer. After sixty days his voice failed, so he began scrawling as rapidly as possible on fine stationery. In the end, he turned to inexpensive scratch pads. Heavy use of cocaine and morphine dulled the pain enough to keep him going.

Somehow, his sense of humor remained intact. After a few weeks of writing he reported, "I will have to be careful; I see every person I give a piece of paper to, puts it in his pocket. Some day, they will be coming up against my English."

Just days before he died on July 23, 1885, Grant completed his part of the deal. His voluminous *Memoirs* were finished, despite the fact that in the process of completing the job he had concluded that "A verb is anything that signifies to be; to do; or to suffer. I must be a verb; I signify all three."

Now the great question was: Could Mark Twain fulfill his part of the bargain?

Already the humorist had begun hiring canvassers, promising them a percentage of their sales. He himself produced a manual telling them "How to Introduce the Personal Memoirs of U. S. Grant." By the time two green-and-gold volumes came from the press, Twain had nearly 10,000 men in the field, ready to go. Many had already taken fifty-cent deposits against future deliveries.

Grant's death created an immediate, immense market for the book so painfully produced. Perhaps because of Twain's lack of experience rather than in spite of it, the humorist-publisher produced America's first great best-seller of its sort. Soon the canvassers no longer had to knock on doors; potential buyers were seeking them out, cash in hand.

As a result, Mark Twain's publishing house presented the Grant estate with a check for $250,000, the first royalty payment of a dead president's life story. Eventually the book earned over $450,000. It had achieved its purpose: to make money.

Early presidents produced voluminous writings, most of which were not intended for commercial publication. However, after the combination of Grant and Twain proved successful, most chief executives have turned out one or more books written chiefly for the financial return.

Woodrow Wilson was an exception to the pattern. Offered $150,000 for his account of the World War I peace conference at which he was a major participant, he said, "No, thank you, my memories are not for sale."

Avid fisherman Herbert Hoover scored a success with his 1963 volume, Fishing for Fun—And to Wash Your Soul. [NEW YORK TIMES PICTURES]

Earlier, Theodore Roosevelt had been paid $1,000 a month by *Outlook* magazine as a contributing editor. His account of hunting big game in Africa brought $50,000 from *Scribner's Magazine.*

Though known as "Silent Cal," Coolidge was relatively fluent on paper. A newspaper column by him, syndicated throughout the nation, earned him $203,000 in 1931. His *Autobiography*—tiny by comparison with Grant's *Memoirs*—added $75,000 to his net worth.

Dwight D. Eisenhower was paid $650,000 for his *Crusade in Europe* and was given special tax treatment for the money. Harry Truman became more than peeved with the Internal Revenue Service when his own profitable *Memoirs* didn't get the same favorable tax treatment.

Herbert Hoover turned out three volumes of memoirs that hardly anyone read, but he hit the literary jackpot with his 1963 book on *Fishing for Fun—And to Wash Your Soul.* Richard Nixon wrote about *The Real War,* and Gerald Ford lent his name to *Portrait of the Assassin.* As the literary pot of gold has become increasingly full, first ladies have also written their memoirs. Rosalynn Carter's autobiography, *First Lady from Plains,* cost $17.95, a figure that would have astounded Mark Twain's canvassers who hawked Grant's *Memoirs* door-to-door.

48

Now Priceless Memorabilia Were Sold as Scrap and Hauled Off as Junk

In 1800, a few months before the end of John Adams's administration, the government moved from Philadelphia to the new capital, Washington, D.C. Thus President and Mrs. Adams were the first occupants of the executive mansion, which had only half a dozen rooms ready for occupancy. Abigail Adams used the large East Room for drying the presidential laundry as there was no drying yard in the swampy landscape surrounding the house.

As soon as the new president, Thomas Jefferson, was chosen by the House of Representatives, after tieing with Aaron Burr for electoral votes, John Adams wrote a polite letter to his successor. Confirming a charge made in Congress, Adams said that all of his horses, carriages, and equipage had indeed been purchased with government money. He added that all seven horses were old and his carriages had been purchased secondhand to save money.

"These may not be suitable for you," he told Jefferson, "but if you find that you can use them, they will certainly save you considerable Expense."

Republican Jefferson wanted nothing to do with Federalist purchases that had already become a political issue, so he decided to keep only a one-horse cart for use in going to market. Everything else left behind by Adams—including silver-mounted harnesses for the horses—was sold in haste.

Deals were consummated with such rapidity that no clear records were kept. Apparently there was little haggling; if a person made an offer for a coach or a set of harness, that offer was accepted on the spot. As a result, now-priceless memorabilia linked with the administration of the second president went to purchasers at bargain basement prices.

Congress gave Andrew Jackson authorization to sell White House "equipage and furniture" he considered "decayed, out of repair, or unfit for use."

Nearly three decades later, in 1829, Congress made the first major appropriation for finishing and furnishing the White House—$14,000. Andrew Jackson was authorized to direct the expenditure of this money and to do the same with "the proceeds of the sale of such furniture and equipage of the said house as may be decayed, out of repair, or unfit for use."

Again, there was no record of the prices secured for relics linked with early presidents—not even a list of items sold. The auction firm of Howard and Shortent filled a Pennsylvania Avenue room with chairs, curtains, chandeliers, lamps, mattresses, bowls, decanters, dishes, eagle ornaments, cornices, and even silver plate. Their November sale, held in time to clean out the White House before Jackson moved into it, was highly successful. As a result, the auctioneers held a second sale in March; at that time they mainly offered linens and curtains.

Martin Van Buren, protégé of Jackson and his successor in the White House, did not like the gaudy and ornate furniture with which Old Hickory had filled the White House. Furthermore, much of it was damaged as a result of Jackson's policy of opening the doors of the mansion to all comers. So for the second time, "decayed furniture" from the White House was sold at auction. During Van Buren's four-year tenure, repeated sales brought $5,680.40. There is no record of the items sold or the presidents with whom they were associated.

James Buchanan, the only bachelor ever to be master of the White House, turned to his niece, Harriet Lane, for help. He made her his official hostess and gave her a free hand with household decisions.

Harriet took one look at the place, says Washington lore, and turned up her nose. She especially disliked the Blue Room furniture that had been purchased in France by James Monroe.

Deciding that the use of gilded furniture would "brighten up the old place," she selected fifty pieces of furniture that she considered to be out of style or unrepairable and had them carted off to the auction house. There is no listing of exactly what was sold.

After his election, but before his move to Washington, Abraham Lincoln advertised a sale in the *Illinois State Journal*. It would be expensive to move household belongings, so he offered to the general public such items as "Parlor and Chamber Sets, Carpets, Sofas, Chairs, Wardrobes, Bureaus, Bedsteads, Stoves, glass, Etc., etc." One bill of sale has been preserved in Lincoln's own handwriting. From Springfield druggist S. H. Melvin, he received $82.25 for "6 chairs, 1 spring mattress, 1 wardrobe, 1 whatnot, 1 stand, 9½ yards of stair carpet, and 4 comforters."

Lincoln's vice president, Andrew Johnson, managed temporarily to save from sale a handmade desk at which Andrew Jackson stood for hundreds of hours. Workmen were carting it off for sale as junk when Johnson stopped them because he revered Old Hickory.

Under Ulysses S. Grant the mansion was stripped of most marble mantels and many chandeliers and mirrors. Wooden mantels replaced those sold as junk.

After Garfield's assassination, former Vice President Chester A. Arthur had been in the White House only a short time before he told house steward William T. Crump to put all other duties aside for at least a full day. With Crump in tow, the new president went through the mansion room by room, examining furniture and pointing—without a word—to each item he wished discarded.

Duncanson Brothers, auctioneers, carted twenty-four wagon loads of furnishings to their establishment. These included many of the gilded chairs bought by Harriet Lane, along with many older pieces that included Andrew Jackson's stand-up desk. Beds, lamps, tables, and curtains filled wagon after wagon.

Ex-president Rutherford B. Hayes, who seems to have been one of the few persons in the nation who sensed that anything linked with a president would some day become valuable, submitted a number of bids. Probably, but not positively, he became the proud owner of mahogany serving tables that had been in the White House half a century at the time he first occupied it.

Yet, as late as 1902 when the executive mansion was extensively remodeled for Theodore Roosevelt, huge quantities of furnishings were sold to the highest bidder at incredibly low prices. Mrs. Roosevelt balked at placing chipped china on sale because she considered

Rutherford B. Hayes submitted bids when 24 loads of White House furnishings were sold to the highest bidder. [BRADY STUDIO PORTRAIT, NATIONAL ARCHIVES]

that to be undignified; so she ordered servants to break up such pieces.

Irwin H. Hoover, an aide who spent nearly half a century in the service of chief executives, is the authority for a tale linked with the administration of Woodrow Wilson. According to him, when the wartime president vacated the executive mansion, staff members "cut at least ten large oil paintings from their frames." The frames were then sold at auction, while staffers kept the paintings.

Herbert Hoover later reported that no one had time to try to sell a collection of presidential busts. Some were made of plaster, others of metal. Therefore a sledgehammer was used to demolish thirty-two of them in a single day, and the scraps were put in trash cans.

Time and time again government-owned presidential carriages, private railway cars, and automobiles were disposed of as casually as though they had belonged to a small-town businessman. At least one presidential yacht, the *Mayflower,* was sold as junk immediately after the vessel was de-commissioned.

Probably because of his frugality rather than concern about preserving historical artifacts, Harry Truman put a stop to indiscriminate sales. When the White House underwent extensive repairs, the former haberdasher insisted that even the scrap building material should be sold to souvenir hunters. All pieces of lumber of any size were made into gavels, and even laths were cut into one-foot pieces and offered at twenty-five cents each.

That meant that custodians of presidential memorabilia had come full circle. In the future, nothing associated in any way with former presidents would be treated as junk.

CHAPTER
49

Presidents Have Had Some Unusual First Paying Jobs

Son of a poverty-stricken farmer, young Richard Nixon often lay in bed dreaming that some day he would become a railroad engineer. That job sounded exotic, especially since he was not paid for work he did at his father's gas pump and small general store. Neither was Richard paid for going to the Los Angeles market to bring produce for his father's customers. At age fourteen he jumped at the chance for a real job that brought him money

His mother and brother Harold were at an Arizona sanitarium, where Richard went for a summer vacation. While there, he found part-time work as barker for the Wheel of Fortune, a game of chance favored by patrons of the Slippery Gulch Rodeo in Prescott.

By comparison, the first president started out quite high on the financial scale. At age seventeen he got his first job as an assistant to surveyors who were laying out the town of Alexandria, Virginia. His pay, seven dollars a day, was high for the time. However, when his surveying job took him into the Shenandoah Valley to help map out new lands on the frontier, young George complained that he was underpaid and did not take up surveying as a vocation.

No one knows how much Abraham Lincoln received for his first paying job. In his own recollections, he confided that after having worked for years as a farm boy he was delighted to earn real money for rowing passengers to a steamboat. At nineteen he helped take a flatboat loaded with farm produce to New Orleans. His first salaried job was in New Salem, Illinois, where he got fifty cents a day plus sleeping accommodations as a clerk in a general store.

Both Millard Fillmore and Andrew Johnson worked outside the family for nothing; they were bound out as apprentices, and fees paid by their employers went to their parents. Both boys ran away, but only Johnson managed to open his own business while a fugitive. (He had

At age sixteen, Andrew Johnson opened a tailor shop, thereby becoming the youngest self-employed future chief executive.

broken a window as a prank and feared arrest.) At age sixteen, he launched a tailor shop in Laurens Court House, South Carolina, having learned the rudiments of the trade during his apprenticeship in Raleigh, North Carolina.

Born into a wealthy family in an upscale New York City suburb, George Bush postponed his matriculation at Yale University to join the navy at age eighteen as an ensign aboard the aircraft carrier *San Jacinto.* After completing service, Bush had a desk at his father's international banking house waiting for him. Instead, Bush spurned Wall Street and headed west to the Texas oil fields for his first civilian job—painting machinery and sweeping floors. Years later he said, "I couldn't have gotten better preparation for the White House."

Bill Clinton's first job, at age ten, was a precursor to his career as a glad-handing politician. Young Bubba was hired by his grandfather, Eldridge Cassidy, to stand at the front door of Cassidy's general store in Hope, Arkansas, and greet incoming customers with a friendly welcome and warm handshake. "I liked telling people 'Hello,' and at quitting time I got paid in all-day suckers," Clinton said.

At the age of five, Jimmy Carter sold boiled peanuts on the street. His nickname was "Hot," short for "Hot Shot."

Calvin Coolidge earned his first cash selling apples and popcorn balls at town meetings. Later, as a pioneer craftsman, he hand-crafted toys in a carriage shop.

Lyndon Johnson started out as a hired hand at a nearby farm in Texas. A printer's devil and shoeshine boy, he found time to trap animals and sell their skins.

By the time he was seventeen, Johnson had a job as a pick and shovel man who also operated a four-mule "fresno" in a road-building project.

Harry Truman, who never came close to achieving the wealth of Johnson, started at better pay. Soon after graduating from high school, he became a timekeeper for a contractor at a salary of thirty-five dollars a month. When that job gave out, he became a newspaper mailroom clerk at seven dollars a week, a level at which he seemed to be stuck since his third job as a bank clerk paid exactly thirty-five dollars a month.

Truman was so efficient that bank executives upped his salary to sixty dollars a month, but that was not enough to hold him. Three years out of high school, he moved to a competing bank as bookkeeper at the whopping salary of seventy-five dollars a month.

Benjamin Harrison, grandson of President William Henry Harrison, looked to the legal world very early and managed to land a job as court crier at $2.50 a day. Three years after being admitted to the bar, the young lawyer wangled an appointment as Indianapolis city attorney at $400 a year.

William Howard Taft, who also turned to law very early, had the advantage of coming from a prominent family with strong political connections. Hamilton County, Ohio, paid him $1,200 a year to work as assistant prosecutor.

After a stint as assistant teacher in an institute for the blind, Grover Cleveland was paid ten dollars a month—plus room and board—in his new job as editor of the *American Shorthorn Handbook*.

Herbert Hoover, who became a millionaire before his White House days, earned his first cash as an orphan farm boy by picking potato bugs from plants at the rate of one dollar per 100 bugs. He also earned spending money by picking strawberries and collecting scrap iron for sale.

James A. Garfield wanted to become a sailor, so at sixteen he hiked from the family farm to Cleveland, Ohio. At the docks he failed to find

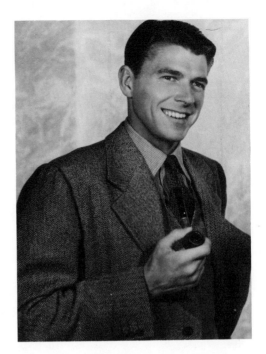

The future actor and president once earned ten dollars for retrieving a swimmer's false teeth from a river.

anyone willing to take him on board as a hired hand, so he became a mule driver on the canal between Cleveland and Pittsburgh. Accident-prone Garfield fell into the canal at least fourteen times during six weeks, miraculously escaped drowning, and decided to quit work and go back to school.

Warren G. Harding was briefly a hired hand for the contractor who graded a roadbed for the Toledo and Central Railroad. More significantly for his future career, he worked a few hours a week as printer's devil at the Caledonia, Ohio, *Argus*. After he learned to run a printing press by watching others do it, he soon landed a job on the Marion *Democratic Mirror* at one dollar a week.

Harding then tried his hand at teaching, largely because the little school outside Marion offered him thirty dollars a month. One term was enough. He quit his job, borrowed $300, bought the Marion *Star*, and became a newspaper publisher at age nineteen.

Others who became chief executives may have earned more money in early jobs, but Ronald Reagan insisted that he "had the best job any boy could want." For six or seven summers he was the lifeguard at a riverfront recreation park near his home town of Dixon, Illinois, where he saved 77 persons from drowning—by his own account.

He also retrieved a man's dentures from the river bottom, for which the grateful swimmer tipped him ten dollars. "The first big money I ever saw," Reagan recalled while sitting in the Oval Office.

50

Gifts and Loans Have Provoked Public Interest

Ronald Reagan's last months in office were marred by revelations that the first lady had broken promises made in 1982 when she said she no longer would accept expensive clothing and jewelry "on loan" because that practice created problems for her husband.

Under the 1978 Ethics in Government Act, federal officials are required to make annual financial disclosures in which gifts are enumerated. The value of gifts accepted by the president and first lady are taxable as ordinary income. According to news accounts, in October 1982 Nancy Reagan had borrowed an estimated one million dollars worth of finery, much of which was never returned. Many in the nation's capital saw no distinction between an outright gift and the loan of a garment.

Responding to questions about a $35,000 Russian sable and a diamond necklace and earrings estimated at $480,000, the first lady tartly responded, "I am not a federal employee; the disclosure requirement does not apply to me."

That answer—technically correct—clearly skirted the law since the first lady personally oversees an East Wing staff whose estimated $500,000 per year payroll comes from taxpayers' money.

Gifts have come to chief executives and their wives since the infancy of the republic. Some presidents have accepted none; others have accepted almost all that were offered. Foreign heads of state have showered White House occupants with expensive baubles, and ordinary American citizens have bestowed many curious gifts, some sent out of admiration and others probably dispatched with an eye upon publicity value. Until modern times, each chief executive decided how to handle this matter; laws governing acceptance of gifts and requiring financial disclosure are quite recent in origin.

During the Reagan years, gifts ranged from the colossal to the comical. Imelda Marcos of the Philippines gave Nancy Reagan two

Nancy Reagan was severely criticized and ridiculed following 1988 disclosures that she had "borrowed" an estimated one million dollars worth of designer clothing and jewelry for her public appearances, much of which was never returned.

gowns—one of black velvet and the other of red silk—valued together at $10,000. Almost simultaneously, her husband received from the Secret Service a chain saw and accessories worth $238.

Burton Associates of California presented the president with hearing aids worth $1,590, but they were topped by a business competitor who sent four of these devices with a market value of $3,000.

Ronald Reagan received from the president of Pakistan an engraved shotgun worth $8,000 and from Bettino Craxi of Italy a brown leather jacket with the initials "R.R." Two riding crops sent from Eduardo Sanchez Junco of Madrid, Spain, were valued at $130, but no one felt competent to estimate the value of a revolver engraved with the president's signature, a gift from Leopold Deters, of Springfield, Massachusetts.

George Washington, first to be confronted with the question of whether or not to accept gifts, took the middle road. He declined some, but accepted others. Financially pinched as a result of having neglected his own affairs to serve as commander-in-chief of the colonial forces, he was voted $20,000 in canal stock by the Virginia Assembly.

"How would this matter be viewed by the eye of the world," he asked in declining the gift, "and what would be its opinion when it comes to be related that George Washington accepted $20,000? However customarily these gifts are made in other countries, if I accepted this should I not henceforth be considered a dependent."

But when King Charles III of Spain, ignoring a law that forbade the exportation of full-blooded jackasses, sent a splendid animal to Washington, he accepted it and named it Royal Gift. Later, the Marquis de Lafayette sent Washington a Maltese jack that the Father of His Country accepted and called Knight of Malta.

Thomas Jefferson flatly refused to accept any gift of any kind, regardless of the giver. His uncompromising stand created a problem in January 1802, when a 1,235-pound cheese reached the executive mansion, courtesy of Jefferson's admirers in West Chester, Pennsylvania. Since the mammoth cheese was already in the capital—drawn there by six horses—it didn't seem sensible to send it back. So out of his own pocket Jefferson paid for it at about 150 percent of the current market price for cheese.

When ambassadors from Tunis solemnly presented a splendid oriental rug, Thomas Jefferson sternly told them to send it back to Tunis. His granddaughter, who sometimes served as hostess of the executive mansion, was in tears when she heard the verdict, but Jefferson refused to budge.

John Quincy Adams faithfully followed Jefferson's example and refused to accept any gift, however small its value. He even planned to return to the maker a gift of soap but relented under the pleading of his wife.

Andrew Jackson followed the example of George Washington and decided the question of gifts on a case-by-case basis. From dairy farmer T. S. Meacham of Oswego County, New York, he accepted a 1,400-pound cheese. But he turned down Philadelphia's offer of eight white horses and Baltimore's gift of a carriage made of hickory wood.

Old Hickory didn't demur, however, when his wife received a pre-inaugural gift of a lavish lace veil from Cincinnati. Using a different pattern of lace for each letter, the veil displayed the name *Jackson*, along with twenty-four stars, one for each of the states then in the Union.

A gift from the emperor of Morocco—two horses and a lion—annoyed Andrew Jackson. Since the animals were already in the country, he decided not to send them back, but he turned them over to Congress with instructions that lawmakers should "do with them as they saw fit."

James K. Polk cited Jefferson as his authority in refusing to accept any gift "of more value than a book or a cane." Following his example, the first lady shook her head when offered bouquets of flowers grown in the conservatory attached to the Patent Office; but she persuaded

Washingtonians flocked to get their share when Andrew Jackson announced that a gift to him of 1,400 pounds of cheese was available to the public "first come, first served."

him to let her keep a silk fan with ivory sticks that displayed portraits of the first eleven presidents.

Although briefed about Andrew Jackson's refusal of elegant transportation, Millard Fillmore accepted from New York admirers "the most splendid carriage seen on Washington's unpaved streets," a green coach fitted out with silver lamps and accessories.

From "the democracy of Savannah, Georgia," Franklin Pierce accepted a six-piece set of sterling silver: a soup tureen, two oyster dishes, two venison dishes, and a fruit bowl.

James Buchanan reverted to the austerity policy of Jefferson and refused to accept any gift, however inexpensive it might be. When Philadelphia makers sent him a splendid set of harness, he inquired its value, decided to keep the gear, and solemnly wrote out a check for $800 in payment.

When the first diplomatic representatives from Japan reached the United States during Buchanan's administration, they created a major problem. They brought along fifteen large boxes packed with gifts of every sort: swords, saddles, screens, bed curtains, writing cases, lacquer ware, and even a teakwood case inlaid with pearls and gold. President Buchanan put a few of the Japanese gifts into the Green Room of the White House, then sent the rest to the Patent Office for sale.

Abraham Lincoln firmly rejected a herd of elephants proffered by the king of Siam but nodded assent when the first lady said she would like to accept "a highly ornamented sewing machine, as a token of esteem" from friends in Springfield, Illinois.

Mrs. Lincoln's strong southern ties were universally known and widely criticized. Still, a unit of Federal Zouaves brought to her a Confederate flag captured from a Louisiana regiment, and the president persuaded her to accept it. Four years later, on the day of his second inauguration, he did not protest when one of his cabinet members presented to the first lady the Bible that Lincoln had kissed when he took the oath of office.

In practice, President Lincoln almost casually decided whether to accept a particular item or to reject it.

Lincoln's successor, Andrew Johnson, took a firm position and did not waver from it: no gifts, under *any* circumstances. Offered by New Yorkers a splendid carriage, with horses and harness Johnson was reminded that Lincoln had accepted just such a gift. "No matter," said the Tennessean. "I am not Lincoln; take them back."

U. S. Grant made a complete about-face with respect to gifts. He accepted almost anything offered. From the Sultan of Turkey, he took a splendid oriental rug and a thirty-two-piece sterling silver coffee set. When Mexico sent dressed leopard skins, the Civil War hero said "Thank you."

As the president's policy became general knowledge, presents showered upon the White House from all parts of the nation: gold-tipped cigars, blooded bull pups, Hambletonian colts, assorted clothing and jewelry, books about the war, Currier and Ives prints, original oil paintings, and rare maps. Grant made no explanation or apology, simply accepting with gratitude whatever came.

Rutherford B. Hayes accepted few personal gifts. He reluctantly agreed to keep an oak desk sent by Queen Victoria and joyfully accepted from members of the twenty-third Ohio Regiment a silver plate with an engraved sketch of his 1863–64 log hut headquarters.

As a Congressman, James A. Garfield was accused of accepting a gift of stock from the Credit Mobilier, a corporation that sought favors from the federal government. Garfield denied the charge, which his accusers were never able to prove.

William McKinley refused most offers of gifts but accepted from admirers in Georgia a 78-pound watermelon. It reached the White House wrapped in an American flag and tied with white ribbon.

Theodore Roosevelt accepted a gold goblet from the San Francisco Chamber of Commerce, but when gifts arrived from Prince Henry of Prussia, he sent them to the Corcoran Gallery of Art.

When Theodore Roosevelt's madcap daughter Alice, for which the popular song "Alice Blue Gown" was written, was married during her father's presidency, she was showered with expensive gifts: a necklace of

Told that Abraham Lincoln accepted numerous gifts in almost casual style, Andrew Johnson shook his head and said, "No gifts; I am not Lincoln. Take them back."

sixty-three matched pearls plus a diamond clasp from Cuba; silks, embroideries, and ivory carvings from the Dowager Empress of China; a rare tapestry from France; chased silver vases from Japan; and hundreds of costly gifts from American corporations and individuals.

Woodrow Wilson's marriage while chief executive also produced a flood of gifts: carpets, silver, glassware, lace, vases, diamond and sapphire jewelry, mahogany furniture, linens, tapestries, clocks, lamps, candy, brooms, brushes, perfumes, even soap and sugared popcorn. Although only the more expensive gifts were acknowledged, all were accepted.

It was Woodrow Wilson who stopped a long-standing practice. Year after year, Andrew Carnegie had kept chief executives supplied with all the Scotch whisky they could use. Wilson let it be known that he would accept no whisky, Scotch or otherwise.

Tainted as he later was by the Teapot Dome scandal, Warren G. Harding took a Spartan view of gifts. However, Evalyn Walsh McLean did succeed in persuading Mrs. Harding to accept from her "a lace boudoir cape, made in the shape of a crown."

Calvin Coolidge accepted one pair of skis and two dozen live chickens during his administration. He had a wire fence put up and let the chickens run free until they were needed for the White House table.

By the time Dwight D. Eisenhower became president, Congress had passed an early conflict of interest law. Ike pointed out that since he was an elected—not an appointed—official, "the conflict of interest law does not apply to me." For his Gettysburg farm he accepted livestock and agricultural machinery estimated by some critics to be worth at least $300,000.

One of Ike's top aides was Sherman Adams, who clearly was subject to the conflict of interest law. Adams impulsively accepted gifts from a Boston businessman, thereby becoming the first top official of the nation to be forced out of office because of a vicuña coat.

During two centuries of the American presidency, attitudes about gifts have swung like a pendulum. Legal restrictions have arisen in an effort to combat undue influence and to protect susceptible chief executives and their wives. Prior to January 20, 1981, however, nothing quite like Nancy Reagan's million dollar "borrowing binge" appears in the record.

INDEX

Names of presidents and their wives are shown in CAPITALS; illustrations are in **boldface**.